THE UNIVERSITY COLLEGE OF
RIPON AND YORK ST. JOHN
RIPON CAMPUS

Please return this book by the date stamped below   tion
- if recalled, the loan is reduced to 10 days

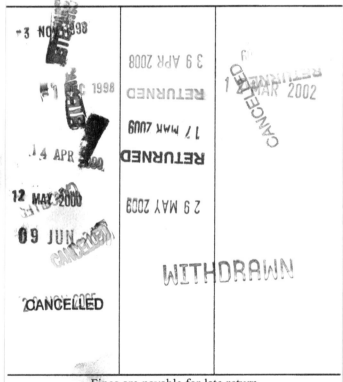

Fines are payable for late return

THE CAMBRIDGE APPLIED LINGUISTICS SERIES

Series editors: Michael H. Long and Jack C. Richards

This new series presents the findings of recent work in applied linguistics which are of direct relevance to language teaching and learning and of particular interest to applied linguists, researchers, language teachers, and teacher trainers.

Power and Inequality in Language Education

Edited by

James W. Tollefson
University of Washington

CAMBRIDGE
UNIVERSITY PRESS

Published by the Press Syndicate of the University of Cambridge
The Pitt Building, Trumpington Street, Cambridge CB2 1RP
40 West 20th Street, New York, NY 10011-4211, USA
10 Stamford Road, Oakleigh, Melbourne 3166, Australia

First published 1995

Printed in the United States of America

Library of Congress Cataloging-in-Publication Data
Power and inequality in language education / edited by James W. Tollefson.
p. cm. – (The Cambridge applied linguistics series)
ISBN 0-521-46266-5. – ISBN 0-521-46807-8 (pbk.)
1. Language and languages – Study and teaching – Social aspects.
2. Language policy. I. Tollefson, James W. II. Series.
P53.8.P68 1995
418'.007 – dc20   94–33478
                                                                CIP

A catalog record for this book is available from the British Library

ISBN 0-521-46266-5 Hardback
ISBN 0-521-46807-8 Paperback

Contents

Contributors

Elsa Roberts Auerbach, University of Massachusetts, Boston
Brian M. Bullivant, Monash University, Melbourne, Australia
Thomas S. Donahue, San Diego State University, California
Ofelia García, City College of New York
David Welchman Gegeo, University of Hawaii at Manoa
Nancy H. Hornberger, University of Pennsylvania, Philadelphia
Marilyn Martin-Jones, Lancaster University, Lancaster, England
Alastair Pennycook, University of Hong Kong
Mukul Saxena, University College of Ripon and York St. John, York,
   England
Selma K. Sonntag, Humboldt State University, Arcata, California
James W. Tollefson, University of Washington
Karen Ann Watson-Gegeo, University of California, Davis

Series editors' preface

Massive population shifts, both voluntary and forced, and a slowly growing recognition of linguistic human rights have combined to give new importance to decisions concerning language policy in a variety of social settings, not least in schools and universities. What are educational language planners to do when confronted with multilingual, multicultural societies, often with several languages and dialects represented in a single classroom, a shortage of teachers and written materials for many of those languages and dialects, and competing political and ideological pressures?

Professor James W. Tollefson has assembled a collection of original papers on these and related issues which should be of value to educators at all levels in such settings, as well as to researchers and graduate students in applied linguistics and sociolinguistics. The authors work in North America, Australia, Europe, Asia, and the Pacific. They treat relationships among policy, curriculum, and classroom procedures; the spread of official language movements and of English as a medium of instruction; the role of corpus planning in policy development; and throughout, the influence of wider issues of ideology and socioeconomic power on language policy at all levels, in governments, schools and universities, and individual classrooms. Explicit attention is also given to methodological issues in future research on these matters.

We think *Power and Inequality in Language Education* is a valuable addition to the applied linguistics literature. Its data-based orientation and academic rigour addressing critical social issues make it an appropriate volume for inclusion in the Cambridge Applied Linguistics Series.

Michael H. Long
Jack C. Richards

Preface

Over the past generation, the development of applied linguistics as a distinct academic discipline has had the unfortunate effect of widening the gap between researchers interested in theories of language and society and teachers interested in the pedagogy of language teaching and learning. Yet a key generalization that has emerged from research in applied linguistics is that power and inequality – important issues in research – are central to language teaching and learning. What happens in the language classroom is intimately linked to social and political forces, and practitioners must understand those links if they are to be fully effective in their work. This volume aims to explore some of the issues of power and inequality in language education, and make available to practitioners current research in this field.

Any book dealing with such a large area must be selective. For this volume, the choice of articles has been guided by my desire to include diverse theoretical perspectives and approaches, as well as a set of topics that illustrate the range of language education issues in which power and inequality are central. Of necessity, important topics have been left out, especially historical analyses of the institutions responsible for the spread of English language education worldwide, and case studies of many of the countries in which language education plays an important role in determining which groups have economic and political power. I hope that the range of topics included here will stimulate readers new to the field to seek out additional published work.

All books are cooperative products. As editor, I am particularly grateful to the authors whose work appears in this collection. Their patience, their prompt and detailed responses to numerous queries, and their efforts to coordinate their articles deserve special praise. I wish to thank also the editorial staff at Cambridge University Press, especially Mary Vaughn, Jane Mairs, and Suzette André, for their professional work on the manuscript. Mike Long was instrumental in bringing this topic to the Cambridge Applied Linguistics series. Partial funding for this project was provided by Joe Norman, Dean of the College of Arts and Sciences at the University of Washington.

James W. Tollefson

Introduction: Language policy, power, and inequality

James W. Tollefson

Until recently, most teacher-preparation programs in language education and English as a second language focused on second language acquisition, teaching methods, and linguistics, without placing these fields in their social, political, and economic context. The result was that many language teachers and other applied linguists lacked an understanding of how language-learning theory and common teaching practices are linked with broader sociopolitical forces. More recently, however, applied linguistics has begun to examine the impact of social, economic, and political forces upon the theory and practice of language teaching and learning (e.g., Fairclough 1989; Pennycook 1989; Tollefson 1991; Williams 1992). A central feature of this examination is a new emphasis upon the role of language policy in language education.

The purpose of *Power and Inequality in Language Education* is to explore the relationship between language policy and language education with a particular emphasis on power and inequality. A key aim of the collection is to link ideology and the analysis of power relations to language policy in education. This book is primarily intended for graduate students in applied linguistics and language teaching, although it will also be useful for undergraduates with a background in these fields.

The articles in *Power and Inequality in Language Education* cover a wide range of topics, yet the researchers whose work is represented here share a common belief that the relationship among language, power, and inequality is central to the fields of applied linguistics and language education. Thus each article examines ways in which language policy and language education around the world are linked with the distribution of political power and economic resources. The collection is international in scope, reflecting our belief that language educators and other applied linguists must have an appreciation for the profound impact of differing sociopolitical contexts upon language policies and practices in education.

The articles in this volume illustrate the range of topics in which language policy, power, and inequality come together. Thus, despite their diversity, they present several recurring themes. Perhaps the most important theme is that research in applied linguistics must incorporate, as a central concept, the issue of *power*. Power can be examined from several

1

perspectives. "Discourse power" refers to encounters between unequal individuals. "State power" refers to control of the armed forces and agencies of government. "Ideological power" refers to the ability to project one's own practices and beliefs as universal and commonsense. (For discussion of these forms of power, see Fairclough 1989; Tollefson 1991.) All of these meanings refer to the capacity to control resources, both tangible economic resources and intangible resources such as language and discourse. A concern with the meaning of the term *power* is explicit in the contributions of Sonntag, Bullivant, and Hornberger. For all of the authors in this collection, power resides not in individuals or groups, but rather within relationships in which struggles over power are won or lost. Thus these articles explore how language policies at all levels, from the national authority to the individual classroom, reflect relationships of unequal power.

A second important theme of this collection is that language policies are both an outcome of power struggles and an arena for those struggles. The articles by Auerbach, Watson-Gegeo and Gegeo, Martin-Jones and Saxena, Sonntag, and Hornberger show how language policies at all levels of the society, from the state to the individual classroom, reflect existing power relationships. Yet, as Auerbach, Pennycook, Watson-Gegeo and Gegeo, and Donahue point out, policy debates also offer a mechanism for minority groups to assert their power and to alter existing power relationships. Thus the articles in this collection illustrate the dynamic tension that exists within the social sciences between an understanding of the impact of social structure on individual choice and action, and an appreciation for the capacity of individuals and groups to challenge and to alter the structure of social systems.

A third theme is that English language teaching must be examined within the context of the spread of English as a world language. The articles by Auerbach, Pennycook, Watson-Gegeo and Gegeo, and García in particular question the widespread ideological view of English as a tool for gaining individual economic opportunity, and instead argue that the spread of English is part of wider social, political, and economic processes that contribute to economic inequalities. Sonntag, Donahue, and García explore these processes in detail, showing the ways in which the spread of English may serve the interests of particular socioeconomic groups.

A fourth theme of this volume is that an understanding of the causes and consequences of migration is important for applied linguists and language teachers. As the number of migrants worldwide has increased, migration has become a permanent feature of the global political economy. Much of the increase in language education and the rising influence of language policies is due to this explosion in migration. Auerbach, Pennycook, Martin-Jones and Saxena, García, and Bullivant ask us to place migrant education programs within their historical context, and to

ask such questions as: What is the function of migrant language programs? Whom do these programs serve? What is their economic and
social impact upon the lives of their graduates? In order to answer these
questions, applied linguistics must confront the connection between language policy and power, and the ways in which language policies contribute to economic, social, and political inequality.

A fifth theme is that state language policies, although often associated
with a rhetoric of "equality" and "opportunity," frequently serve to
channel migrants and other linguistic minorities into low-paying jobs in
the peripheral economy. Auerbach, Martin-Jones and Saxena, García,
Bullivant, and Hornberger examine the consequences of such policies and
programs. Several articles, including those by Auerbach, Watson-Gegeo
and Gegeo, and Martin-Jones and Saxena, analyze alternative policies and
programs that may better serve the interests of linguistic minorities.

A sixth and final theme of this collection is that the fields of applied
linguistics and language teaching must undertake a critical self-
examination. Pennycook argues that central concepts in applied linguistics reflect a particular ideological view of the power relationships that
exist in social institutions. He points out that English language educators
too often adopt uncritical assumptions about the value of English –
assumptions that are self-serving and that do not reflect the reality of the
lives of many English language learners. Bullivant traces the fundamentally ideological underpinnings of social scientific debate over Australian
language policy, and speculates that these policies may ultimately undermine the goals of those who favor a multicultural social system. Auerbach
shows how "commonsense" assumptions about teaching and learning
and about the roles of teachers and students are rooted historically in the
relationships of unequal power that characterize contemporary society.
Martin-Jones and Saxena suggest that the focus on interaction in applied
linguistics research has had the effect of removing language specialists
from policy debates. Hornberger shows how a narrow focus on "corpus"
planning, removed from historical context and without an analysis of the
interest groups involved in corpus-planning debates, may fail to capture
the social, political, and economic consequences of corpus-planning decisions. Sonntag and Donahue warn that many analyses of language-policy
debates fail to capture the underlying political strategies and motivations
of individuals and groups involved in the policy-making process. All
authors in this volume argue implicitly that the historical development of
applied linguistics and key concepts within the discipline of language
teaching may limit the kinds of analyses that are carried out and also may
lead applied linguists to adopt perspectives that serve the interests of
groups that dominate state policy making. The articles in this collection
are examples of the kind of critical self-examination essential for the
growth and development of the field of applied linguistics.

The individual articles in *Power and Inequality in Language Education* illustrate the range of issues currently being debated in language policy and language education. The first article, Elsa Roberts Auerbach's "The Politics of the ESL Classroom: Issues of Power in Pedagogical Choices," focuses on language and power in individual classrooms. Auerbach has been at the forefront of efforts to critically examine widely used curricula and materials for immigrants in the United States. In this article, she analyzes pedagogical choices confronting teachers of adult immigrants and refugees in North America in light of their implications for students' roles in the broader social order. Auerbach shows that choices within the classroom reflect social relations and processes outside the classroom. Focusing on curriculum development, instructional content, materials, and language choice, Auerbach compares choices within dominant, mainstream approaches to adult ESL with alternative approaches. How do commonsense notions about the social roles of *teacher* and *student* determine what happens in individual classes? How are curricula, materials, classroom practices, even the physical arrangement of space a reflection of unspoken assumptions about power in the society outside the classroom? Auerbach asks whether a rethinking of the roles of teacher and student can lead to new ways to organize language classes. Accordingly, she examines alternatives to traditional practices, including the participatory approach and "classrooms without walls," which seek to transform classes. Finally, Auerbach challenges English language educators to apply the "problem-posing" approach to critically examine their own profession, one in which teachers work long hours for low wages, often in part-time jobs with few benefits.

While Auerbach focuses on the microsocial order of the classroom in order to link it to broader sociopolitical forces, in "English in the World/ The World in English," Alastair Pennycook explores those broader social forces directly. In his wide-ranging discussion, Pennycook critically examines the predominant view in the social sciences that the spread of English is neutral, natural, and beneficial – a view that is concerned primarily with questions of multiple or single standards and the description of new Englishes. Believing that language is always "engaged with the realities of power" (Terdiman 1985:38), Pennycook outlines an alternative "critical perspective" toward the spread of English, which focuses on how English threatens other languages, operates as a gatekeeper to positions of wealth and privilege, and plays a role in the unequal distribution of global economic and cultural resources. Pennycook suggests that the spread of English is, in part, due to deliberate policies of English-speaking nations to spread the language in order to protect and promote their own interests. Thus he explores the connections between English and the discourses of development, democracy, capitalism, and modernization. Yet Pennycook rejects theories of structural determinism, arguing instead that the role of English-in-the-world and the-world-in-English permits "counter-discourses" in which existing power relationships may be challenged. Pennycook's macroanalysis shows how important it is for language teachers to become knowledgeable about the role of language in the struggle over global resources.

Karen Ann Watson-Gegeo and David Welchman Gegeo present a case study of the devastating impact of the spread of English and other recent social changes upon the education of children in the Solomon Islands. Their article, "Understanding Language and Power in the Solomon Islands: Methodological Lessons for Educational Intervention," focuses on the widespread school failure of rural children in the Solomon Islands, where more than seventy indigenous languages compete with Solomons Pijin and English. Watson-Gegeo and Gegeo raise important questions of social science methodology in their study of educational policy in the Solomon Islands. They are interested in the link between research and educational intervention, specifically aimed at reducing the school failure of rural children. When intervention is the goal, they argue for a research methodology of "thick explanation," which involves the integration of both micro- and macrolevels of contextualized data, within a qualitative, ethnographic framework.

Also interested in issues of research methodology in applied linguistics, Marilyn Martin-Jones and Mukul Saxena examine a specific form of educational provision developed for bilingual children in primary schools in Britain, known as "bilingual support." Their article, "Supporting or Containing Bilingualism? Policies, Power Asymmetries, and Pedagogic Practices in Mainstream Primary Classrooms," examines teaching/ learning situations in mainstream British classes in which bilingual teachers or assistants use both English and the language of bilingual learners to assist them in all areas of the curriculum. The purpose of this assistance is to facilitate the learners' transition to monolingual English education. Martin-Jones and Saxena trace the historical development of the policy of bilingual support and place this educational provision within the wider context of educational policy in the United Kingdom since the early 1970s. Their article then summarizes their two-year ethnographic study of bilingual support in a local education authority in northwest England. Like Watson-Gegeo and Gegeo, Martin-Jones and Saxena argue that a combination of micro- and macrolevel data is necessary if the impact of language policy in individual classrooms and schools is to be understood. Moreover, they are critical of the dominance of ahistorical, microethnographic, interactionist research in applied linguistics, which they believe serves to minimize the contribution of applied linguists to debates about educational policy (cf. Strubell 1990).

Two articles examine the rise of official language movements from different perspectives. First, Selma K. Sonntag's "Elite Competition and

Official Language Movements" explores one way in which language policy may be an arena for challenges to the existing power structure: through the role that official language movements play in political strategies of emerging elite groups in multinational states. Sonntag argues that emerging elites may favor official language policies as a strategy for realigning cleavage lines within the population, in order to undermine the existing politico-economic power structure. Through her examination of official language movements in Belgium, India, the former Soviet Union, and the United States, Sonntag outlines the specific conditions under which official language movements may have this function. Her article shows that debates about language policy often cannot be understood unless the interest groups involved in the debates are identified and their strategies for gaining greater power are understood.

The second article about official language movements, Thomas S. Donahue's "American Language Policy and Compensatory Opinion," examines in detail the political role of U.S. English, the major interest group favoring an official English policy in the United States. Donahue, who has followed the work of U.S. English for nearly a decade, places the official English movement within the context of the economic restructuring taking place in U.S. society. Donahue's analysis demonstrates that official language movements, when placed within their historical and structural contexts, can be understood as part of broad struggles over the distribution of "life chances." Moreover, Donahue challenges us to consider whether some language policy debates may be diversions from more important struggles over the (re)distribution of wealth and the (re)structuring of the class system. In his provocative conclusion, Donahue asks whether the official English debate may not be a "phony issue," irrelevant to more important policies affecting economic and social mobility in the United States.

In "Spanish Language Loss as a Determinant of Income among Latinos in the United States: Implications for Language Policy in Schools," Ofelia García presents both qualitative and quantitative data to examine the link between the ability to speak English and the economic well-being of Spanish speakers in the United States. Her article challenges the widespread assumption that income among Spanish speakers is determined by their competence in English. Based upon her studies, García rejects what she calls the "myth" that the economic failure of many Latinos in the United States is a result of their refusal to "relinguify" from Spanish to English. García's critique of this myth shows that the belief that language and income are linked can serve as a justification for policies that restrict minority languages. García examines in particular the case of Spanish in Dade County, Florida, arguing that the economic value and prestige of a language is not a static characteristic, but instead part of the dynamic and negotiable relationship between minority and majority language groups.

Brian M. Bullivant's "Ideological Influences on Linguistic and Cultural Empowerment: An Australian Example" offers a historical analysis of the political and ideological considerations that have influenced provisions for language education in Australia. By examining programs for both English as a second language and languages other than English, Bullivant traces the emergence of the concept of a "multicultural Australia" in the 1970s following a period of assimilationist and Anglo-conformist rhetoric and policy in education and social welfare. Bullivant describes the evolution of what he calls "naive or Utopian multiculturalism" in the late seventies, through several crises, into "neo-multiculturalism" in the late 1980s. He argues that the current "economics of multiculturalism," which sees multicultural ideology as playing an important role in the economic restructuring of Australia, involves an ambitious program to improve national economic competitiveness through a National Language Policy, which emphasizes in particular the teaching of languages. The ideological shift from microlevel, individual empowerment to macrolevel, collective empowerment may lead, Bullivant speculates, to a postpluralist period, in which national economic concerns take precedence over ethnic interests. Bullivant's critique of the ideology of multiculturalism in Australia suggests that debates over "empowerment," "equal opportunity," and "diversity" are often distractions from central economic issues of language policy and language use. Bullivant argues that debates over the ideology of multicultural education in Australia usually ignore the historical and structural basis for economic inequality, focusing instead on educational reforms that cannot resolve problems (such as the school failure of linguistic minorities) that have deep historical and structural roots. He suggests that applied linguists and other educators too often focus on debates over "culture" that ignore socioeconomic inequality and class issues.

The final article in the collection, by Nancy H. Hornberger, focuses on an example of "corpus planning," in which language planners make decisions about the structure of the Quechua language in Peru. In "Five Vowels or Three? Linguistics and Politics in Quechua Language Planning in Peru," Hornberger explores the language-planning issue of whether the official Quechua alphabet in Peru should have five vowels or three. First emerging as a policy controversy in 1983, when the Workshop on Quechua and Aymara Writing recommended three vowels, this debate may seem at first glance to be a minor technical one, of interest only to professional linguists. But, as is often the case in language planning around the world, the controversy has complex social, cultural, and political implications. In her analysis, Hornberger shows how this seemingly trivial debate in fact involves important questions about the structure of Quechua, the language-planning process in Peru, the basis for authority on language, and the purity, authenticity, and autonomy of Quechua; as well as questions about a wide range of educational issues, including texts and materials, curricula, teacher preparation, and access to literacy. By examining the views of these issues held by the competing interest groups in Peru, Hornberger shows that the Quechua vowel controversy reflects major sociocultural and politico-economic divisions in Peruvian society, as well as efforts to challenge those divisions. Hornberger concludes her critique of the five-or-three-vowel debate with a call for greater involvement of those individuals most often ignored in the policy-making process – speakers of the Quechua language. Hornberger's call for a more democratic, participatory policy-making process is one echoed by the other authors as well in *Power and Inequality in Language Education*.

References

Fairclough, N. 1989. *Language and power.* London: Longman.

Pennycook, A. 1989. The concept of method, interested knowledge, and the politics of language teaching. *TESOL Quarterly* 23(4): 589–618.

Strubell, M. 1990. Code-switching in the classroom: Comments. *European Science Foundation Network on Code-Switching and Language Contact – Papers of the Workshop on "Impact and consequences: Broader consequences," Brussels, November, 1990.* Strasbourg: European Science Foundation.

Terdiman, R. 1985. *Discourse/Counter-discourse.* New York: Cornell University Press.

Tollefson, J. W. 1991. *Planning language, planning inequality: Language policy in the community.* London: Longman.

Williams, G. 1992. *Sociolinguistics: A sociological citique.* London: Routledge.

1 The politics of the ESL classroom: Issues of power in pedagogical choices

Elsa Roberts Auerbach

Close your eyes and imagine an ESL classroom. My guess is that the picture in your mind's eye includes a teacher, a group of learners, some desks, chairs, a blackboard, books, papers, four walls, and a door. Have you drawn anything outside the walls of the classroom? Are there any visible ways in which relations of power or authority show up in your picture?

If the learners' relation to the social order outside the classroom is not immediately apparent in your picture, you are probably not alone. Although issues of power and politics are generally seen as inherent in language policy and planning on a macrolevel, classrooms themselves may be seen as self-contained, autonomous systems, insulated from external political concerns. The actual teaching that goes on behind closed doors is often conceived of as a neutral transfer of skills, knowledge, or competencies, to be left in the hands of trained professionals whose job it is to implement the latest methods and techniques. Language acquisition is seen as little more than a tool in service of other goals, to be used for whatever purposes the learner chooses, but generally leading toward greater economic access.

The central argument of this chapter is that although dynamics of power and domination may be invisible, they permeate the fabric of classroom life. The day-to-day decisions that practitioners make inside the classroom both shape and are shaped by the social order outside the classroom. Pedagogical choices about curriculum development, content, materials, classroom processes, and language use, although appearing to be informed by apolitical professional considerations, are, in fact, inherently ideological in nature, with significant implications for learners' socioeconomic roles. Put simply, our choices as educators play a role in shaping students' choices. In this chapter, I will examine how the classroom functions as a kind of microcosm of the broader social order, by unpacking some of the assumptions implicit in these choices as they relate to adult ESL/literacy instruction in the U.S. context; similar analyses apply to other second language teaching contexts as well (Cummings and Gregory 1984; Quinn 1986; Spener 1988).

The theoretical framework

In examining how politics and power enter into language teaching, the first question we must ask is: What is power and how does it manifest itself? Fairclough (1989) argues that dominant classes exercise power in two basic ways – through coercion and through consent – either by forcing others to go along with them or by convincing them that it is in their best interest to do so. Consent, however, is not necessarily the result of conscious choice, but rather an unconscious acceptance of institutional practices:

Institutional practices which people draw upon without thinking often embody assumptions which directly or indirectly legitimize existing power relations. Practices can often be shown to originate in the dominant class or the dominant bloc, and to have become naturalized. (Fairclough, 1989:33)

Fairclough calls this "power to project one's practices as universal and 'common sense'" *ideological power* and attributes to it a central role in ensuring control by consent. He argues that discourse practices are a particularly important mechanism for exercising this control: authority and power are manifested and perpetuated by the ways language is used and the purposes for which it is used. These everyday, taken-for-granted practices permeate all the institutions that make up the fabric of society, not only those that are overtly political (e.g., governmental or legal). Thus, the political must be seen as "involving all relationships within a society" (Pennycook 1989:590).

That education in general, and literacy education in particular, are among the primary institutions that promulgate ideological power is by no means a new argument. An enormous body of literature (too large to cite here) documents the role of education in socializing learners for particular life roles, not just on the level of policy and planning (e.g., through practices like tracking [Oakes 1985]), but through differential content and processes of educational interactions (e.g., Anyon 1980). Freire (1985) argues that, in fact, *all* educational practice implies an ideological stance:

The critical analyst will discover, in the methods and texts used by educators and students, practical value options that betray a philosophy of man, well or poorly outlined, coherent or incoherent. . . . technique itself as an instrument of men in their orientation in the world is not neutral. (p. 43)

According to Freire, education inevitably either serves to perpetuate existing social relations or to challenge them:

Education either functions as an instrument which is used to facilitate the integration . . . into the logic of the present system and bring about conformity to it, or it becomes the "practice of freedom," the means by which men and

women deal critically and creatively with reality and discover how to participate in the transformation of their world. (Schaull in Freire 1970:15)

The very way that knowledge is defined in relation to learners reflects a
position about power and the social order. Questions such as: Whose
experience is valid? What counts as legitimate knowledge? and How is
this knowledge transmitted/constructed? are central to understanding
how power manifests itself in educational practice. In the dominant approach to education, which Freire (1970) calls the *banking model,*
knowledge itself is presented as neutral and objective, scientifically-
based, a commodity to be transmitted from teacher to learner. Learners
are seen as empty vessels who passively receive "deposits" of knowledge
in an uncritical one-way transfer. Since the goal of this type of education
is to assimilate learners into the logic of the dominant system, Freire calls
it a domesticating process.

Critics of the banking approach argue that knowledge is neither objective nor static; it always serves particular interests and is situated in a
specific context. Summarizing this perspective, Pennycook says:

[A]ll knowledge is produced within a particular configuration of social, cultural, economic, political and historical circumstances and therefore always
both reflects and helps to (re)produce those conditions. Furthermore, since all
claims to knowledge represent the interests of certain individuals or groups,
we must always see knowledge as interested. (1989:595)

Further, not to recognize that knowledge is inherently interested and
situated serves the important ideological function of legitimating certain
forms of knowledge and educational practice over others, which, in turn,
assures the dominance of those in power (Pennycook 1989:591). To the
extent that it is the knowledge, life experience, and language and
discourses of the dominant class that are valued in educational institutions, it is their power that is perpetuated. Street (1984) extends this
analysis to conceptions about literacy, arguing that the fact that traditionally literacy has been seen as a set of universal, decontextualized
cognitive skills that exist independently of how, where, why, and by
whom they are used is no accident: It is a way of privileging one group's
literacy and discourse practices over others', and it is, as such, a mechanism for perpetuating the status quo. Recognizing one culture-specific set
of literacy practices (namely those of the mainstream, dominant culture)
and elevating it to universal status gives differential access to those who
use it. Instructional approaches that claim that knowledge is neutral
"tend to verify, legitimize and reinforce the language and literacy related
experiences . . . and the cultural capital of the white (mostly male),
English-speaking middle classes . . ." with the result that "class, racial/
ethnic and gender stratifications are exacerbated." Thus, whereas literacy

is touted as a key to access, access to literacy development is limited by unequal power relations (Walsh 1991:9).

Within this framework, classrooms can be seen as sites of struggle about whose knowledge, experiences, ways of using language, literacy, and discourse practices count. Giroux (1983) argues that whenever the educational agenda is shaped by the dominant classes and the goal is to reproduce existing social relationships, there is resistance to this agenda. This resistance may take the form of overt rejection of teacher authority, refusal to learn in prescribed ways, or dropping out (McDermott 1977; Ogbu 1991); classrooms thus become battlegrounds in culture wars (Shor 1986).

Freire (1970, 1981, 1985) argues that it is only when the education of subordinated peoples directly addresses issues of power and the learners' role in the social order that it can cease to be domesticating. In this view, serving the interests of the learners cannot be separated from challenging their marginalization through both the content and processes of education. In terms of content, the more mechanical aspects of literacy acquisition must always be connected to the learners' social reality; "reading the word" and "reading the world" must go hand in hand (Freire and Macedo 1987). It is the teacher's job to investigate and re-present this reality in problematized form to the learners: Rather than solving problems for learners, the teacher poses problems and engages students in dialogue and critical reflection (a process that Freire calls *conscientization).* The classroom becomes a context in which students analyze their reality for the purpose of participating in its transformation. They address social problems by sharing and comparing experiences, analyzing root causes, and exploring strategies for change. Knowledge, rather than being transmitted from teacher to student, is collaboratively constructed, involving the transformation of traditional teacher-student roles.

Looking at the classroom through a new lens

Once we begin looking at classrooms through an ideological lens, dynamics of power and inequality show up in every aspect of classroom life, from physical setting to needs assessment, participant structures, curriculum development, lesson content, materials, instructional processes, discourse patterns, language use, and evaluation. We are forced to ask questions about the most natural-seeming practices: Where is the class located? Where does the teacher stand or sit? Who asks questions? What kinds of questions are asked? Who chooses the learning materials? How is progress evaluated? Who evaluates it?

The physical setting, for example, is an obvious metaphor for the students' status in society as well as in the classroom. When adult ESL classes take place in borrowed space, in church basements or preschool classrooms with child-size chairs, or have to move from site to site depending on what space is available, messages about students' marginalization, the lack of importance of their education, and their reduction to childlike status are clear. When the seats are arranged in rows with the teacher standing at the front of the room, his or her role as the source of knowledge and manager of interactions takes physical form. The teacher's positioning in turn shapes discourse patterns, controlling who talks and how talk is regulated. The next sections will examine some less visible and more fundamental ways in which power relationships within the classroom reflect and prepare students for those outside the classroom.

Curriculum development

The curriculum is often seen as the driving force for instructional practice, the framework within which day-to-day decisions are made. Typically, programs are mandated to provide written curricula that are to guide teachers' practice. But where do these curricula come from? On what assumptions are they based? How are they developed? Who decides their shape and content?

In the *ends-means* model, which has come to be the dominant, commonsense model of curriculum development for adult ESL, curriculum goals are formulated in terms of scientific assessment of learners' language needs in relation to societal institutions; grammar-driven curricula have increasingly been superceded by situational, survival-oriented models focusing on language skills or competencies deemed necessary to fit in or function "successfully" within particular institutions (e.g., the workplace) or in relation to a range of interactional contexts (e.g., banking, health care, or consumer relations).

Often the curriculum development process starts with experts researching and identifying the body of "knowledge" (ways of using language in particular contexts) to be covered. A salient example is the Texas Adult Performance Level Study (Northrup 1977) in which university-based researchers surveyed literacy usage in a wide variety of contexts and identified sixty-five competencies that they claimed were characteristic of successful functioning in society; a host of adult literacy/ESL curricula and texts have since been developed from it. More recently, ethnographers have begun going into the workplace and documenting the ways in which reading and writing are used on the job, developing literacy inventories, or "audits," that then inform curriculum development. Needs assessment often involves surveying institutional representatives (e.g., supervisors) about what they want learners to do as a result of classes. Content identified in this way is then organized into a sequence of topics or units broken down according to what is to be covered at each level. Within this framework, the syllabus becomes a prescription, or blueprint, for the direction of instruction (Candlin 1984); any deviations from it – spontaneous classroom discussions or issues unrelated to the "lesson" – are seen as aberrations, not counting as legitimate parts of learning.

It is no accident that this model of curriculum development is increasingly being mandated by funders – employers, governmental agencies, and private foundations – whose overriding concern is linking instruction to employability and economic self-sufficiency; funding legislation is framed in terms of terminating refugees' "dependence" on government support as quickly as possible and linking education to the particular job skills required by business and industry (Hudson Institute 1987). A recent proposal in Massachusetts, for example, would have entirely shifted adult ESL out of the Department of Education and into Employment and Training. Within this climate of concern with accountability, the specification of content, linguistic/behavioral tasks, and outcomes and performance standards has become, if anything, more detailed than before; increasingly, "positive outcomes" are measured in terms of job and job-training placements. In some cases, programs are paid retroactively on a piece-work basis according to the number of students placed, thereby forcing programs to limit enrollment to those who can be quickly and easily made job-ready and thus excluding those whose language or literacy needs are greatest.

Thus, despite the fact that it is couched in scientific terms, the ends-means approach serves as a mechanism of social control, disempowering for both students and teachers. Its underlying assumption is that learners should assimilate into preexisting structures and practices without questioning the power relations inherent in them. To the extent that objectives are framed in terms of the needs and demands of institutions rather than learners, and content is limited to knowledge necessary to function according to externally defined norms, relations of domination and subordination are reinforced. Further, the central responsibility for curriculum development lies with outside experts who determine *for* learners what is important for them to learn and how they should learn it. Even these experts' supposedly neutral and technical state-of-the-art research tools, such as the literacy audit, are in reality intensely ideological, taking place, as AFL-CIO official Tony Sarmiento (1989) argues, within a highly politicized context – that of unequal power relations between workers and management:

Do downsizing, streamlining, and changes in ownership characterize its recent past and immediate future? What are the management styles and behaviors that typify the company's relationship with its employees? How open is the information-sharing and dialogue between supervisors and hourly workers?

. . . It is within this broader context of history and relationships that workers will view a literacy audit or job task analysis. (p. 1)

Given the dominance of this ends-means approach, teachers are faced with a dilemma: Either they can impose the externally defined mandate, ignoring or suppressing student-determined needs, topics, and issues (in which case they become agents of the dominant ideology), or they can respond to student initiatives (in which case they are not doing what they are supposed to be doing and may face funding consequences). The reality is that program staff are often forced to spend long hours developing elaborate competency-based curricula that bear little resemblance to what they actually do in the classroom. Thus, they are forced to engage in a kind of charade (claiming to be doing one thing, while in fact doing something different) in order to keep their jobs. Nevertheless, although these curricula are artificial constructs whose primary purpose is to satisfy external requirements, once they have been developed, they inevitably shape day-to-day classroom practice to some extent, becoming a mechanism through which the funders' agenda permeates classroom life.

During the past two decades, North American literacy and ESL educators have developed an alternative approach to adult ESL curricula based on Freire's work (e.g., Wallerstein 1983; Faigin 1985; Barndt 1986; Auerbach and Wallerstein 1987; Auerbach 1989; Nash et al. 1989); this approach aims not to fit learners into the existing order, but to enable them to critically examine it and become active in shaping their own roles in it. This participatory approach starts with the assumption that if language/literacy instruction is to be meaningful to participants and enable them to shape their realities, it must be centered on issues of importance to them. Connecting the *word* and the *world* involves finding out what the world – the lived experience – is for participants. Are they working or on welfare? Do they have children? Are they immigrants or refugees? Do they live in public housing? Because their concerns and needs will vary depending on the answers to these questions, instructional content must to some extent be tailored to each group of students. Although there may be general conditions and concerns common to most immigrants and refugees, it is not possible to know which of these will be "hot" for any given group before interacting with them.

Although the teacher is no longer armed with predetermined lesson sequences or competencies in a participatory approach, this does not mean that he or she comes into the classroom empty-handed, waiting for issues to fall from the sky. Instead, this approach provides the teacher with procedural guidelines and tools for finding student themes, for developing language and literacy around them, and for using them to affect change outside the classroom (Barndt 1987; Auerbach 1989). The process starts with collaborative investigation of what is important to students as an integral component of instruction. Themes may be identified through formal or informal means, by consciously listening for hot issues or by presenting catalyst activities designed to elicit them. Once themes or issues from students' lived experience are identified, participants explore them through dialogue; thus, analysis of students' concerns becomes the context for language and literacy learning. Barndt and others go even further than Freire in suggesting that students should also be increasingly involved in deciding not only *what* is to be explored, but *how* to explore it: As they participate in choosing classroom processes and creating their own forms for literacy development (e.g., drawings, photos, drama, stories, music), they assume more control of the learning process. Learners can then go on to apply what they have learned in the classroom to situations outside the classroom – to work together, for example, to change some aspect of their working conditions or their involvement with their children's schooling.

In this model, the direction of the process is *from the students to the curriculum* rather than *from the curriculum to the students*. As such, the curriculum is *emergent,* arrived at through a process of investigation and exploration (Candlin 1984). As Barndt (no date) says, students discover their own knowledge, create new knowledge, and act on this knowledge. Knowledge is produced rather than received by learners. It is elicited rather than transmitted by teachers. The syllabus, in this model, becomes a retroactive account – a description of what actually happens as a result of this process – rather than an a priori blueprint or prescription; it is a *syllabus of how* rather than a *syllabus of what* (Candlin 1984). As in the ends-means approach, the content and processes rehearse learners for roles outside the classroom, but for very different kinds of roles. In this case it prepares them for proactive, critical participation rather than passive assimilation: As learners become increasingly involved in directing their own education, they practice active participation in other areas of their lives.

An example from family literacy work serves to illustrate the differences between the two approaches to curriculum development. Presenters at a TESOL Convention (Adams and Bitterlin 1988) described interviewing school personnel to ascertain problematic areas in teacher-parent communication and then drawing up an itemized list of parental behaviors deemed inappropriate by teachers; these included parents' sending children to school too early, sick, dirty, or improperly clothed and, further, their nonparticipation in conferences, failure to sign and return report cards, and attempts to tell teachers what to do. The educators then prepared lessons, including worksheets, role plays, and problem-solving activities, designed to address these concerns (Adams and Bitterlin 1988). The explicit goal was to enhance communication between parents and teachers; the implicit goal was to teach parents to conform to the school's expectations.

An activity from the classroom of a teacher with a participatory perspective (McGrail cited in Auerbach 1989:57) illustrates an alternative: In this situation, a student came to class with a flyer that she had received from her child's school. She indicated that she was perplexed by it. The flyer presented a list of things that parents should do to help their children with homework, written in very small print, with complicated syntax and vocabulary. The teacher framed the class discussion about this flyer with the following questions: "Which of these things do you already do? Which would you like to do? Which do you think are ridiculous, impossible, or not useful? What do you already do that's not listed on the flyer?" The questions catalyzed discussion of cultural differences in teachers' versus parents' roles, parents' own strengths, and further options. In this case, the topic was initiated by a student and was presented in a problematized way: Rather than aiming to get the parents to adopt or assimilate into externally defined norms, the teacher invited reflection, cultural comparison, and exploration of possible new practices, thus handing the power back to the participants and enabling them to maintain a stance of independence and choice in the learning process.

Instructional content

Whereas the previous section looked at power implications in how content is selected, this section will examine ideological issues embedded in the content itself. Within the context of the funding mandates outlined above, adult ESL curriculum content usually focuses on employment, functional survival skills, and/or citizenship. Work-oriented content often is geared, on the one hand, toward specific job-related vocabulary and literacy tasks (reading time cards or pay stubs) and, on the other, toward "appropriate" attitudes and behaviors and their concomitant language functions or competencies (learning how to call in sick, request clarification of job instructions, make small talk, follow safety regulations). Sometimes students are explicitly instructed that workers must be obedient and do what the boss asks (see examples in Auerbach and Burgess 1985:485). Often the messages are more subtle, implying, by the types of roles and workplaces depicted, that regardless of their educational background, students' only options are entry-level jobs in the service or manufacturing sectors – a discussion question in a refugee camp curriculum guide, for example, asks, "Why do refugees have to start their jobs at the bottom?" (Experiment in International Living 1983:387). Social control is exerted not just by what is taught, but by what is omitted: Students are rarely taught how to complain, file a grievance, challenge poor safety conditions, organize a union, or get a union to defend their rights (Auerbach and Burgess 1985; Tollefson 1989).

The content of survival curricula generally emphasizes "the way we do things here" – cultural information that claims to characterize norms for American life. Students are taught about tying up garbage, using deodorant, and making shopping lists. McGroaty (1985), comparing ESL texts of the early 1900s with contemporary ones, notes that where earlier texts emphasized lessons on civic responsibility, the virtues of democracy, and the benefits of paying taxes, the focus has now shifted to consumer skills – with lessons on unit pricing, shopping at sales, and layaway plans. This itself is education for a particular kind of citizenship: Students are taught to "participate in the life of the community not through the democratic process but through enlightened market behavior" (p. 22). Of course, with the recent federal legislation mandating ESL for those seeking amnesty, there has been a resurgence of the emphasis on citizenship programs, with content focusing on traditional civics topics: knowledge of government structures, American history, names of presidents, to name a few. Choices about content are often shaped by questions in the citizenship interview. Thus, the instructional content is directly tied to a gatekeeping function: Getting legal status depends on completing a certain number of hours of ESL instruction and passing a test.

In the case of survival curriculum content, the political agenda is less overt. Critics argue that erroneous assumptions about immigrants' and refugees' needs mask a hidden agenda, one of preparing learners for subordination (whether or not this is intentional). Weinstein-Shr (1991), for example, claims that refugees are already skilled survivors: "The [Southeast Asian] families we have worked with made it here despite unbelievable odds and they continue to use their survival resources to manage in difficult conditions . . . [They] have been ingenious in their strategies for dealing with problems" (p. 3). Ethnographic investigation of their actual language and literacy uses reveals that they have developed elaborate systems in which "families divide the language and literacy labor" (p. 3), enabling them to accomplish day-to-day survival tasks such as buying stamps, filling out forms, and shopping (Weinstein 1984 ; see also Klassen 1987).

Teaching survival competencies thus, according to Tollefson (1989), serves quite a different function, that of overtly promoting assimilation into the "American way" while covertly assimilating students into subservient roles. Housing lessons, for example, teach students their responsibilities as tenants, but not their rights or how to respond when landlords do not fulfill their obligations. Often the implication is that people who know what to ask landlords succeed in finding apartments (or people who know how to fill out application forms get jobs). In a social reality where refugees often live in inhuman housing conditions, pay excessive rents, and are the victims of harassment or even arson, the message that survival depends on being a "good" tenant is more than an oversight. In fact, according to Tollefson, the message that survival depends on behaving according to American norms and expectations serves an important ideological function: It promotes the myth that "refugees' ability to solve their social, psychological, physical, and economic problems is directly related to their degree of cultural assimilation" and hence, if they do not "succeed," it is their own fault (1989:57). This myth legitimizes their incorporation into the economic ladder at its bottom rungs.

Although topics in a participatory approach may appear similar (e.g., housing, citizenship, work, and so on), there are fundamental ideological differences in the ways they are actualized in the classroom. The first is that *content draws from and validates what students already know and bring to learning* rather than focusing primarily on what they do not know; this means, for example, that exploration of the new culture is contextualized in comparison with the learners' native culture. The second is that *content is presented descriptively rather than prescriptively:* It focuses on learners' lived experience rather than on idealized projections of that experience. The third is that *content is problematized:* For example, housing may be addressed in terms of housing shortages or tenants' rights, or work may be presented in terms of figuring out what to do about health and safety problems; but more importantly, it means that the way these issues are presented is open-ended without particular behaviors or solutions implied by the teacher or materials. Students examine the various complex and contradictory aspects of each issue in order to both understand it and develop their own strategies for addressing it. Finally, *language work (grammar/competencies) is contextualized in relation to issues* and taught in service of addressing them.

It is difficult to discuss these differences without repeating what I have said in the section on curriculum development since the content in a participatory approach cannot be separated from the process for determining it. The teacher may start this process by bringing in catalysts based on what he or she knows about students' concerns through prior investigation or discussion; the catalysts may take the form of photos, dialogues, drawings, or even structured grammar activities with loaded content (see Auerbach 1990). The purpose of these *codes* (Wallerstein 1983), or *tools* (Barndt 1986), is to activate discussion, elicit participants' knowledge or experience, and prompt reflection. For example, a teacher might ask the question, What made it difficult for you to come to class last week? in order to find out about issues students are dealing with outside the classroom (e.g., child care, transportation, or health problems). Based on what students say, the teacher may, for example, bring in a photo or drawing of a hospital emergency room full of waiting people. This in turn might become the basis of sharing experiences in dealing with the health care system in the United States (including issues of insurance, lack of translators, expense of medicines, and so on) and comparing it to health care in the participants' homelands.

Hemmindinger (1987) proposes two models for generating content, the first starting with cultural sharing and moving on to problem posing, the second starting with problem posing and incorporating cultural sharing later. An example of the former occurred when she discovered that one of her Hmong students was a naturopath, prompting her to elicit input about a range of Hmong medical practices from the class. This in turn led to discussions of medical practices in the dominant, North American context (e.g., having babies in the hospital), a comparison of the two sets of practices (e.g., the use of drugs versus herbal remedies), and the identification of problems in the dominant culture (e.g., following orders on prescriptions). Students then discussed a range of ways to work through these problems (transposing strategies from work and home contexts) and developed language activities related to the problems that had been raised (e.g., calling the emergency room). Finally, the students wrote and role-played dialogues about another incident involving a health care problem.

An example of the second model involved building a lesson sequence around a workplace problem that students brought to class one night: In this case, the teacher learned that most of the students worked as worm pickers and that their employer was cheating them by undercounting the worms they picked. With the class, she wrote a story about this problem (incorporating language functions that she had planned to teach), which students then acted out. The students went on to explore other related issues about the conditions of their work, discussed possible solutions to the original problem, and rewrote the story with a new ending. They decided to work with others in their community to take the farmer to small-claims court and eventually won back wages.

Materials

Materials can be seen as the most concrete physical representation of these differing perspectives on curriculum development and content, with related questions of power embedded in their selection and use. Who decides what materials should be used? On what basis are they selected? Who wrote them and for what purpose? Whose voice do they represent? How is their content related to the reality of students' lives? What are students asked to do with them? What kinds of responses are expected? Most importantly, how are the materials integrated into the rest of the curriculum?

One of the most basic commonsense assumptions about materials is that it is the teacher's job to select them. It is part of his or her professional responsibility to know what is available and appropriate for a particular group of students. Embedded in this assumption is the further assumption that once the right textbook has been chosen, the rest will fall into place: The text is seen to be the backbone of the curriculum (and in some cases, it actually *becomes* the curriculum). Often, the more that a text covers, the better it is seen to be. Publishers are only too happy to provide comprehensive series that attempt to cover every possible situation, grammar point, competency, and skill; one recent adult ESL series, for example, includes books for six levels, with three books (reading/writing, listening/speaking, and grammar) for each level. Even teachers' frequent complaints about how difficult it is to find a good textbook rest on the same assumption about the centrality of texts for curriculum development.

There are a number of ways in which this approach to material selection can be disempowering for students. First, excluding students from the selection and evaluation of materials reinforces the authority of both teacher and text. The assumption is that students do not know enough to participate in these processes; yet, they do so daily by their implicit responses – their silence, their confusion, their side discussions, their absenteeism, or, alternatively, their active engagement and enthusiastic involvement. Not to make their reactions an explicit and valued part of classroom interaction sends the message that if there are problems, they probably lie with the students: Their memories are bad, their comprehension is poor, they are not motivated, and so forth (rather than that the texts were inappropriately selected, do not correspond to students' experiences, or are boring).

Further, reliance on a single text (or group of texts) diminishes the possibility of a student-driven curriculum. The danger is that the text dictates instructional content: The goal becomes to *cover* the material rather than to *uncover* what is important to students. The direction is from the text to the students rather than the reverse. Evaluation, both subjective (in terms of students' sense of accomplishment) and objective (in terms of external measures of progress), tends to be framed in terms of "how far you get." The more comprehensive a text is, the less space there is for students to contribute their experiences and generate content.

In addition, individual text exercises often focus more on rehearsing correct forms than on generating new meanings or sharing information, opinions, and experiences, more on practicing language use for functional purposes in specific situations than on using language to create or exchange ideas. The circumscribed nature of the exercises (which leave minimal space for student contributions) precludes what Bakhtin calls true "appropriation" of the language:

[The word in language] becomes "one's own" only when the speaker populates it with his own intention, his own accent, when he appropriates the word, adapting it to his own semantic and expressive intention. Prior to this moment of appropriation, the word . . . exists in other people's mouths, in other people's contexts, serving other people's intentions: it is from there that one must take the word, and make it one's own. . . . Language is not a neutral medium that passes freely and easily into the private property of the speakers' intentions; it is populated – overpopulated – with the intentions of others. Expropriating it, forcing it to submit to one's own intentions and accents, is a difficult and complicated process. (1981:293–94)

The benign justification for the approach just described is that it is both necessary and desirable: Students cannot use language for creative and communicative purposes until they have mastered the basics (vocabulary, sentence structure, and the language of survival); further, this is what students need and want. A more critical interpretation is that discourse practices embodied in these texts promote what Fairclough (1989:75) calls "inculcation" into existing norms and social relations rather than the power that comes with using language for authentic "communication":

[Inculcation] attempts to *naturalize* partial and interested practices to facilitate the exercise and maintenance of power. Broadly speaking, inculcation is the mechanism of power holders who wish to preserve their power, while communication is the mechanism of emancipation and the struggle against domination.

It is this sense of communication – of language as a tool for struggle, for solving problems, and for taking on the challenges of a complex and hostile system – that learners themselves often mention when they talk about reasons for wanting to study ESL/literacy. Their responses go beyond survival to include issues of self-esteem, self-expression, and, significantly, power (Weinstein-Shr 1991). Latinos interviewed by Klassen (1987), for example, repeatedly used the word *defenderse* 'to defend oneself' in talking about why they need literacy. Thus, by focusing only on functional/strategic competencies in relation to particular contexts, texts may constrain learners, stopping short of allowing language to be used for creative or critical purposes.

As a teacher and a textbook writer, I certainly do not want to argue that all texts are bad or that there is no place for them in the classroom; clearly students like them and teachers need them. The issue is not whether to use them, but which ones to use and how to use them. Although this is not the place for an extensive analysis of currently popular adult ESL texts (see, for example, Auerbach and Burgess 1985; McGroaty 1985), I want to look here at how the relationship between learners, teachers, and texts might be changed so that it promotes communication in Fairclough's sense.

The starting point for text selection is ascertaining whether a text allows *space* for exploration of learners' own lived experience. Does it include provocative catalysts to elicit students' ideas, stories, knowledge (e.g., pictures of actual housing conditions, stories about workplace dilemmas)? Does it invite students' contributions and reactions? Does it problematize the representation of reality, presenting its complex and contradictory aspects in order to provide a context for the exchange of ideas and opinions? Does it invite students to compare their experiences? Does it include the voices of immigrants and refugees presenting their own accounts of the realities of everyday life? Does it invite students to think? Does it leave room for them to use language creatively in generating their own meanings? The common underlying theme of these questions is whether the text is structured to *draw out* from students rather than *put into* them.

Students themselves can be involved in this process of evaluating and selecting materials. Let me tell a story here: Recently in a tutor-training seminar, I asked tutors to respond to one of two work-related excerpts from ESL texts; one was a typical, simplified, idealized story about a day at work; the other was the following quote from an immigrant worker:

You work, you eat, you care for your children, and then you must start again to work. Part of you changes and dries up. You are not whole anymore. It is as if you are here to do what you can to be allowed to exist. (Barndt, Cristall, and Marino 1982:50)

Although most of the tutors chose to respond to the second excerpt, some argued that the first was more appropriate for their ESL students because it was simpler, more basic, and "what they need." I then invited them to do the same exercise with their students. The students overwhelmingly chose to respond to the second piece; when asked why they liked it better, they said it was "real," it was "true." Further, the tutors were surprised by the quality of the language in the students' written responses, which were significantly more sophisticated than those done in response to textbook exercises.

This story raises the point that often students respond best to materials that mirror their experiences and voices – that seem least textlike. This means that textbooks should perhaps be demoted from their status as the primary source of materials, becoming instead only one among many kinds of materials brought in as resources. Although text excerpts may continue to be used in response to particular needs that have been identified through classroom interaction (e.g., to teach a grammar point), other authentic materials (written for some purpose other than to teach language) are brought in as well. These may include excerpts from literature, autobiographical accounts of immigrant experiences, newspaper articles, and publications of student writings, as well as materials that students themselves bring in (bills, letters, and so on). The complaint that there are no good materials rapidly vanishes when one begins to look in places other than ESL catalogs. (See Auerbach 1989 for reviews of a range of such materials.)

Once materials have been selected, it is important to continue to engage students in their evaluation so that the everyday use of materials itself takes on a critical dimension. Rather than just attempting to get the students to do what the text asks, this approach suggests making the text accountable to the students. Excerpts can be measured against students' reality by asking questions such as: Does this seem real? Would this really happen? Has anything like this ever happened to you? Inviting students to critique lessons from the perspective of their experience both validates the experience and gives them a sense of authority vis-à-vis texts.

A final way that the basic orientation to materials can be changed is by involving students in their actual production. This involvement can range from using student language to create reading material (i.e., through the Language Experience Approach), to using students' issues and ideas in teacher-generated texts, to using student writing as texts, and ultimately, to going through all the steps of the production process from prewriting to publication with students. Barndt (no date) describes a number of projects in which students developed photo-stories, socio-dramas, videos, and songs that reflected their social reality (economic relationships, workplace problems, family roles, discrimination). She sees the production of these tools not just as a way to change participants' relation to materials, but, more importantly, as a concrete framework for analyzing and potentially changing their relation to the social order. Following a similar approach, Walsh (1991) worked with a group of low-literate Latino high school students who had been marginalized physically, socially, and academically in a special classroom. Through the production of a photo-novella about a teenager who was considering dropping out of school, they explored issues of discipline and discrimination, using literacy for the first time in a meaningful way for their own purposes. According to Walsh, "This process demonstrated alternative forms of knowledge production that led to a realization for many that the established discourse, meanings, relations and conditions for Latinos in the school did not necessarily have to be taken for granted" (p. 23). She reported that the students were listened to for the first time by school administration as a result of the project.

Language choice

While power dynamics enter into many other domains in ESL education (e.g., needs assessment, evaluation), there is one final question that I would like to consider here – the question of which language should be used in ESL classes. Of course, the commonsense perspective has come to be that English is the only acceptable medium of communication once ESL students enter the door of the classroom. The rationale for this view, often justified with reference to immersion research, is framed in pedagogical terms: Adult ESL students need to learn English as quickly as possible for survival reasons; the more they are exposed to English, the more quickly they will learn; as they hear and use English, they will internalize it and begin to think in English; the only way they will learn it is if they are forced to use it. This view has become almost axiomatic: Teachers devise elaborate games, signals, and penalty systems to enforce the use of English only. For example, an article in a recent issue of the *TESOL Newsletter* (June 1990) extols the virtues of *fining* students for committing "crimes" against the teacher's first language, including the crime of using their first language; the teacher told students, "This is an English-only classroom. If you speak Spanish or Cantonese or Mandarin or Vietnamese or Thai or Russian or Farsi, you pay me 25 cents. I can be rich" (Weinberg 1990:5).

It is not clear, however, that the rationale and research used to justify English-only in the classroom apply to adult ESL students: First, immersion research focuses on second language acquisition among children; second, the research clearly indicates that immersion programs are effective for learners from dominant language groups whose L1 is valued and supported both at home and in the broader society, whereas bilingual instruction is more effective for language minority students who do not fit this profile (Cummins 1981); finally, there is evidence that strong L1 literacy and schooling are key factors in successful L2 acquisition (Cummins 1981; Robson 1981). A growing percentage of students in adult ESL classes come from precisely the groups shown to benefit most from a bilingual approach – subordinated minority language groups and those with limited L1 literacy/schooling backgrounds. Further, what little research has been done concerning the use of L1 as a bridge to L2 for this population of adult ESL students indicates that the bilingual model may be more appropriate than the immersion model (Burtoff 1985; Rivera 1988). Since L1 literacy/schooling seems to be among the strongest determinants of progress in ESL classes (Robson 1981; Klassen 1987), adult educators are increasingly advocating L1 literacy instruction as a basis for ESL acquisition for nonliterate immigrants and refugees and bilingual ESL instruction on beginning levels for others (Rivera 1988). Once again, it seems that a commonsense practice (in this case, exclusive use of English) is based on questionable assumptions, justified in pseudoscientific terms and uncritically accepted as universally applicable.

What are the effects of enforcing the use of English-only in the ESL classroom? For beginning ESL students with little L1 literacy background, the effect may be to completely preclude participation and progress. Bilingual tutors working with such students in a University of Massachusetts project commonly reported that the learners told them that they had no idea what was going on in their classes ("I am always lost." "I waste my time.") (Auerbach 1990). In fact, without first language literacy, Klassen (1987) reports that ESL classes were virtually inaccessible to the low-literate Latinos in Toronto. Typically, students in this situation respond by becoming completely silenced, making virtually no progress, and often dropping out. At the same time, monolingual teachers report enormous frustration at their inability to make breakthroughs and at being forced to reduce lesson content to the most elementary, childlike uses of language. Whether or not students drop out, the result of a monolingual approach is often that they suffer severe consequences in terms of self-esteem and self-confidence; powerlessness is reinforced either because learners are de facto physically excluded from the classroom or because their knowledge, life experience, and language resources are excluded from classroom discourse.

When the L1 is used (either for initial literacy instruction or as a bridge to ESL), teachers report quite different results. Hemmindinger (1987) claims that not only is language shock alleviated by use of the L1, but progress in ESL is faster; the bilingual classroom allows for the transition from L1 to L2 in a safe setting. Further, if the goal is to foster language as a tool for critical thinking, for making sense of and acting on issues of importance in one's life (with content deriving from learners' reality), then use of the L1 may be critical for identifying those issues; it may facilitate more meaningful interaction in the L2, becoming one tool among many in the process of constructing meaning. Even beyond the beginning levels, use of the L1 can be seen as a resource rather than an obstacle. Collingham (1988) lists a range of ways the L1 can be used in teaching the L2, including: to negotiate the syllabus, to develop ideas as a precursor to expressing them in the L2, to reduce inhibitions or affective blocks to L2 production, to elicit language and discourse strategies for particular situations, to provide explanations of grammar and language functions, to teach vocabulary, and to keep records.

Teachers from Centro Presente, an ESL program for Central Americans in Boston, report that the selective use of Spanish helps to increase the level of trust and student motivation; their students often say that they have dropped out of English-only ESL classes because they felt intimidated or lost. Centro teachers use Spanish to monitor comprehension, to give instructions, to talk about metacognitive aspects of language acquisition, to elicit issues from students, to make comparisons between the two languages, to aid in pronunciation (by writing English words phonetically in Spanish), and most importantly, to create a positive atmosphere, allowing for cooperation and peer teaching. Students often say, "I can't say this in English, but I really want to say it"; once ideas have been expressed in Spanish, the group can help the learner express them in English. Centro teachers argue that since students do not just start by thinking in the L2, allowing for the exploration of ideas in the L1 supports a gradual, developmental process in which use of the L1 drops off naturally as it becomes less necessary. Even in multilingual classes, students can use the L1 for peer teaching, which can then become a basis for peer teaching via the medium of English.

Others similarly have found pedagogical benefits to providing the option of L1 use. Strohmeyer and McGrail (1988) found that allowing for the exploration of ideas in the L1 served to enhance students' ESL writing. When they invited students to decide for themselves which language to use for a photography/writing project, some of the more advanced ESL students chose to write first in Spanish and then went on to write much more developed pieces in English. Shamash (1990) describes a process of teaching ESL that might be considered heretical by some: Students can choose to write in their first language, creating texts that are truly meaningful since they reflect the learners' experiences; these texts are then translated with the help of bilingual tutors or learners and become the bridge into English.

Despite the fact that use or prohibition of the L1 is often framed in purely pedagogical terms, clearly it is also an ideological issue. Ironically, often the very people who argue vehemently against the English-Only movement on a societal level insist on the exclusive use of English at the classroom level. My point here is that they are two sides of the same coin: Insistence on English in the classroom may result in slower acquisition of English, a focus on childlike and disempowering approaches to language instruction, and ultimately a replication of relations of inequality outside the classroom, reproducing a stratum of people who can do only the least skilled and least language/literacy-dependent jobs (Skutnabb-Kangas 1979; Spener 1988). As Collingham (1988) says:

To treat adult learners as if they know nothing of language is to accept the imbalance of power and so ultimately to collude with institutional racism; to adopt a bilingual approach and to value the knowledge that learners already have is to begin to challenge that unequal power relationship and, one hopes, thereby enable learners to acquire the skills and confidence they need to claim back more power for themselves in the world beyond the classroom. (p. 85)

Thus, central to the dynamics of language usage is the question of choice, which in turn reflects broader issues of power: Who gets to decide and enforce classroom rules for language use? Clearly, if the teacher unilaterally determines and enforces language-use rules, differential power relations are perpetuated. Even when the teacher sees the benefits of L1 usage but students are divided on the issue, it is important to involve students in determining classroom guidelines. It is not unusual for L1 use to become a source of classroom tension, with some students feeling that it is a waste of time (or exclusionary, in multilingual classes), and others seeing it as a necessary support. Central to acquiring the skills and confidence for claiming more power outside the classroom is a shift of power inside the classroom. Thus, rather than teachers making informed decisions (either for or against use of the L1) on the basis of pedagogical criteria, the issue of language choice must be posed back to students for reflection and dialogue. As such, this issue itself can become content for language and literacy work: Students can discuss the advantages and disadvantages of L1 versus L2 use and the functions of each in different contexts, and can establish their own rules for the classroom, deciding when it is and is not productive to use the L1. Certainly, teachers can contribute their own knowledge and opinions in this exchange, but what is important is a shift toward shared authority.

Ultimately, this process for making decisions in the classroom is more important than the outcome – not because it is a neat mechanism for classroom management, but because it models a way of addressing problems and shifting power that can be extended more broadly. The tools that students develop for thinking critically, exploring alternatives, and making choices prepare them for addressing the issues that they confront in everyday life. The same process can be applied with any other issue of classroom dynamics and learning: If there are attendance problems, or if students want traditional grammar-based lessons, involving them in the exploration of underlying issues fosters critical thinking and a sense of control over their own learning. This, in turn, becomes a kind of rehearsal for and model of the process of changing power relations outside the classroom.

Classrooms without walls

The essence of my argument until now has been that issues of power are embedded in both the content and the processes of ESL pedagogy: In order to challenge existing relations of inequality outside the classroom, curriculum content must include explicit analysis of the social context, and students must be invited to participate in making pedagogical choices inside the classroom. Some adult educators, however, have gone a step further, arguing that it is not enough to rehearse for changing social roles through classroom-based changes; rather, transformations in relations must extend beyond traditional classroom boundaries to include learner participation in program administration and decision making.

Curriculum specialists from the International Ladies Garment Workers' Union's (ILGWU) Worker Family Education Program, for example, talk about their program in terms of "classrooms without walls," in which students are involved in many interrelated learning contexts, from union activities, to workplace experiences, to a student council (La Mar 1991). In the ILGWU program, students have become active participants in making decisions about class and program activities, curriculum, and evaluations and are currently exploring the possibilities for extending this participation to hiring and program management. They organized themselves against a much-hated standardized test (about which teachers had also complained, but had done little to change); the student council was able to convince program coordinators to create and implement an alternative assessment and intake procedure that is administered along with the other test. They have formed a curriculum committee that developed a curriculum guide to the ESL classes offered by the program; they have participated in teacher hiring. Student workers have begun training other workers in their rights. Most important, they regularly practice democracy as they campaign for student council offices, elect delegates, run meetings, debate issues, establish committees, organize events and projects, and evaluate program activities. All of these forms of participation are seen as integral aspects of their overall learning experience, contexts for language acquisition, and ultimately, steps toward redefining their roles as workers in some of the lowest paying, most marginalized positions in the U.S. labor force.

Getting from here to there

What is the reality for adult ESL teachers who want to begin to make some of the changes discussed in this chapter? On the one hand, the participatory approach puts a heavy burden on practitioners, demanding a level of critical inquiry, creativity, and productivity that is beyond that required with a text-based or predetermined curriculum. Teachers must identify issues, create materials, and constantly reinvent the curriculum. On the other hand, they typically work long hours, with minimal pay and no benefits, often patching together several part-time jobs, and they rarely have job security. There are few opportunities for professional development, and those that do exist rarely focus on participatory approaches to teaching. Although the burden for change is on practitioners, there is little support for them to make changes; like their students, they are disempowered and marginalized at the lowest ranks of their profession.

Perhaps the only way to address this dilemma is by applying the same problem-posing model to the work of ESL educators that is advocated here for work with students. This model rests on two fundamental concepts: that of critical social analysis and that of collective action for change. Applied to practitioners' work, this means that reflecting on classroom-based practices and becoming aware of their implicit messages about power and social relations can be a starting point for changes. It means asking questions such as: Why are ESL teachers so marginalized? What is it that funders are asking with their mandates for job placements and functional and competency-based curricula? What is the relationship between students' disempowerment and practitioners' disempowerment? (See Auerbach 1991 for a fuller discussion of these issues.)

Beyond the level of building critical understanding, however, it also means teachers and students working together for better conditions, more autonomy in curriculum development, and so on. Ironically, to the extent that practitioners give up the "power" to unilaterally make pedagogical choices and share these choices with students, they gain the power to implement changes. Just as the ILGWU students were successful in getting rid of a mandated test when teachers had failed to do so, the combined strength of students and teachers can begin to address issues of inequality that both groups face. Just as collective action is a tool for students in dealing with problems in their workplaces, it is a tool for teachers in their workplaces. These actions may range from site-based collaborations to citywide organizing. Some centers, for example, have weekly teacher-sharing meetings in which practitioners share materials and ways of approaching classroom issues; others have developed center-wide files of materials and resources that teachers have used to address the particular themes of the students in their community so that teachers don't always have to generate new materials as concerns come up; in Boston, part-time adult literacy teachers have begun organizing for union membership.

Finally, individual actions and changes must be seen in the context of a larger struggle between perspectives; this means recognizing that change is a long process that may start with rearranging seats, using grammar exercises to find out about housing problems, initiating dialogue journals, or debating the role of the first language in the classroom. Each of these individual, incremental changes contributes to a broader process of re-thinking pedagogy and shifting power relations.

References

Adams, M., and G. Bitterlin. 1988. Curriculum materials for helping parents communicate with personnel at children's schools. Presentation at 22nd Annual TESOL Convention, Chicago.

Anyon, J. 1980. Social class and the hidden curriculum of work. *Journal of Education* 162(1): 67–92.

Auerbach, E. (Ed.). 1989. Book notices: Non-traditional materials for adult ESL. *TESOL Quarterly* 23(2): 321–35.

1990. *Making meaning, making change: A guide to participatory curriculum development for adult ESL and family literacy.* Boston: University of Massachusetts.

1991. Politics, pedagogy and professionalism: Challenging marginalization in ESL. *College ESL* 1(1): 1–9. .

Auerbach, E., and D. Burgess. 1985. The hidden curriculum of survival ESL. *TESOL Quarterly* 19(3): 475–95.

Auerbach, E., and N. Wallerstein. 1987. *ESL for action: Problem-posing at work*. Reading, Mass.: Addison-Wesley.

Bakhtin, M. 1981. *The dialogic imagination*. Austin: University of Texas.

Barndt, D. 1986. *English at work: A tool kit for teachers*. North York, Ontario: CORE Foundation.

1987. *Themes and tools for ESL: How to choose them and use them*. Toronto: Ministry of Citizenship.

no date. *Just getting there: Creating visual tools for collective analysis*. Toronto: Participatory Research Group.

Barndt, D., F. Cristall, and d. marino. 1982. *Getting there: Producing photostories with immigrant women*. Toronto: Between the Lines.

Burtoff, M. 1985. *Haitian Creole literacy evaluation study. Final Report*. Washington, D.C.: Center for Applied Linguistics.

Candlin, C. 1984. Syllabus design as a critical process. In C. J. Brumfit (Ed.), *General English syllabus design*. Oxford: Pergamon Press.

Collingham, M. 1988. Making use of students' linguistic resources. In S. Nicholls and E. Hoadley-Maidment (Eds.), *Current issues in teaching English as a second language to adults* (pp. 81–85). London: Edward Arnold.

Cummings, R., and S. Gregory. 1984. The politics of teaching English as a second language. Colloquium at the 18th Annual TESOL Convention, Houston, Tex.

Cummins, J. 1981. The role of primary language development in promoting educational success for language minority students. In *Schooling and language minority students: A theoretical framework*. California State Department of Education. Los Angeles: California State University.

Experiment in International Living. 1983. *Opening lines: A competency-based curriculum in English as a second language*. Brattleboro, Vt.: The Experiment in International Living.

Faigin, S. 1985. Basic ESL literacy from a Freirean perspective: A curriculum unit for farmworker education. M. Ed. thesis, University of British Columbia, Vancouver.

Fairclough, N. 1989. *Language and power*. London: Longman.

Freire, P. 1970. *Pedagogy of the oppressed*. New York: Seabury Press.

1981. *Education for critical consciousness*. New York: Continuum.

1985. *The politics of education: Culture, power and liberation*. South Hadley, Mass.: Bergin-Garvey.

Freire, P., and D. Macedo. 1987. *Literacy: Reading the word and the world*. South Hadley, Mass.: Bergin-Garvey.

Giroux, H. 1983. *Theory and resistance in education: A pedagogy for the opposition*. South Hadley, Mass.: Bergin-Garvey.

Hemmindinger, A. 1987. Two models for using problem-posing and cultural sharing in teaching the Hmong English as a second language and first language literacy. M.A. thesis, St. Francis Xavier University, Antigonish, Nova Scotia.

Hudson Institute. 1987. *Workforce 2000*. Monograph. Boston: Towers Perrin.

Klassen, C. 1987. Language and literacy learning: The adult immigrant's account. M.A. thesis, University of Toronto.

La Mar, M. 1991. ILGWU Worker Family Education Program. Presentation at 25th Annual TESOL Convention, New York.

McDermott, R. P. 1977. The cultural context of learning to read. In S. F. Wanat (Ed.), *Issues in evaluating reading* (pp. 10–18). Washington, D.C.: Center for Applied Linguistics.

McGroaty, M. 1985. Images of the learner in English language texts for adults: From citizen to consumer. *Issues in Education* 3(1): 13–30.

Nash, A., A. Cason, M. Rhum, L. McGrail, and R. Gomez-Sanford. 1989. *Talking shop: A curriculum sourcebook for participatory adult ESL*. Boston: University of Massachusetts.

Northrup, N. 1977. *The adult performance level study*. Austin: University of Texas.

Oakes, J. 1985. *Keeping track: How schools structure inequality*. New Haven: Yale University Press.

Ogbu, J. 1991. Cultural diversity and school experience. In C. Walsh (Ed.), *Literacy as praxis: Culture, language, and pedagogy* (pp. 25–50). Norwood, N.J.: Ablex.

Pennycook, A. 1989. The concept of method, interested knowledge, and the politics of language teaching. *TESOL Quarterly* 23(4): 589–618.

Quinn, D. 1986. Using Freirean methods in educating the technical elite. Paper presented at the 20th Annual TESOL Convention, Anaheim, Calif.

Rivera, K. 1988. Not "either/or" but "and": Literacy for non-English speakers. *Focus on Basics* 1(3/4): 1–3.

Robson, B. 1981. *Alternatives in ESL and literacy: Ban Vinai*. Asia Foundation Final Report. Arlington, Va.: Center for Applied Linguistics.

Sarmiento, A. 1989. Workplace literacy and workplace politics. *Work America* 6(9): 1–2.

Shamash, Y. 1990. Learning in translation: Beyond language experience in ESL. *Voices* 2(2): 71–75.

Shor, I. 1986. *Culture wars: School and society in the conservative restoration, 1969–1984*. Boston: Routledge and Kegan Paul.

Skutnabb-Kangas, T. 1979. *Language in the process of cultural assimilation and structural incorporation of linguistic minorities*. Rosslyn, Va.: National Clearinghouse for Bilingual Education.

Spener, D. 1988. Transitional bilingual education and the socialization of immigrants. *Harvard Educational Review* 58(2): 133–53.

Street, B. 1984. *Literacy in theory and practice*. Cambridge: Cambridge University Press.

Strohmeyer, B., and L. McGrail. 1988. *On FOCUS: Photographs and writings by students*. Boston, Mass.: El Centro del Cardenal.

Tollefson, J. 1989. *Alien winds: The reeducation of America's Indochinese refugees*. New York: Praeger.

Wallerstein, N. 1983. *Language and culture in conflict: Problem-posing in the ESL classroom*. Reading, Mass.: Addison-Wesley.

Walsh, C. 1991. Engaging students in their own learning: Literacy, language and knowledge production with bilingual communities. Paper presented at Biliteracy: Theory and Practice Colloquium. Washington, D.C.: National Clearinghouse on Literacy Education.

Weinberg, J. 1990. Pennies from He Vinh. *TESOL Newsletter* 24(23): 5.
Weinstein, G. 1984. Literacy and second language acquisition: Issues and perspectives. *TESOL Quarterly* 18(3): 471–84.
Weinstein-Shr, G. 1991. Literacy and second language learners: A family agenda. Paper presented at Biliteracy: Theory and Practice Colloquium. Washington, D.C.: National Clearinghouse on Literacy Education.

2 English in the world/The world in English

Alastair Pennycook

Various right-wing intellectuals in the United States have recently been arguing that we are now witnessing the "end of history," that the rapid reorientations in Eastern Europe represent a final victory for the West and for capitalist democracy. Although such claims are clearly naive, it is nevertheless evident that we are passing through a time in which many of the distinctions that have helped us to divide and explain the world appear to be crumbling. The preeminent symbol of this process was perhaps the pulling down of the Berlin Wall, bringing with it a series of implications both for the erosion of the communist/capitalist divide and for the possibilities of a restructuring of Europe. Large-scale structures, such as the Soviet Union and its sphere of influence, are disintegrating, and as they do so, many new and local concerns are coming to the fore. In Canada, the failure to find an agreement between the federal and provincial governments in the Meech Lake Accord, for example, has raised many questions about provincial concerns, the status of Quebec, women's issues, and the rights of Aboriginal people within the larger construct of a nation state.

"Think globally, act locally" we are urged by environmentalist groups, suggesting a view of the world that bypasses the state and sees global problems as solvable by local, individual action. At the same time as these moves towards decentralization and fragmentation are occurring, however, new large-scale structures are developing, most notably with the reshaping of Europe, the growth of Southeast Asia as an economic and political force, and the complex challenges posed by the Muslim world. Distinctions such as that between 'East' and 'West' are shifting as global communications redefine cultural and political relations and as countries such as Japan start to straddle the divide. As Clifford (1988) has pointed out, the West refers to a technological, economic, and political force that no longer radiates from a discrete geographical or cultural centre, but rather is disseminated in a diversity of forms from multiple centres (including Japan, Australia, the now former Soviet Union, and China).

These changes are difficult to comprehend, not just because of the rapidity with which they have been happening or because of their scale,

34

but because many have challenged the premises according to which we have understood the world. And as I watch these shifts and changes – the turmoil of the world towards the end of the twentieth century – I am struck by the fact that English seems to be bound up in it all. Turn on the television news, and everywhere there will be something going on in English: signs and placards in English at a demonstration for Estonian independence or for political change in China, an interview with King Hussein of Jordan in English, a speech by Nelson Mandela in English to a packed stadium in Soweto. With the recent changes in Eastern Europe, there has been a rush to learn English, and such organizations as the British Council are scrambling to secure that market. Meanwhile, the private English language school business in Japan is now worth several billion dollars.

Just as I am both fascinated and troubled by these global changes, intrigued on the one hand by the possibilities brought about by these rapid shifts in international relations and our understanding of global order, but disturbed on the other by the implications of the continued power of international capitalism and "free world" ideology for the current massive global inequalities, poverty, starvation, exploitation, and pollution, so I am concerned by the relationship of English to all these changes. What I would like to explore here, then, is the *worldliness* (cf. Said 1983) of English. I want to maintain the ambiguity of this term – worldliness in the sense of being in the world and worldliness in the sense of being global – and to argue that English is inextricably bound up with the world: English is in the world and the world is in English. Following Said's (1983:35) question as to whether there is a way to deal fairly with a text without either on the one hand reducing it to its worldly circumstances or on the other leaving it as a hermetic textual cosmos, I want to ask how we can understand the relationship between the English language and its position in the world in such a way that neither reduces it to a simple correspondence with its worldly circumstances nor refuses this relationship by considering language to be a hermetic structural system unconnected to social, cultural, and political concerns.

This chapter, therefore, will seek to draw relations between global inequalities and the English language. I will also be trying to work out ways of thinking about this relationship that avoid the pitfalls of structuralist determinism. I think it is of great importance in looking at questions of language, power, and inequality that we examine very carefully the critical frameworks we employ. In the next sections I shall review the predominant paradigm of writing on English as an International Language (EIL) before discussing more critical work that has raised numerous questions about the global spread of English. This will be followed by a discussion of ways of understanding the world and language before returning to a discussion of how we can conceptualize the question of the world being in English, and also of how opposition to the power of English and Western discourses can be formed.

The predominant paradigm

Otto Jespersen ([1938] 1968) estimated speakers of English to have numbered 4 million in 1500, 6 million in 1600, 8.5 million in 1700, between 20 and 40 million in 1800, and between 116 and 123 million in 1900. As we approach the end of the twentieth century, the number of speakers of English appears to have increased almost tenfold since 1900. Today, rough agreement can be found on figures that put the total number of speakers of English at between 700 million and 1 billion. This figure can be divided into three roughly equal groups: native speakers of English, speakers of English as a second (or intranational) language, and speakers of English as a foreign (or international) language. It is this last group that is the hardest to estimate but clearly the fastest-growing section of world speakers of English. Beyond these crude figures, a measure of the extent of the spread of English can be found by its varying uses around the world. For some time now, there has been circulating a range of descriptions of and statistics on the use of English, which have now become enshrined in the *Cambridge Encyclopedia of Language*:

English is used as an official or semi-official language in over 60 countries, and has a prominent place in a further 20. It is either dominant or well established in all six continents. It is the main language of books, newspapers, airports and air-traffic control, international business and academic conferences, science, technology, medicine, diplomacy, sports, international competitions, pop music, and advertising. Over two-thirds of the world's scientists write in English. Three quarters of the world's mail is written in English. Of all the information in the world's electronic retrieval systems, 80% is stored in English. English radio programmes are received by over 150 million in 120 countries. Over 50 million children study English as an additional language at primary level; over 80 million study it at secondary level (these figures exclude China). In any one year, the British Council helps a quarter of a million foreign students to learn English, in various parts of the world. In the USA alone, 337,000 foreign students were registered in 1983. (Crystal 1987:358)

There also seems to be fairly broad agreement on the reasons for and the implications of this spread. Although perhaps not all would agree with Hindmarsh's (1978) bland optimism that "the world has opted for English, and the world knows what it wants, what will satisfy its needs" (p. 42), this view is nevertheless not too distant from the predominant view. Although few today would overtly cling to the common nineteenth-century arguments that England and the English language were superior and thus intrinsically worthy of their growing preeminence, the spread of

English is today commonly justified by recourse to a functionalist perspective, which stresses choice and the usefulness of English, and suggests that the global spread of English is natural (although its spread was initiated by colonialism, since then it has been an accidental by-product of global forces), neutral (unlike other, local languages, English is unconnected to cultural and political issues), and beneficial (people can only benefit by gaining access to English and the world it opens up). Platt, Weber, and Ho (1984), for example, introducing the question of the "new Englishes," deal with the spread of English thus: "Many of the New Nations which were once British colonies have realised the importance of English not only as a language of commerce, science and technology but also as an international language of communication" (p. 1). Similarly, Kachru (1986) argues that "English does have one clear advantage, attitudinally and linguistically: it has acquired a *neutrality* in a linguistic context where native languages, dialects, and styles sometimes have acquired undesirable connotations. . . . It was originally the foreign (alien) ruler's language, but that drawback is often overshadowed by what it can do for its users. True, English is associated with a small and elite group; but it is in their role that the *neutrality* of a language becomes vital" (pp. 8–9). He goes on to suggest that "whatever the reasons for the earlier spread of English, we should now consider it a positive development in the twentieth-century world context" (p. 51).

The main issue of debate is whether efforts should be made to maintain a central standard of English or whether the different varieties of English should be acknowledged as legitimate forms in their own right. The popular view, according to Crystal (1988), is that "while all mother-tongue speakers inevitably feel a modicum of pride (and relief) that it is their language which is succeeding, there is also an element of concern, as they see what happens to the language as it spreads around the world. . . . Changes are perceived as instances of deterioration in standards" (p. 10). Mazrui (1975) sums up this attitude: "In spite of the phenomenal spread of the language, the British at home seem to look on it at best as an amusing phenomenon, and at worst as something which is tending to pollute and corrupt the language" (p. 75). The two ideologies – one or multiple standards – can be clearly seen in the title change of the leading journal on English as a world language: When its editorialship moved from W. R. Lee in Britain to Braj Kachru and Larry Smith in the United States, its title also changed from *World Language English* to *World Englishes*. In academic circles, the two leading figures in this debate have been Kachru (e.g., 1985) and Quirk (e.g., 1985), the former arguing, for example, that "native speakers of this language seem to have lost the exclusive prerogative to control its standardization" (p. 30), and the latter maintaining, for example, that "the existence of standards . . . is an endemic feature of our mortal condition and that people feel alienated and disorientated if a standard seems to be missing in any of these areas" (pp. 5–6).

Apart from some work on the sociological and social psychological implications of the spread of English (see Fishman, Cooper, and Rosenbaum 1977), which has also suggested that English is a neutral tool of international communication, the principal focus of work on EIL has been on questions of standards or on descriptions of varieties of English. The key issues, then, as represented in Kachru's important edited volume, *The Other Tongue: English Across Cultures,* are questions of models, standards, and intelligibility (e.g., Kachru 1982a, 1982b; Nelson 1982), and descriptions of the new forms of English: Nigerian English (Bamgbose 1982), Kenyan English (Zuengler 1982), Singapore English (Richards 1982), and so on.

The view that the spread of English is natural, neutral, and beneficial also seems to hold sway for many people more directly involved in English language teaching. Naysmith (1987) suggests that there is a "cosy, rather self-satisfied assumption prevalent at successive national and international conferences that ELT [English Language Teaching] is somehow a 'good' thing, a positive force by its very nature in the search for international peace and understanding" (p. 3). With the extent of the debate on the role of English in the world being between a conservative view on standards and a more liberal pluralist concept of variety, and with the primary concerns being those of intelligibility and description, most people in English language teaching have been poorly served by academic work that fails to address a far more diverse range of questions that might encourage a reassessment of our role as teachers of English in the world. It is to some of the critical work that has sought to address these issues that I shall turn in the next section.

Critical views on English in the world

What I think is sorely lacking from the predominant paradigm of investigation into English as an international language is a broad range of social, historical, cultural, and political relationships. There is a failure to problematize the notion of choice and an assumption that individuals and countries are somehow free of economic, political, and ideological constraints; there is a lack of historical analysis that would raise many more questions about the supposed naturalness of the spread of English during both the colonial and neo-colonial eras; there is a view of language that suggests that it can be free of cultural and political influences and therefore neutral; and there is an adherence to positivist and structuralist paradigms of analysis, with their emphasis on description and objectivity.

As I have argued elsewhere (1989a, 1990b), this divorce of language from broader questions has had major implications for teaching practice and research. A similar criticism has been leveled at the positivistic approach to language planning. Luke, McHoul, and Mey (1990) suggest that even in this highly political domain of applied linguistics, a technical discourse of norms and treatment was adopted from structural-functionalist sociology, thus allowing language planners to overlook the immensely political nature of their work. Many language planners, assuming their task to be an ideologically neutral one entailing the description and formalization of language(s) (corpus planning) and the analysis and prescription of the sociocultural statuses and uses of language(s) (status planning), embraced the "presupposition that the linear application of positivist social science could transform problematic, value-laden cultural questions into simply matters of technical efficiency" (p. 25).

Similar shortcomings can be found in much educational theory, where, as Giroux (1983) suggests, the predominant "culture of positivism" allowed for analysis only of questions of efficiency in learning and teaching, and not of questions such as the extent to which "schools acted as agents of social and cultural reproduction in a society marked by significant inequities in wealth, power, and privilege" (p. 170). English language teachers, therefore, have been poorly served by the limited analysis of EIL provided by mainstream applied linguistics. There has been little opportunity to speculate on questions other than structural varieties of English. As Phillipson (1988) suggests, the "professional training of ELT people concentrates on linguistics, psychology and education in a restricted sense. It pays little attention to international relations, development studies, theories of culture or intercultural contact, or the politics or sociology of language or education" (p. 348). Before going on in the next section to explore issues in international relations, development, international communication, and education, I shall turn in this section to critical analyses of English in the world.

Cooke (1988) has described English as a Trojan horse, arguing that it is a language of imperialism and of particular class interests. Both he and Judd (1983) draw attention to the moral and political implications of English teaching around the globe in terms of the threat it poses to indigenous languages and the role it plays as a gatekeeper to better jobs in many societies. First of all, then, English poses a threat to other languages. This is what Day (1980, 1985) has called linguistic genocide. In his study of the gradual replacement of Chamorro in Guam and the North Marianas, Day (1985) concludes pessimistically that "as long as the Marianas remain under the control of the United States, the English language will continue to replace Chamorro until there are no native speakers left. This has been American policy and practice elsewhere, and there is no reason to believe that Guam and the North Marianas will be an exception" (p. 180). Although this may of course seem to be an extreme case, we should nevertheless acknowledge the widespread threat that English presents. If it is not posing such a threat to first languages, as a universal second language it is constantly replacing other languages in daily use and school curricula. In bilingual or multilingual societies, for example, the prevalence of English can easily lead to the disregarding of one or more other languages.

The second major issue raised here is the extent to which English functions as a gatekeeper to positions of prestige in society. With English taking up such an important position in many educational systems around the world, it has become one of the most powerful means of inclusion into or exclusion from further education, employment, or social positions. In many countries, particularly former colonies of Britain, small English-speaking elites have continued the same policies of the former colonizers, using access to English language education as a crucial distributor of social prestige and wealth. Ngugi (1985) describes his experiences in Kenya, where not only was his native language proscribed with humiliating punishments (similar punishments and proscriptions were also the norm in schools for Canada's Aboriginal peoples) but English became "*the* main determinant of a child's progress up the ladder of formal education" (p. 115):

[N]obody could go on to wear the undergraduate red gown, no matter how brilliantly they had performed in all the papers in all other subjects, unless they had a *credit* (not even a simple pass!) in English. Thus the most coveted place in the pyramid and in the system was only available to holders of an English-language credit card. English was the official vehicle and the magic formula to colonial elitedom. (ibid., 115)

Tollefson's (1986) study of leftist opposition to English in the Philipines gives further evidence of these connections between English and the social and economic power of elites. Whereas many studies of English language use in the Philippines have concentrated on questions such as integrative or instrumental motivation, leftist policies on language suggest a different orientation in the support for English or Pilipino. The increased emphasis on English during the martial law restrictions from 1972 to 1983, Tollefson argues, underlined the degree to which English plays a major role in "creating and maintaining social divisions that serve an economy dominated by a small Philippine elite, and foreign economic interests" (p. 186). What emerges here is the clear suggestion that we cannot reduce questions of language to such social psychological notions as instrumental and integrative motivation, but must account for the extent to which language is embedded in social, economic, and political struggles. Therefore in arguing against the standard interpretation of the language situation in the Philippines, which tends to ascribe instrumental value to English and to see the struggle to maintain Pilipino as a sign of its symbolic and integrative role, Tollefson makes it clear that "consistent leftist opposition to English in the Philippines should not be viewed as an effort to adopt Pilipino as a symbol of national unity and identity, but rather as part of a program to change the distribution of political power and material wealth" (p. 186).

The extent to which English is involved in the political, educational, social, and economic life of a country is clearly a result of both the historical legacy of colonialism and of the varying success of countries since independence in warding off the threats of neo-colonialism. The different roles of English and Swahili in Kenya and Tanzania, for example, need to be seen with respect to both their colonial pasts and the different educational and development policies in the two countries (Zuengler 1985). In Tanzania, Swahili has become widely used as the national and official language due in no small part to Nyerere's insistence on "education for self-reliance," a policy that emphasized the need for each stage of schooling to be complete in itself and to prepare Tanzanians to participate in the socialist development of the country. In Kenya, by contrast, although Swahili is also the official national language, English remains the dominant language of Kenya's economic and legal spheres, as it is the dominant language of much schooling, especially in Nairobi, within an educational system that has sought more to prepare an elite few for higher education than to educate a citizenry capable of maintaining a policy of socialist self-reliance.

If English thus operates as a major means by which social, political, and economic inequalities are maintained within many countries, it also plays a significant role as a gatekeeper for movement between countries, especially for refugees hoping to move to the English-speaking countries. In his extensive studies of the English language programmes in the Southeast Asian refugee processing centers, Tollefson (1988, 1989) has suggested that they "continue to limit refugees' improvement in English language proficiency, capacity for cultural adaptation, and preemployment skills, thereby contributing to the covert goal of ensuring that most refugees will only be able to compete effectively for minimum-wage employment" (1988:39). These programmes then, although ostensibly providing immigrants with English language education to prepare them for their immigration to the United States, serve as centres for the preparation of a workforce to suit the U.S. economy. They are constantly oriented towards the Americanization of immigrants, a process that assumes that American society has little or nothing to learn from immigrants' cultures and that "immigrants' primary civic responsibility is to transform themselves by adopting that society's dominant values, attitudes, and behaviors" (1989:58).

The central belief here is that the cultures of immigrant peoples are the principal hindrance to their future prospects in North America, and that the American ideologies of individualism, self-sufficiency, and hard work as a guarantor of success need to be inculcated in these future citizens of the United States before their arrival: "Today's refugee program assumes that there is a unified American culture and character; that the refugees' cultures and characters are the source of their social, psychological, and economic problems; and that the purpose of the program therefore is reeducation: to teach the refugees to give up their old ways of thinking, believing, and behaving" (1989:59–60). This discussion starts to raise questions not only about the connections between English in the world and social and economic power but also about the relationship between English and various cultural forms.

Ndebele (1987:4) suggests that "the spread of English went parallel with the spread of the culture of international business and technological standardization." Later in this paper, I shall explore in more detail the links between language, culture, and discourse – the extent to which the world is in English rather than just English being in the world – but at this juncture I shall merely address the question, similar to the ones already discussed with reference to social, economic, and political power, of the *parallel* spread of English and various forms of culture and knowledge. Most important in this respect is the dominance of English in the domains of business, popular culture, and international academic relations. As Flaitz (1988) has shown, it is through popular music that English is making a major incursion into French culture. As this study also shows, there is a deep split between the attitudes of various members of the French elite, with their constant attempts to lessen the effect of English on the French language, and those of a broader section of the population, who welcome the conjunction of popular culture and English. As Flaitz (1988:201) points out, this study clearly refutes claims such as Fishman's that English is not "ideologically encumbered."

In international academic relations, the predominance of English has profound consequences. A large proportion of textbooks in the world are published in English and designed either for the internal English-speaking market (United Kingdom, United States, Australia, and so forth) or for an international market. In both cases, students around the world are not only obliged to reach a high level of competence in English to pursue their studies, but they are also dependent on forms of Western knowledge that are often of limited value and extreme inappropriacy to the local context. As Jernudd (1981) suggests, the modern discipline of linguistics, with its very particular ways of studying formal properties of language, generally serves needs different from those of many Third World countries, where diverse questions concerning language use are often far more appropriate. Yet, as he explains, linguistics is often exported to and taken up in those countries "because it is an internationally visible, modern approach to the study of language (and that not the least because it is available through the medium of English), and because the new countries' universities model themselves on Western counterparts" (p. 43). Similarly, Altbach (1981) argues that much technological expertise in India has been inappropriate because "much of Indian science is oriented toward metropolitan models, because of the use of English, because of the prestige of Western science, and because of the foreign training of many key Indian researchers" (p. 613).

Other writers have claimed an even more fundamental role of English in the (re)production of global inequalities. Naysmith (1987), for example, suggests that English language teaching "has become part of the process whereby one part of the world has become politically, economically and culturally dominated by another" (p. 3). The core of this process, he argues, is the "central place the English language has taken as *the* language of international capitalism" (ibid., 3). Such a position, which suggests that English is an integral part of the global structures of dependency, has been explored at length by Robert Phillipson. He argues that *linguicism* – "the ideologies and structures which are used to legitimate, effectuate and reproduce an unequal division of power and resources (both material and non-material) between groups which are defined on the basis of their language (i.e., of their mother tongue)" (1988:339) – is best seen within the broader context of *linguistic imperialism*, "an essential constituent of imperialism as a global phenomenon involving structural relations between rich and poor countries in a world characterised by inequality and injustice" (ibid., 339).

Most significantly, Phillipson's work demonstrates the limitations of arguments that suggest that the current position of English in the world is an accidental or natural result of world forces. Rather, through his analysis of the British Council and other organizations, Phillipson makes it clear that it has been deliberate government policy in English-speaking countries to promote the worldwide use of English for economic and political purposes. The British Council report for 1960–61, for example, draws a direct parallel between the advantages of encouraging the world to speak English (with the help of American power) and the history of U.S. internal policies for its immigrant population: "Teaching the world English may appear not unlike an extension of the task which America faced in establishing English as a common national language among its own immigrant population" (cited in Phillipson 1988:346). Ndebele (1987) also suggests that "The British Council . . . continues to be untiring in its efforts to keep the world speaking English. In this regard, teaching English as a second or foreign language is not only good business, in terms of the production of teaching materials of all kinds. . . , but also it is good politics" (p. 63). Given the connections outlined in this section between English and the export of certain forms of culture and knowledge, and between English and the maintenance of social, economic, and political elites, it is evident that the promotion of English around the world may bring very real economic and political advantages to the promoters of that spread. Indeed, Skutnabb-Kangas and Phillipson (1989) conclude that "it has been British and American government policy since the mid-1950s to establish English as a universal 'second language', so as to protect and promote capitalist interests" (p. 63).

Of primary importance to those of us working in English language teaching is the connection between our work and this global spread of English. Phillipson (1986) states that a primary purpose of his work is to gauge "the contribution of applied linguists and English Language Teaching Experts in helping to legitimate the contemporary capitalist world order" (p. 127). As I have suggested elsewhere (1990b), it is incumbent on applied linguists to explore the interests served by our work. If we start to accept some of the critical perspectives outlined here, we must surely start to raise profound questions about our own practices. Certainly, these perspectives suggest that we must be highly suspicious of claims that the spread of English is natural, neutral, or beneficial. In the next sections, I shall explore these questions further, by reexamining the ways in which we understand international relations, and by exploring questions of language and discourse. In doing so, I will raise not only the issue of English being in the world but also the extent to which the issue of the world being in English can be taken up. I hope both to draw attention to some of the limitations of the work I have summarised in this section and to extend the analysis by exploring the relationship between language, culture, and discourse.

Understanding the world

Although there is of course a vast range of writing on the questions of international relations, development, and international communication, it is possible to establish two broad orientations. The first, which is still by far the predominant one and has been variously labeled as traditionalist, realist (as opposed to idealist), conservative, liberal, or bourgeois, has its origins in European post-Renaissance thought, especially the work of Kant, Rousseau, and Hobbes. It takes the principal actors in the world to be aggressive nation states (inherently aggressive because of natural human aggression in the Hobbesian view, aggressive as a result of social corruption of the noble primal state according to Rousseau, or aggressive to the extent that the regime was corrupt in Kant's view), and the major concern in international relations to be that of avoiding war through strategic weapon deployment or diplomacy (see Holsti 1985).

After the Second World War, this view of the world was coupled with a notion of development that divided the world into developed and underdeveloped nations, with the process of development assumed to be a linear evolutionary path involving the development of industry and technology and a set of 'modern' values in the population. This road to development included the learning of modern forms of governmental organization (capitalist/democratic or socialist/democratic depending on whether the "aid" came from the First or the Second World) and the need to overcome the limitations of "primitive" or "traditional" cultures. (This same orientation can be seen in the programmes for refugees described by Tollefson [1989] in the previous section.) This could be achieved, it was thought, by helping to provide industrial equipment and advanced technology and by setting up mass education and communication systems that would help inculcate the modern values deemed necessary to develop.

Although this view of the world is still the predominant one in much of the "developed" world, there has been one major challenge to its conception of global relations. This came about in part because of a crisis in U.S. relationships with the world after Vietnam and a shift in confidence in academic circles during the 1960s; but most of all it was the result of the realization in much of the Third World that development aid was not all that it claimed to be. As Gibbons (1985) puts it, "The Third World itself began to experience a measure of disenchantment, when it discovered that development aid was not really aid, but a business investment camouflaged to look like development aid" (p. 40). From these concerns, a critical response emerged that drew largely on neo-Marxist analyses of the distribution of global wealth. The principal questions came to be problems of modernization, exploitation, and inequality within a world capitalist system. *Dependency theory* suggests that within a global capitalist system, development and underdevelopment are inversely related within and between nations. Dependency, therefore, describes the causal relationship between the development of the central/metropolitan areas at the expense of the concomitant underdevelopment of the peripheral/satellite areas of the globe (see Frank 1966; Galtung 1971; Preston 1986) .

From this perspective, then, the focus shifted from competing nation states to unfair distribution of wealth within a global capitalist system; barriers to development were no longer internal limitations imposed by culture and knowledge but rather external conditions imposed by the global economy; the prime actors were no longer political elites but rather class dynamics within center-periphery relations. This raised important questions about the role of education and international communication in the maintenance of global inequalities. Writers such as Carnoy (1974) argued that educational institutions in the Third World were largely forms of neo-colonial domination, continuing to serve the interests of the former colonizers and the central nations. Altbach (1981) argued that current intellectual centers have a massive influence over the international academic system, providing educational models, publishing books and journals, and setting the research agenda, thus reducing universities in many parts of the world to little more than "distributors of knowledge" (p. 602). Profound questions were also raised about international communications, with analyses showing that both in terms of quantity – a massive flow from First to Third World countries – and in terms of quality – representations of the Third World showed it as violent, backward, and disease-ridden as opposed to the modern, clean, and democratic First World – there was once again a colossal structure that maintained global inequalities (see Galtung 1985; Gibbons 1985; Schiller 1985; Mowlana 1986; Meyer 1988).

This second major framework, then, has raised questions of neo-colonialism and imperialism in the world, suggesting that there is a constant reproduction of economic, political, educational, cultural, and communication inequality. Although I think such analyses have far more to say about global relations than the states-centric conservative and liberal analyses, they also have a number of shortcomings, and it is important to try to overcome these. I now wish to try to go beyond this socioeconomic determinism in a way that will allow me not only to locate English critically in the world but also to locate the world critically in English. As Walker (1984) has suggested, in the neo-Marxist framework there is a "radical reduction of all human action to the same common denominators required by a positivist conception of knowledge" (p. 191). I feel that if we are to move towards an understanding of English in the world, we need to avoid the limitations of structuralism and positivism not only in our views of language but also in our understanding of the world.

The general epistemological crisis in the social sciences has also started to effect how we conceptualize global order. In the era of postmodern and poststructuralist thought, when fundamental questions are being raised about the whole Enlightenment project and the very notion of modernity and its most cherished beliefs in positivism, in the rational, unified subject, in the dichotomy between knowing subject and known objects, and in universal truths, it is not only the traditional understanding of world order that is coming under scrutiny, but also the deterministic and reductionist views of more critical thinking. A diverse range of critical work from the philosophy of science, feminist theory, Third World scholars, and other critical theorists has opened up fundamental questions as to the nature of the predominant paradigms of Western knowledge. It has been convincingly argued that the unitary concept of progress and development, the predominance of positivism in the social sciences, and the claims made to forms of rationality and objectivity, are all modes of thought particular to the European origins of the Enlightenment and to the social, cultural, and political conditions that gave rise to that mode of thinking. In attempts to show how all our thinking is constructed by particular social, cultural, and historical forces, rather than reflecting some universal truths, there has been a recognition of the fundamental roles of language and culture. Walker (1984), for example, argues that in looking at international relations we must start with the assumption that "social and political change is both reflected and constituted by language" (p. 185).

In his study of global relations, Worsley (1985) suggests that "the concept of culture has been virtually ignored by those social scientists who reduce the study of society to political economy or the study of social structure" (p. 41). Furthermore, in going beyond the predominant social scientist paradigms, we need, as Worsley (1985) and Wuthnow, Hunter, Bergesen, and Kurzweil (1984) argue, to avoid not only the view that culture is separate from the social but also the view that it is causally *secondary,* being in Marxist terms part of the superstructure, which is dependent on the socioeconomic realities of the infrastructure. What I am referring to, then, is not the conservative elitist view that identifies culture with a small range of aesthetic products, not the Marxist view that reduces culture to a reflection of socioeconomic relations, and not the liberal pluralist view common in much English language teaching, which takes cultures to be sets of stable beliefs, values, and behaviour that can be taught as an adjunct to a language syllabus. Rather, I am referring to a sense of culture as the process by which people make sense of their lives, a process always involved in struggles over meaning and representation.

Once we elevate culture to a prominent position in our understanding of the world, a number of key issues arise. Of great significance have been the implications of Said's (1978) seminal work on Orientalism, in which he shows how the "Orient" was constructed in the discourse of Western writers as an essentialized and homogeneous entity. As Walker (1984) suggests, this thinking has posed fundamental questions about how we understand culture, how we view the problem of the dominance of modes of Western thought, how, in looking at the Other, we often do little more than reconstruct ourselves. Once we start to see all knowledge as socially constructed, then, as Gendzier (1985), for example, has shown, it becomes clear how North American thinking on development and modernization has reflected Cold War ideology and liberal democratic theory far more than it has ever reflected the lived realities of the people and cultures with which it has purported to deal. Clifford (1988) asks whether it is indeed possible "to escape procedures of dichotomizing, restructuring, and textualizing in the making of interpretive statements about foreign cultures and traditions" (p. 261).

Although Clifford suggests that the "culture concept" may have "served its time" (p. 274), and should perhaps be replaced by a vision of "powerful discursive formations globally and strategically deployed" (ibid., 274), he nevertheless suggests some hope if we consider culture not so much as organically unified or traditionally continuous, not just as received from language, tradition, or environment, but as a "negotiated, present process," as "*made* in new political-cultural conditions of global relationality" (pp. 273–74). In considering the importance of culture in global relations, it is important, too, to consider that, as I suggested in the introduction, the traditional boundaries of the world are slipping. Thus, as Appadurai (1990) argues, "The new global cultural economy has to be seen as a complex, overlapping, disjunctive order, which cannot any longer be seen in terms of existing center-periphery models" (p. 6). I am suggesting, therefore, that the tendencies towards socioeconomic determinism and universality in dependency theory run the risk of assuming that a universal theory of socioeconomic relations can account for all global relationships and that people are passive consumers of hegemonic cultural forms.

I am arguing here for an avoidance of totalizing theories of social and cultural reproduction in favour of a critical paradigm that acknowledges human agency and looks not only at how people's lives are regulated by language, culture, and discourse but also at how people both resist those forms and produce their own forms. Important to this discussion are the particular interests of the international discourses on development, democracy, freedom, modernization, education, politics, and so on, in structuring the way people make sense of and act in the world. Interesting new directions for work can be seen, for example, in Escobar's (1985) argument that by using Foucault's insights into the nature of discourse as a conjunction of power/knowledge relationships, and by conducting a genealogy (rather than just an archaeology) of the discourse of development, we can come to a radical reinterpretation of the effects of development theory and practice:

Without examining development as discourse we cannot understand the systematic ways in which the Western developed countries have been able to manage and control and, in many ways, even create the Third World politically, economically, sociologically and culturally; and that, although underdevelopment is a very real historical formation, it has given rise to a series of practices (promoted by the discourses of the West) which constitute one of the most powerful mechanisms for insuring domination over the Third World today. (p. 384)

It is Escobar's contention, then, that not only does this discourse of development constitute a powerful means of effecting domination and economic exploitation, but that it is also only through the dismantling of this discourse and constructing of a counter-discourse that Third World countries will be able to pursue some different form of development.

In light of Escobar's comments, it is tempting to consider the whole global system in terms of Foucault's (1979) powerful metaphor of the *panopticon*, the "transparent, circular cage, with its high tower, powerful and knowing" (p. 208). Thus, we can see how the Third World is subjected to a form of *surveillance* – a "normalizing gaze" that "compares, differentiates, hierarchizes, homogenizes, excludes" (1979:183) – by the "powerful and knowing" central tower, the Western intellectual and political institutions that construct discourses on the Third World, and which, by the nature of their surveillance, lead the objects of that surveillance to become the "principle of [their] own subjection" (p. 203). And, just as Rahim (1986) suggests that English became the language of the panopticon in colonial India, so I would like to suggest that English today is the language of the global panopticon. (It is also perhaps not entirely coincidental that the great Utilitarian, Jeremy Bentham, not only gave us the concept and the word panopticon but was also the originator of the word *international*.)

Of significance to the issues I wish to address in this paper are, on the one hand, the continued acknowledgement of inequalities and dependencies between First and Third World countries, and on the other, an attempt to conceptualize these relationships in a way that avoids the reductionist and deterministic tendencies inherent in looking predominantly at socioeconomic relationships. Of fundamental importance is the elevation of notions of culture and discourse as principal factors in our understanding of the world. Although not belittling the importance of economic and material inequalities, I would argue that it is also crucial to understand how discourses construct and regulate our realities and operate through a diverse range of international institutions. Once we move beyond a view of the world as made up of competing states or as reducible to a set of socioeconomic relations, in favour of a view that also tries to account for diverse cultures and discourses constituting our subjectivities, then it also starts to become clear that language, and especially any international language, may play a far greater role in the world than had heretofore been considered. Importantly, too, this view suggests that people around the world are not merely passive consumers of culture and knowledge but active creators. In the next section I shall explore the relationship between international discourses and English, and I shall discuss the importance of counter-discourses formed in English.

Discourse, counter-discourse, and the world in English

Now that I have outlined the limitations that I see with some of the critical approaches to international relations and have suggested some directions that I wish to pursue in conceptualizing the globe, it may be reasonably clear that some of the critical perspectives on EIL are also open to similar criticisms. Thus Phillipson's (1986) theory of linguistic imperialism, based as it is on Galtung's (1971, 1980) theory of structural imperialism, runs the risk of becoming deterministic in its reliance on infrastructural determinants of language rights. Although I want to acknowledge the very great importance of work such as Phillipson's in its description of the structures of global language inequality, I also want to avoid what seems to be a foreclosure of discussion and possibilities by naming the spread of English as linguistic imperialism.

Phillipson describes a massive structure of linguistic imperialism and suggests ways of trying to counter this through language-planning policies. My position, however, is that we cannot reduce language spread to an imperialism parallel to economic or military imperialism. What I want to examine are the *effects* of the spread of English, how people take up English in their daily lives, what is done with "the world language which history has forced down our throats" (Achebe 1975:220). By taking up the concept of discourse I am suggesting that the implications of the spread of English may be even greater than suggested in structuralist analyses because of the connection between English and international discourses, and that it may be almost impossible to solve these problems through language-planning policies since, as Luke, McHoul, and Mey (1990) argue, "while language . . . can be 'planned', discourse cannot." And yet I also want to suggest that the concept of discourse allows for the construction of counter-discourses in English and may offer remarkable potential for change.

Language plays a central role in how we understand ourselves and the world and thus all questions of language control and standardization have major implications for social relations and the distribution of power. I think Shapiro's (1989) discussion of "language purism," a particular aspect of language planning and standardization, states this issue clearly:

At many levels, a society's approach to the Other is constitutive of the breadth of meaning and value it is prepared to tolerate. Language purism is a move in the direction of narrowing legitimate forms of meaning and thereby declaring out-of-bounds certain dimensions of otherness. It is not as dramatic and easily politicized as the extermination of an ethnic minority or even so easily made contentious as the proscription of various forms of social deviance. But the Other is located most fundamentally in language, the medium for representing selves and other. Therefore, any move that alters language by centralizing and pruning or decentralizing and diversifying alters the ecology of Self-Other relations and thereby the identities that contain and animate relations of power and authority. (p. 28)

Once we start to deal with language as always political, never neutral, its relationship to other forms of power becomes easier to perceive.

Kachru (1986) quotes the Nigerian novelist Chinua Achebe (1975) in support of his arguments for the legitimation of the new Englishes. Achebe argues that it is neither necessary nor desirable for an African

writer to be able to use English like a native speaker. Rather, he argues
that English "will be able to carry the weight of my African experience.
But it will have to be a new English, still in communion with its ancestral
home but altered to suit its new African surroundings" (p. 223). But what
do we mean when we talk about a new English? I want to argue that this
is a far more complex question than simply a case of new words, new
syntax, or new phonology, that Achebe is concerned not so much with the
structural diversity of English as with the cultural politics of new meanings, the struggle to claim and to create meanings in the political arenas of
language and discourse. Significantly, Achebe's remark follows a quota-
tion from the African-American writer James Baldwin, who argues that

My quarrel with English has been that the language reflected none of my experience. But now I began to see the matter in quite another way. . . . Perhaps
the language was not my own because I had never attempted to use it, had
only learned to imitate it. If this were so, then it might be made to bear the
burden of my experience if I could find the stamina to challenge it, and me, to
such a test. (Cited in Achebe 1975:223)

   Achebe and Baldwin are referring to a political struggle over meaning,
and it is in this domain that the notion of new Englishes becomes interesting. As Mazrui (1975) demonstrates, the relationship between English
and politics is always complex. Although English has been one of the
major languages of colonialism and neo-colonialism in Africa, a language
linked to oppression, racism, and cultural imperialism, it was also the
language through which opposition to the colonizers was formed.
"Among the functions of the English language in the Commonwealth
must indeed be included a function which is unifying. What are often
overlooked are some of the *anti*-Commonwealth tendencies which are
also part of the English language" (1975:191). On the eve of an election
in Nairobi, Mazrui relates, the Kenyan political leader Tom Mboya stood
in front of a vast crowd and recited the poem "If" by Rudyard Kipling.
What are we to make of the use of a poem by one of the great apologists
of imperialism in a political speech by a vehement opponent of imperialism and colonialism? According to Mazrui, "The cultural penetration of
the English language was manifesting its comprehensiveness. That was in
part a form of colonization of the African mind. But when Rudyard
Kipling is being called upon to serve the purposes of the Africans themselves, the phenomenon we are witnessing may also amount to a
decolonizing of Rudyard Kipling" (p. 209).
   What starts to emerge from these instances is a sense that language is a
site of struggle, that meanings are always in flux and in contention. The
process of using language against the grain, of the empire writing back to
the centre (see Ashcroft, Griffiths, and Tiffin 1989), of using English to
express the lived experiences of the colonized and to oppose the central

meanings of the colonizers, is a crucial aspect of global language use. In the rarefied atmosphere of structuralist linguistics, especially transformational grammar, the creation of new meanings is merely a result of the generation by an internal language machine of new sentences. If, however, language is seen in its cultural and political context, meanings are forged in the contested terrain of social interaction. "Engaged with the realities of power," Terdiman (1985:38) argues, "human communities use words not in contemplation but in *competition*. Such struggles are never equal ones. The facts of domination, of control, are inscribed in the signs available for use by all members of a social formation." Thus, as Morgan (1987) puts it, the world is always/already in the word.

In looking, therefore, at postcolonial literature, at forms of "writing back" in the language of the colonizers, I wish to avoid the same liberal pluralism of the writing on the new Englishes that we looked at earlier and that takes as its central concerns a notion of diversity and the legitimation of other standards. I am not here concerned with legitimating other forms of Commonwealth literature or "New literatures in English" so that they can be incorporated into the canon of English. Rather, I am interested in the ways in which these literatures in English are rich in struggles over meaning and opposition to the central definitions. As Ashcroft, Griffiths, and Tiffin (1989:189) suggest, "A canon is not a body of texts *per se,* but rather a set of reading practices." Thus, the question is not so much one of replacing, validating, or incorporating new forms of English language or literature, but rather of rethinking our understanding of language practices.

I am trying to articulate here a relationship between English and global relations that avoids reducing it either to a coincidental conjunction – English just happens to be the language in which various discourses are expressed – or to a structural determinism – the nature of the English language determines what discourses can be expressed. Rather, the power/knowledge relationships of discourse operate according to or in conflict with the power relationships always/already in the words of the language. This relationship is of course constantly in flux, and since it suggests that both language and discourse are constitutive of as well as constituted by each other, it also implies that language and discourse have been constituted by and have been constitutive of the history of their connections as well as the present process of their conjunction. Neither can be separated from their present cultural and political context or from their historical formation.

Discourses and languages can both facilitate and restrict the production of meanings. When we look at the history and present conjunction of English and many discourses of global power, it seems certain that those discourses have been facilitative of the spread of English and that the spread of English has facilitated the spread of those discourses. It is in this sense that the world is in English. The potential meanings that can be articulated in English are interlinked with the discourses of development, democracy, capitalism, modernization, and so on. And if we accept the argument that subjectivities are constructed in discourse (see, for example, Weedon 1987), then we can see how the spread of English is not only a structural *reproducer* of global inequalities, but also *produces* inequality by creating subject positions that contribute to their own subjectification. But it is also at this point that possibilities for resistance present themselves in alternative readings of Rudyard Kipling, postcolonial struggles in English, and the formation of counter-discourses.

Ashcroft, Griffiths, and Tiffin (1989) identify two elements to writing back: *abrogation*, a denial and refusal of the colonial and metropolitan categories, of the standards of normative or 'correct' usage, of the claims to fixed meanings inscribed in words; and *appropriation*, the process by which the language is seized and replaced in a specific cultural location. This is similar to what I have elsewhere (1990a) called a diremptive/redemptive project, diremption being the challenge to the hegemonizing character of prevailing Western discursive practices, and redemption being the emancipation of subjugated knowledges and identities that have been submerged beneath or marginalized by the predominant discursive practices and power/knowledge relationships. It is by engaging in the struggle to oppose the centre's claim to control over meaning and to create new meanings in opposition to the hegemonizing character of Western discourses and English that counter-discourses can be formed. It is at this moment, Ashcroft, Griffiths, and Tiffin (1989:87) suggest, as "the myth of centrality embodied in the concept of a 'standard language' is forever overturned . . . that English becomes *english*."

I have been trying to suggest in this section, then, that if we elevate language, culture, and discourse to a central role in the (re)production of global inequalities, the relationship between English and these inequalities becomes on the one hand stronger but on the other more open to resistance. If we see the relationship between power/knowledge in discourse and the power inscribed in words and produced in the struggle over meaning, we can start to understand not only the extent to which English is in the world and the extent to which it appears to run parallel to many forms of global oppression, but also the ways in which the world is in English, the ways in which the history of conjunctions between various discourses and English creates the conditions for people's complying with their own subjugation. Thus, I have tried to maintain many of the critical elements of more structuralist descriptions of the world, while linking English more closely to forms of ideological coercion and allowing at the same time for ways of understanding resistance and other possibilities. In the final section I shall try to suggest what implications such a view holds for teaching English around the world.

English teachers and the worldliness of English

I have suggested that the predominant paradigms of analysis of the spread of English around the world have by and large failed to problematize the causes and implications of this spread. They have dealt primarily with descriptions of varieties of English and have paused only to debate the questions of standardization and intelligibility. The spread of English is taken to be natural, neutral, and beneficial. English language teachers, therefore, have been poorly served by a body of knowledge that fails to address the cultural and political implications of the spread of English. More critical analyses, however, show that English threatens other languages, acts as a gatekeeper to positions of wealth and prestige both within and between nations, and is the language through which much of the unequal distribution of wealth, resources, and knowledge operates. Furthermore, its spread has not been the coincidental by-product of changing global relations but rather the deliberate policy of English-speaking countries protecting and promoting their economic and political interests. Thus, I have argued, English is in the world and plays an important role in the reproduction of global inequalities.

I have also suggested that when we consider the importance of language, culture, and discourse in how we make sense of the world (and how the world makes sense of us), another aspect of the worldliness of English emerges: the extent to which the world is in English. By considering the relationship between language and discourse, it is possible to go beyond an understanding of the structural concordance of English and forms of global inequality to understand how people's subjectivities and identities are constituted and how people may comply with their own oppression. This, however, is by no means a deterministic thesis; it is not the structure of English that is important here but the politics of representation. And it is in this locus of struggle over meaning that counter-discourses can be formulated.

Peirce's (1990) explanation of the difference between predominant views of EIL and a view that deals with the politics of meaning illustrates the issue well:

To interpret People's English as a dialect of international English would do the movement a gross injustice; People's English is not only a language, it is a struggle to appropriate English in the interests of democracy in South Africa. Thus the naming of People's English is a political act because it represents a challenge to the current status of English in South Africa, in which control of the language, access to the language, and teaching of the language are entrenched within apartheid structures. (p. 108)

What, then, are the implications of all this for teachers and applied linguists? Rogers (1982) argues that, given the falsity of the hopes that

English teaching provides, we should try to discourage the teaching of English. As the responses to Rogers's article rightly suggest, however, to deny people access to English is an even more problematic solution (Abbott 1984; Prodromou 1988). Although I think we should support language-planning policies aimed at maintaining languages other than English, there are also limits to the effectiveness of such policies. Phillipson's (1988:353) "anti-linguicist strategies" may only be part of the picture. As long as English remains intimately linked to the discourses that ensure the continued domination of some parts of the globe by others, an oppositional programme other than one that seeks only to limit access to English will be necessary.

Elsewhere (Pennycook 1989b), I have argued that local forms of opposition can indeed be taken up. Following Foucault's (1980:81) formulation, I suggested that by asking what forms of knowledge have been disqualified and subjugated by the dominant discourses, we could attempt to bring about the "insurrection of subjugated knowledges." More generally, I would suggest that counter-discourses can indeed be formed in English and that one of the principal roles of English teachers is to help this formulation. Thus, as applied linguists and English language teachers we should become political actors engaged in a critical pedagogical project to use English to oppose the dominant discourses of the West and to help the articulation of counter-discourses in English. At the very least, intimately involved as we are with the spread of English, we should be acutely aware of the implications of this spread for the reproduction and production of global inequalities.

References

Abbott, G. 1984. Should we start digging new holes? *ELT Journal* 38(2): 98–102.

Achebe, C. 1975. English and the African writer. In A. Mazrui, *The political sociology of the English language* (Appendix B, pp. 216–23). The Hague/Paris: Mouton.

Altbach, P. G. 1981. The university as center and periphery. *Teachers College Record* 82(4): 601–22.

Appadurai, A. 1990. Disjuncture and difference in the global cultural economy. *Public Culture* 2(2): 1–24.

Ashcroft, B., G. Griffiths, and H. Tiffin. 1989. *The empire writes back: Theory and practice in post-colonial literatures.* London and New York: Routledge.

Bamgbose, A. 1982. Standard Nigerian English: Issues of identification. In B. J. Kachru (Ed.), *The other tongue: English across cultures* (pp. 99–111). Urbana: University of Illinois Press.

Carnoy, M. 1974. *Education as cultural imperialism.* New York: David McKay.

Clifford, J. 1988. *The predicament of culture: Twentieth century ethnography, literature and art.* Cambridge, Mass.: Harvard University Press.

Cooke, D. 1988. Ties that constrict: English as a Trojan horse. In A. Cumming, A. Gagne, and J. Dawson (Eds.), *Awarenesses: Proceedings of the 1987 TESL Ontario conference* (pp. 56–62). Toronto: TESL Ontario.

Crystal, D. 1987. *The Cambridge encyclopedia of language.* Cambridge: Cambridge University Press.

1988. *The English language.* Harmondsworth: Penguin.

Day, R. 1980. ESL: A factor in linguistic genocide? In J. C. Fisher, M. A. Clarke, and J. Schachter (Eds.), *On TESOL '80. Building bridges: Research and practice in teaching English as a second language.* Washington, D.C.: TESOL.

1985. The ultimate inequality: Linguistic genocide. In N. Wolfson and J. Manes (Eds.), *Language of inequality* (pp. 163–81). Berlin: Mouton.

Escobar, A. 1985. Discourse and power in development: Michel Foucault and the relevance of his work to the Third World. *Alternatives* 10:377–400.

Fishman, J. A., R. L. Cooper, and Y. Rosenbaum. 1977. English around the world. In J. A. Fishman, R. W. Cooper, and A. W. Conrad (Eds.), *The spread of English* (pp. 77–107). Rowley, Mass.: Newbury House.

Flaitz, J. 1988. *The ideology of English: French perceptions of English as a world language.* Berlin/New York/Amsterdam: Mouton de Gruyter.

Foucault, M. 1979. *Discipline and punish: The birth of the prison.* New York: Vintage.

1980. *Power/knowledge: Selected interviews and other writings, 1972–1977.* Edited by Colin Gordon. New York: Pantheon.

Frank, A. G. 1966. The development of underdevelopment. *Monthly Review* (Sept): 17–30.

Galtung, J. 1971. A structural theory of imperialism. *Journal of Peace Research* 8(2): 81–117.

1980. *The true worlds: A transnational perspective.* New York: The Free Press.

1985. Social communication and global problems. In P. Lee (Ed.), *Communication for all: New world information and communication order* (pp. 1–16). Maryknoll, N.Y.: Orbis.

Gendzier, I. 1985. *Managing political change: Social scientists and the Third World.* Boulder, Colo.: Westview Press.

Gibbons, A. 1985. *Information, ideology and communication: The new nations' perspectives on an intellectual revolution.* Lanham, Md.: University Press of America.

Giroux, H. A. 1983. *Theory and resistance in education: A pedagogy for the opposition.* South Hadley, Mass.: Bergin and Garvey.

Hindmarsh, R. X. 1978. English as an international language. *ELT Documents: English as an international language* 102:40–43.

Holsti, K. J. 1985. *The dividing discipline.* Boston: Allen and Unwin.

Jernudd, B. 1981. Planning language treatment: Linguistics for the Third World. *Language in Society* 10(1): 43–52.

Jespersen, O. [1938] 1968. *Growth and structure of the English language.* Toronto: Collier-Macmillan.

Judd, E. L. 1983. TESOL as a political act: A moral question. In J. Handscombe, R.A. Orem, and B. P. Taylor (Eds.), *On TESOL '83* (pp. 265–73). Washington, D.C.: TESOL.

Kachru, B. 1982a. Introduction: The other side of English. In B. J. Kachru (Ed.),

The other tongue: English across cultures. Urbana: Univ. of Illinois Press.

1982b. Models for non-native Englishes. In B. J. Kachru (Ed.), *The other tongue: English across cultures* (pp. 31–57). Urbana: University of Illinois Press.

1985. Standards, codification and sociolinguistic realism: The English language in the outer circle. In R. Quirk and H. G. Widdowson (Eds.), *English in the world*. Cambridge: Cambridge University Press.

1986. *The alchemy of English: The spread, functions and models of non-native Englishes*. Oxford: Pergamon.

Luke, A., A. McHoul, and J. L. Mey. 1990. On the limits of language planning: Class, state and power. In R. B. Baldauf, Jr., and A. Luke (Eds.), *Language planning and education in Australasia and the South Pacific* (pp. 25–44). Clevedon: Multilingual Matters.

Mazrui, A. 1975. *The political sociology of the English language*. The Hague/Paris: Mouton.

Meyer, W. H. 1988. *Transnational media and Third World development: The structure and impact of imperialism*. New York: Greenwood Press.

Morgan, B. 1987. Three dreams of language, or no longer immured in the Bastille of the humanist word. *College English* 49(4): 449–458.

Mowlana, H. 1986. *Global information and world communication*. New York and London: Longman.

Naysmith, J. 1987. English as imperialism? *Language Issues* 1(2): 3–5.

Ndebele, N. S. 1987. The English language and social change in South Africa. *The English Academy Review* 4:1–16.

Nelson, C. 1982. Intelligibility and non-native varieties of English. In B. J. Kachru (Ed.), *The other tongue: English across cultures* (pp. 58–73). Urbana: University of Illinois Press.

Ngugi wa Thiong'o. 1985. The language of African literature. *New Left Review* 150(March/April): 109–27.

Peirce, B. N. 1990. The author responds. *TESOL Quarterly* 24(1): 589–618.

Pennycook, A. 1989a. The concept of method, interested knowledge, and the politics of language teaching. *TESOL Quarterly* 23(4): 589–618.

1989b. *English as an international language and the insurrection of subjugated knowledges*. Paper presented at the Fifth International Conference of the Institute of Language in Education, Hong Kong, 13 December 1989: "LULTAC '89."

1990a. The diremptive/redemptive project: Postmodern reflections on culture and knowledge in international academic relations. *Alternatives* 15(1): 53–81.

1990b. Towards a critical applied linguistics for the 1990s. *Issues in Applied Linguistics* 1(1): 9–29.

Phillipson, R. 1986. English rules: A study of language pedagogy and imperialism. In R. Phillipson and T. Skutnabb-Kangas (Eds.), *Linguicism rules in education* (pp. 124–343). Roskilde University Centre, Denmark.

1988. Linguicism: Structures and ideologies in linguistic imperialism. In J. Cummins and T. Skutnabb-Kangas (Eds.), *Minority education: From shame to struggle*. Avon: Multilingual Matters.

Platt, J., H. Weber, and M. L. Ho. 1984. *The new Englishes*. London: Routledge and Kegan Paul.

Preston, P. W. 1986. *Making sense of development.* London and New York: Routledge and Kegan Paul.

Prodromou, L. 1988. English as cultural action. *ELT Journal* 42(2): 73–83.

Quirk, R. 1985. The English language in a global context. In R. Quirk and H. G. Widdowson (Eds.), *English in the world.* Cambridge: Cambridge University Press.

Rahim, S. A. 1986. Language as power apparatus: Observations on English and cultural policy in nineteenth-century India. *World Englishes* 5(2/3): 231–239.

Richards, J. C. 1982. Singapore English: Rhetorical and communicative styles. In B. J. Kachru (Ed.), *The other tongue: English across cultures* (pp. 154–67). Urbana: University of Illinois Press.

Rogers, J. 1982. The world for sick proper. *ELT Journal* 36(3): 144–51.

Said, E. 1978. *Orientalism.* New York: Random House.

    1983. *The world, the text and the critic.* Cambridge, Mass.: Harvard University Press.

Schiller, H. I. 1985. Strengths and weaknesses of the new international information empire. In P. Lee (Ed.), *Communication for all: New world information and communication order* (pp. 17–32). Maryknoll, N.Y.: Orbis.

Shapiro, M. J. 1989. A political approach to language purism. In B. H. Jernudd and M. J. Shapiro (Eds.), *The politics of language purism.* Berlin: Mouton de Gruyter.

Skutnabb-Kangas, T., and R. Phillipson. 1989. Wanted! Linguistic human rights. *Rolig Papir.* (Roskilde Universitetscenter) 44.

Terdiman, R. 1985. *Discourse/counter-discourse.* Ithaca, N.Y.: Cornell University Press.

Tollefson, J. W. 1986. Language planning and the radical left in the Philippines: The New People's Army and its antecedents. *Language Problems and Language Planning* 10(2): 177–89.

    1988. Covert policy in the United States refugee program in Southeast Asia. *Language Problems and Language Planning* 12(1): 30–42.

    1989. *Alien winds: The reeducation of America's Indochinese refugees.* New York: Praeger.

Walker, R. B. J. 1984. World politics and Western reason: Universalism, pluralism, hegemony. In R. B. J. Walker (Ed.), *Culture, ideology and world order.* Boulder, Colo.: Westview Press.

Weedon, C. 1987. *Feminist practice and poststructuralist theory.* Oxford: Basil Blackwell.

Worsley, P. 1985. *The three worlds: Culture and world development.* London: Weidenfeld and Nicholson.

Wuthnow, R., J. Hunter, A. Bergesen, and E. Kurzweil. 1984. *Cultural analysis.* London: Routledge and Kegan Paul.

Zuengler, J. E. 1982. Kenyan English. In B. J. Kachru (Ed.), *The other tongue: English across cultures* (pp. 112–24). Urbana: University of Illinois Press.

    1985. English, Swahili, or other languages? The relationship of educational development goals to language of instruction in Kenya and Tanzania. In N. Wolfson and J. Manes (Eds.), *Language of inequality* (pp. 241–54). Berlin: Mouton.

3 Understanding language and power in the Solomon Islands: Methodological lessons for educational intervention

Karen Ann Watson-Gegeo and David Welchman Gegeo

Schooling is often talked about as being the key to well being and prosperity. It is an irony of modern Solomon Islands history that it has instead become for many people an occasion of failure and disappointment, a sign of their exclusion from the development to which they aspire. (Wasuka 1989:99)

Robert B. Kaplan (1990:9) states that in an ideal environment, language planning would be a "function of government at the highest level" rather than of a country's education sector, but that a clear-cut separation of functions is often not the case in real environments. Kaplan's statement appears consistent with the macrosocietal, top-down perspective held by high governmental officials with whom language planners often consult, and with the typically macrolevel approaches of language-planning research. One also detects here the lower esteem in which educational practice and local-level points of view are held vis-à-vis high-level policy making. From the perspective of effective and meaningful education, however, the separation of planning and implementation is neither possible nor desirable. Language and education are highly political because they involve significant outcomes for people's lives and futures. Even reasonably well-informed outside consultants rarely have in-depth knowledge of local conditions. They may be advising heads of departments or ministries who are shuffled from one portfolio to another, with little or no expertise related to their current assignment. Communities and on-line educators may well have the kind of knowledge essential to formulating meaningful policy.

The focus of this chapter, however, is not who should be making language policy. In fact, we begin at the opposite end from Kaplan, with a concern for improving educational practice. But the issue raised by Kaplan's comment is closely related to our focus: the need to integrate micro- and macrolevels of contextual data, collected and analyzed in a qualitative, ethnographic framework, to achieve a more holistic under-

We wish to thank the teachers and headmasters at the school where we observed and/or interviewed in 1981, 1987, and 1990, and the families who participated in our study of Kwara'ae children's language socialization over the past several years. The work reported in this chapter has been supported in part by the National Institute of Mental Health, Spencer Foundation, National Science Foundation, Fulbright, and East-West Center.

standing of language and power as it relates (in our case) to schooling and educational intervention.

For over 10 years we have conducted ethnographic and sociolinguistic research in rural Kwara'ae district of Malaita in the Solomon Islands, with the aim of improving educational practice in rural schools, where dropout and failure rates are high. This chapter traces the evolution of that research to illustrate the problems of deciding on where explanation is located, and the resulting implications for intervention. We begin with a brief discussion of ethnography and the micro-/macrolevel of contextual data issue.

Ethnography and micro-/macrolevels of analysis

A form of qualitative research, *ethnography* is the study of people's behavior in naturally occurring, ongoing settings, with a focus on the cultural interpretation of behavior (Watson-Gegeo 1988:576). The goal of ethnography is to provide a descriptive, interpretive, and explanatory account of behavior in a given setting. To this end, the researcher carries out systematic, intensive, detailed observation and in-depth interviewing, examining how behavior and interaction are socially organized, and the social rules, interactional expectations, and cultural values underlying them (ibid., 577).

Depending on setting and research questions, many kinds of data may be collected in an ethnographic project (e.g., observations, interviews, audio- or videotapes of events, documents, historical accounts, artifacts), and analysis may involve quantitative (e.g., frequency counts, tests of significance, multivariate analysis) as well as qualitative methods. Ethnographic projects are typically several months to a year or more long, during which the researcher moves back and forth between more comprehensive and macrolevel versus more topic- or hypothesis-oriented and microlevel data collection and analysis.

Micro and *macro* are comparative or relational terms meaningful only when defined and applied in a specific context (DeWalt and Pelto 1985:1). The same phenomenon can be treated as either micro or macro, depending on a researcher's focus (which, in ethnography, may change over time). For example, a researcher interested in instructional and non-instructional talk between teacher and student will probably treat individual interactions as micro and the classroom as a whole as macro. For a researcher examining school governance, however, the classroom is likely to be one microenvironment among several within the larger school or school district. Micro/macro relationships are typically formulated with regard to scales that are spatial (e.g., individual, group), causal, or temporal (e.g., synchronic, diachronic).

Social scientists have not adequately addressed how small-scale, or microlevel, and large-scale, or macrolevel, events and processes are inter-related, or how they are to be meaningfully linked in an explanation (DeWalt and Pelto 1985). Few methodological guidelines exist for making the nature of the links explicit (but see the DeWalt and Pelto volume for essays in that direction). An analytic model would need to be interactive and dynamic (Bennett 1985).

We have found Giddens's (1979) theoretical work on structuration to be particularly useful for thinking about how micro- and macrolevels in behavior and society are interrelated (see also Friesen 1986 for an excellent study applying Giddens's theoretical framework to integrating micro- and macrolevels in the study of labor mobility and economic transformation in the Solomon Islands). Giddens (1979) is concerned with how individuals and society create each other through praxis (action or practice):

> The concept of structuration involves that of the *duality of structure,* which relates to the *fundamentally recursive character of social life, and expresses the mutual dependence of structure and agency.* I mean that the structural properties of social systems are both the medium and the outcome of the practices that constitute those systems (italics in original). (p. 69)

Giddens's formulation is instructive for what we take to be a primary goal of ethnography, holism: i.e., that an aspect of culture or behavior must be described and explained in relation to the whole system of which it is a part (Watson-Gegeo 1988, drawing on Firth 1961; Diesing 1971). An alternative way of expressing this principle is that an adequate ethnographic analysis must account for both the behavior and the context in which the behavior occurred. Context and behavior are seen as mutually causal. Here, "context" includes not only the immediate circumstances in which an activity or interaction occurred (micro), but also relevant socio-cultural relationships and institutions (macro).

Levels of context may be thought of as concentric spheres of influence surrounding the events or behavior on which a study focuses. Another metaphor we have found useful is that of *horizontal* and *vertical* levels or dimensions of context (Watson-Gegeo and Ulichny 1988). By horizontal we mean behavior, interactions, and events as they unfold in time, together with the immediate circumstances affecting them. Horizontal context is usually the referent when research claims to take context into account and be what psychologists call ecologically valid. The scope of ecologically valid research, however, is often limited to relatively short segments of time. An adequate ethnographic description requires examining events and behavior in light of both the long-term history of relationships in the immediate setting and the relevant larger historical processes related to vertical levels.

By vertical levels of context, we mean institutional arenas of activity within the larger culture and society that may appear to be outside the immediate context, but that shape behavior in profound ways. For instance, whatever participants themselves bring to an interaction from their previous experiences and learning has been shaped by the society's socialization practices at home, at school, and in the community. Similarly, classroom interactions are strongly influenced by the characteristics of schools as social institutions (e.g., McNeil 1986). Despite the fact that they are not directly observable and may be poorly understood or even unknown to the interactants, vertical levels of context have great significance for explaining behavior.

Attention to contextual levels and holism as requirements of an adequate ethnographic analysis may be conceptualized as *thick explanation*. In laying out a framework for the ethnographic analysis of culture through participant observation, Geertz (1973) emphasized the importance of going beyond behavioristic, or "thin" description of people's actions to include information on indigenous interpretations, values, and processes of making sense of interactions and events – which together with careful description of the observed behavior constitute rich, or "thick," description. We argue that thick description can still lead to thin explanation. In our view, thick explanation means taking into account all relevant, theoretically salient micro- and macrocontextual influences, whether horizontal or vertical, that stand in a systematic relationship to (i.e., are part of a system with; see Diesing 1971:137–41) the behavior or event(s) one is attempting to explain. A systems approach helps to delimit boundaries for the study. It is also useful to apply Glaser and Strauss's (1967) notion of *theoretical saturation* in category development to the problem of deciding how many levels need to be included for the explanation to be thick. Here, saturation would mean the point at which no additional levels are found that *substantially* contribute to the explanation.

Our concern with micro/macro dimensions of analysis grows out of the problem of accounting for why children in rural areas of developing countries such as the Solomon Islands do not succeed in school. We turn now to an account of our research – why we began as we did, how we have defined *micro* and *macro* at different stages of the research, and what we have learned about language, schooling, and educational intervention.

Cultural congruence and language socialization

Located in the southwest Pacific, Solomon Islands is a culturally diverse multilingual nation. In a population of about three hundred thousand (Groenewegen 1989), over seventy indigenous languages are spoken

(Tryon 1979). We have worked primarily in rural Kwara'ae district on the island of Malaita. Kwara'ae is the language with the largest number of speakers in the Solomons, but it is only one language among ten on Malaita (population sixty thousand). D. W. Gegeo, who speaks Kwara'ae natively, grew up in West Kwara'ae and attended primary school there.

Solomon Islands faces many of the problems typical of Third World nations, including rapid sociocultural change, a high birthrate, rural and urban poverty, malnutrition, and low literacy rates. On Malaita, the provincial government headquarters and primary urban area are located in West Kwara'ae, which has been a center for intense mission and development activity over the past 50 years. However, West Kwara'ae villagers' level of schooling remains low, and villages are economically poor. Kwara'ae children typically have little or no exposure to English (the medium of instruction in schools), to Solomon Islands Pijin (an English-based pidgin/creole variety used nationally as a lingua franca), or to literacy materials prior to schooling. Their fathers usually have had two to three years of schooling, but their mothers are often nonliterate.

Our initial research questions were tied to two overlapping areas in the sociolinguistic and educational literature. First, various studies and theoretical articles have suggested that prior to schooling, minority and Third World children lack experience with 'decontextualized' discourse (involving abstraction, generalization, and a focus on relationships among words disembodied from their referents; see Wertsch 1985) and with related metalinguistic skills necessary for acquiring literacy in school (Scollon and Scollon 1979). Book reading, question/answer routines, and other language activities typically found in white American middle-class caregiver-child interactions are often said to be essential to success in school (Snow 1983).

Second, other studies have proposed the "cultural mismatch hypothesis" for why minority and Third World children fail in school: i.e., that classroom organization, discourse forms, teaching strategies, and values differ in important ways from these children's home cultures and prior experiences with language use (Cazden, John, and Hymes 1972; Erickson and Mohatt 1982; Boggs 1985).

With these issues in mind, we asked: What patterns of teaching and learning occur in the homes and communities of Kwara'ae children during the important preschool years? How do patterns of home and classroom language use differ? And how can classrooms be made more culturally congruent? Exploring these questions entailed examining children's language learning and socialization at home, together with the cognitive skills they develop there, as well as classroom interactional patterns and the cognitive skills children are expected to display in school. Our thinking was guided by the experience of the Kamehameha Early Education Program (KEEP) in Hawai'i, which developed classroom reading lessons based on talk-story speech events in the Hawaiian community (Boggs 1985). Talk-story routines (originally studied by Watson-Gegeo; Watson 1975) involve exploring ideas and meanings through conarration and linking associated topics and ideas rather than centering on a single topic (Watson-Gegeo and Boggs 1977). These routines violate such classroom discourse rules as "one speaker at a time" and "stick to the main topic." However, when first-grade reading lessons were redesigned around talk-story routines and other culturally congruent organizational changes were made in the classroom, Hawaiian children's scores on standardized reading tests rose dramatically (Au and Jordan 1977). We hoped to discover a corresponding speech event in Kwara'ae that, like talk-story, could be adapted for classroom use.

For this stage of our research, we defined the community (several villages and a school) as macrosocial and the family as microsocial units. During 3-month field visits in 1978 and 1979, we collected data on social structure and organization, language use and discourse, beliefs and values, and subsistence and economic activities at the community level, supplemented by Gegeo's cultural knowledge. We then conducted an intensive study of nine families, focusing on thirteen children from birth to 9 years of age, in a cross-age, semi-longitudinal design. The study, which took place over four field periods (2 periods totalling 7 months in 1981, and 3 months each in 1984 and 1987), examined children's language learning and socialization in adult-child and child-child interactions.

Many findings during this stage of the study were contrary to our original expectations. For instance, previous research in similar communities elsewhere (e.g., Howard 1970; Levy 1973) had found that children learn primarily through observation rather than through direct teaching, and that teaching/learning interactions rely on demonstration more than verbal explanation. But we found that from the age of 6 months, Kwara'ae children experience direct, verbally mediated teaching of many intellectual and cultural skills, in both the immediate context of use and in temporally and spatially distant contexts (Watson-Gegeo and Gegeo 1986a, 1986b). Children are pushed toward adult standards of speech, behavior, and responsibility very early: They begin productive work and participate in important social exchanges by 3 years of age. Many Kwara'ae caregiver-child routines resemble those used by white American middle-class caregivers to teach their children language and to prepare them for school.

Of particular interest is the special kind of teaching, beginning around 18 months of age, called *fa'amanata'anga* 'shaping the mind'. Fa'amanata'anga speech events occur in a formal, serious-to-sacred context and combine direct teaching with interpersonal counseling (Watson-Gegeo and Gegeo 1989; Watson-Gegeo 1990). They are built on abstract discussion and the teaching of reasoning skills through question/answer pairs, rhetorical questions, tightly argued sequences of ideas and premises, comparison and contrast, and cause and effect. Comprehension, inferencing, and creative use of metaphors and examples to develop points and illustrate them are emphasized in these events. In short, fa'amanata'anga teaches children universal reasoning skills. In Kwara'ae culture, the cognitive and interactional skills demonstrated and practiced in fa'amanata'anga sessions are essential for effective performance in testimony, oratory, and debate in public meetings and court hearings, and for being recognized as an elder at mid-life.

Close study of twenty-five tape-recorded fa'amanata'anga sessions involving young children revealed that children as young as 3 years of age can understand and participate appropriately in the complex reasoning of these sessions (Watson-Gegeo and Gegeo, 1989). Our findings led us to question the notion that language socialization in preliterate societies necessarily fails to prepare children cognitively for schooling. The next step was to compare patterns of teaching and language use in home and community with those in the classroom.

Language and interaction in the classroom

We observed language arts lessons in several classrooms at a school attended by most of the children we studied. Our observations, together with interviews of parents, headmasters, and teachers, gave us insights into differences in discourse and values between home and school.

As of the mid-1980s, the only language officially allowed in the classroom was English. However, rural teachers often have poor English skills themselves. As might be expected in this situation, the discourse used in lessons and for classroom control is highly formulaic. A typical reading lesson in first grade involves isolated English sentences divorced from any context whatsoever, designed to demonstrate abstract notions of grammar and vocabulary. Some of these sentences depict cultural scenarios unfamiliar to the children (e.g., "Ken is playing with ice cream"). Others are highly problematic because they violate local cultural values or expectations: e.g., "He's only a little boy and he can't help his father" stands in marked contrast to the local cultural emphasis on family interdependence and early adultlike work behavior. Similarly, "Maxie the hen was proud of her feathers," which attributes human emotions and behavior to a symbolically unimportant bird, is illogical and silly to Kwara'ae children, whom we saw laugh in embarrassment when it was first read in class. By school age, Kwara'ae children have been taught at home that knowledge must have meaning and applicability to be of value.

Rural teachers' pedagogical strategies are primarily whole-group drill and practice with individual oral recitation, and simple worksheets. Children memorize the singsong phrases and often recite with no apparent attention to meaning. Worksheets in the early primary grades typically involve picture-word pairs, but we have found that many children who score 100 percent correct on a series of redundant vocabulary worksheets are unable to read the words if we cover up the pictures.

A thin explanation of Kwara'ae children's school failure points to the differences between home and school language use, the submersion of their first language, their immersion in a restricted version of English, pedagogically inadequate and irrelevant materials, and poorly trained teachers. We believe that these children should receive their initial education in their first language, and that teaching/learning patterns in the home and community (particularly fa'amanata'anga) could be adapted to classrooms to make education more meaningful for them.

However, given that home experiences with language, although different from school experiences, involve intense training in universal reasoning skills, we began to wonder why these children seem unable to transfer what they know to school learning. This question arose from considering the links between contexts in the child's interactional world: In what ways are they continuous? Disjunctive? Where are cognitive, linguistic, and interactional skills learned, and where are they then used? Even without a focus on children's learning at school, such questions would have required that we move out of the micro- and macrocontexts of the children's primary culture, and into the macrocontexts – which we have labeled vertical – in which their society and culture articulate with national and international institutions and culture(s). The other question raised during the first two stages of our work also required examining the relationships between local schools and macro economic and political factors: Why is teaching in rural Solomon Islands' schools so poor?

Institutional constraints past and present

The third stage of our study began with extending the horizontal dimension to trace Solomons history through the macro (societal) processes of colonialism, missionization, World War II, and accelerated economic development since independence in 1978. We examined how these historical events and processes have contributed to dramatic social and political changes over the past 80 years, and the proactive and reactive ways in which schooling – including debates over the language of instruction – has contributed to many of these changes. Language has played an important and highly political role in the history of the Solomons, contributing to the undermining of traditional sources of knowledge, growing inequities between urban and rural areas, and the emergence of social classes. Since the British established hegemony over the Solomons in the mid-nineteenth century, language has been a tool for both colonial suppression and resistance, and for attempts to form a nation out of disparate societies while at the same time emphasizing religious, cultural, and class divisions (for a detailed discussion of the politics of language in historical perspective, see Watson-Gegeo 1987; Watson-Gegeo and Gegeo 1992).

Current institutional practices at the national and provincial level with regard to education are continuous with Solomons colonial history. Primary among these has been the continuation of English as the official national language and sole medium of school instruction. English is spoken (with varying degrees of fluency) by probably no more than 10 to 15 percent of Solomon Islanders, yet all middle to higher echelon jobs in the private and public sectors require both spoken and written English skills. Upward mobility depends on acquiring proficiency in English in a situation in which competition for the relatively few good jobs is very keen.

Limitations of space prevent an in-depth presentation of the complex ways in which micro- and macrocontextual levels intersect and interact. A thick explanation of schooling failure in the Solomons is at least a book-length project. Instead, we will examine selected micro/macro linkages that illustrate how societal processes and institutional practices shape interactions in the classroom and community.

The rapid expansion of primary schools since 1970 to meet development goals, the rising number of school-age children due to the Solomons' high birthrate, and the replacement of expatriate teachers with local teachers after independence have all negatively affected the quality of instruction over the past two decades. Island teachers sent to rural areas rarely have a good command of English, and as of 1987 school leavers with the equivalent of an American tenth-grade education were still being posted to rural primary schools without any teacher training. These problems reflect the difficulty of recruiting and training enough teachers to keep up with the expanding population in an economy in which teacher salaries are low in comparison to jobs in the private sector. Many untrained teachers posted to rural areas are waiting to be recalled for government-sponsored teacher training, after which they hope to be posted to an urban school. Often they are not committed to rural education.

To retain teachers, prevent *wantok* (shared native language) favoritism, expand teachers' experiences, and expose students to the varied knowledge of different teachers, the national and provincial policy through the mid-1980s has been to rotate teachers and headmasters frequently from one area of the country or province to another. An unintended outcome of this practice has been to undermine staff attempts to create a coherent program in any particular school. Teachers burn out easily and tend to resist being involved in program planning because they feel it is a waste of time.

Teachers' career aspirations are one factor creating strain in their relationships with parents. Parents regard teachers as temporary residents of their community, and complain that they are not committed to the children. Because teachers are there temporarily, they come to know their students' abilities and characteristics only superficially. Relationships between the school and community, and between teacher and student in the classroom may become tense and distant. Parents often resent being called to repair buildings, cut the grass, or supply food to school feasts because they do not regard the school as truly their own. They often complain that teachers are getting a salary whereas they are not, so why must they give further of time and resources to the school? These attitudes are openly expressed in the presence of children and probably affect their attitude toward school.

Parents' attitudes also reflect the decline in status of teaching as a vocation since colonial times. In the past, school teachers were equated with traditional knowledge specialists, and were accorded respect, high status, and almost a sacred role. In mission times, being a teacher was equal in status to being a priest or minister. With the decline of respect for traditional culture, and the rise of new white-collar professions in the wake of economic development, the importance of teaching has been devalued. Many teachers in fact leave teaching to take up positions in the churches as ministers or priests.

The few materials available in most rural schools are outdated castoffs from abroad, culturally biased in format and content. Budget problems and the need to stay on good terms with foreign aid donors mean that donations of outdated texts and materials sent (often in incomplete sets) from schools or agencies in Western countries must be accepted and distributed to schools, whether or not ministry officials or teachers think the materials are worthwhile. Such materials are forwarded to rural schools without instructions for their use. One rural headmaster told us, "We get the students' books without the teacher manual, or the teacher manual without the students' books – it seems we hardly ever get both."

The short supply and poor quality of materials we observed in rural schools is partly due to national financial constraints and inadequate planning, but also to deliberate favoring of urban schools. National government officials (and even provincial officials) often show a disinterest in rural areas altogether, as if "Solomon Islands" referred only to Guadalcanal, or really only to Honiara, the capital.

With poor training and few materials, school administrators and teachers can only repeat their own schooling experience. Education under these circumstances becomes the presentation of "school knowledge" in simplified bits of unrelated information packaged in ritualized lesson formats (McNeil 1986), based on what Freire (1970) calls the banking model of education – this is what many parents, teachers, and administrators believe school learning is about. Their view is reinforced by the national examination system. Teachers' primary responsibility is to prepare children to take the exams that control entrance into the proportionately few secondary school placements. They must be sure that students are prepared for the kinds of information and formats expected on the exam. Teachers who see beyond the exam-based vision of teaching quickly become demoralized by their own poor training and the lack of institutional support, so that their creativity is suppressed and they, too, resort to remaining within the narrow confines of the available texts.

The conditions of rural schools are thus not merely the result of cultural differences or of poor teacher training. Nor are they accidental. Another macrolevel factor implicated in rural school failure is the growing class division in the Solomons and the related growing inequity between urban and rural areas (Connell and Curtain 1982). As in many colonial and postcolonial settings, schooling has assisted both processes by imparting European values and culture (Boutilier 1978), in line with Collins's (1985:73) observation that schools everywhere primarily "teach particular status cultures." Now as in the colonial past, rural areas are associated with notions of primitiveness and urban areas with sophistication. Education is viewed as the path to economic advancement via urban employment, to a European lifestyle, and to political power. Academically inferior rural schools are functional in a system in which the urban elites want to make certain that their own children will favorably compete for the limited number of secondary school slots, thereby perpetuating the elite group in the next generation.

All of these factors infuse rural classrooms and communities with a particular atmosphere, of which everyone participating in local education – whether headmaster, teacher, parent, or child – is aware. Parents' knowledge of how the educational system works against rural areas is one way macrolevel influences become instantiated at the moment of socializing interactions between parents and children. We observed that, directly and indirectly, rural parents communicate to their children the likelihood of failure at school, even as they try to prepare and encourage their children to succeed. This communication often comes in fa'amanata'anga sessions that are affectively intense and symbolically loaded.

The undervaluing of local knowledge vis-à-vis school knowledge has meant that some parents are abandoning traditional teaching of universal reasoning skills at home because they have come to accept the postcolonial elite view that schools control all the knowledge that is worth knowing. We suspect that if traditional teaching methods are abandoned, children will be even less prepared for school than they have been up to now.

To a Kwara'ae child competent at age 6 or 8 in household and subsistence tasks, whose village world is complex, challenging, and interesting, school lessons with their fragmented, simplistic information may be boring and meaningless. Going to school may carry positive symbolic meaning for such a child: We see children proudly setting off for school in their uniforms each morning, carrying pencils and exercise books, and looking forward to some sort of desk job when they grow up. But studying and learning in school may not be meaningful to children, nor do some of them understand that success in school requires it. Everyone in the surrounding villages knows who is taking the examination when it is given, and failure brings embarrassment for the child's whole family as well as defeat for the family's hopes of economic advancement. The majority do fail and stay in the village, work on plantations, or seek low-skilled jobs in town, often with the strong sense of defeat described by Solomons educator Moffat Wasuka (quoted at the beginning of this chapter).

Conclusion

We have attempted to accomplish two goals in this chapter: first, to argue for the need to integrate micro- and macrocontextual levels of information in the study of language, education, and power; and second, to briefly illustrate the usefulness of such an integration to an explanation of rural children's school failure in the Solomon Islands. We have argued that a thick explanation for school failure requires a holistic analysis. In fact, we have been unable in the space of a chapter to discuss all of what we know to be significant at a variety of levels for children's school failure.

For the Solomons as elsewhere, the educational questions of the 1990s will be: What is a good education, and what is it for? Who should define it? Will it be defined nationally, provincially, or locally? How are policies and programs to be designed? It seems clear to us that educational intervention will have to occur across the levels we outlined, if it is to be successful. The answer to the well-known dilemma, should educational intervention be top-down or bottom-up, is obviously both, and simultaneously so. Similarly, a vision of what education should become must be worked out across the levels we have identified rather than dictated from a government ministry.

References

Au, K. H-P., and C. Jordan. 1977. Teaching reading to Hawaiian children: Finding a culturally appropriate solution. In C. Jordan, R. G. Tharp, K. H-P. Au,

T. S. Weisner, and R. Gallimore, *A multidisciplinary approach to research in education: The Kamehameha Early Education Program.* Technical Report No. 81. Honolulu: Kamehameha Schools/Bishop Estate, Kamehameha Early Education Program.

Bennett, J. W. 1985. The micro-macro nexus: Typology, process, and system. In B. R. DeWalt and P. J. Pelto (Eds.), *Micro and macro levels of analysis in anthropology: Issues in theory and research.* Boulder, Colo.: Westview Press.

Boggs, S. T. 1985. *Speaking, relating and learning: A study of Hawaiian children at home and at school.* Norwood, N.J.: Ablex.

Boutilier, J. A. 1978. Missions, administration, and education in the Solomon Islands, 1893–1942. In J. A. Boutilier, D. T. Hughes, and S. W. Tiffany (Eds.), *Mission, church, and sect in Oceania.* ASAO Monograph No. 6. New York: University Press of America.

Cazden, C. B., V. P. John, and D. Hymes. (Eds.). 1972. *Functions of language in the classroom.* New York: Teachers College Press.

Collins, R. 1985. Functional and conflict theories of educational stratification. In J. H. Ballantine (Ed.), *Schools and society: A reader in education and sociology.* Palo Alto: Mayfield.

Connell, J., and R. Curtain. 1982. Urbanization and inequality in Melanesia. In R. J. May and H. Nelson (Eds.), *Melanesia: Beyond diversity.* Vol. 2. Canberra: Research School of Pacific Studies, Australian National University.

DeWalt, B. R., and P. J. Pelto. 1985. Microlevel/macrolevel linkages: An introduction to the issues and a framework for analysis. In B. R. DeWalt and P. J. Pelto (Eds.), *Micro and macro levels of analysis in anthropology: Issues in theory and research.* Boulder, Colo.: Westview Press.

Diesing, P. 1971. *Patterns of discovery in the social sciences.* Chicago: Aldine.

Erickson, F. D., and G. Mohatt. 1982. Cultural organization of participation structures in two classrooms of Indian students. In G. Spindler (Ed.), *Doing the ethnography of schooling: Educational anthropology in action.* New York: Holt, Rinehart and Winston.

Firth, R. 1961. *Elements of social organization.* Boston: Beacon.

Freire, P. 1970. *Pedagogy of the oppressed.* New York: Continuum.

Friesen, W. D. 1986. Labour mobility and economic transformation in Solomon Islands. Ph.D. diss., University of Auckland, New Zealand.

Geertz, C. 1973. *The interpretation of cultures.* New York: Basic Books.

Giddens, A. 1979. *Central problems in social theory: Action, structure and contradiction in social analysis.* Berkeley: University of California Press.

Glaser, B. G., and A. L. Strauss. 1967. *The discovery of grounded theory: Strategies for qualitative research.* Chicago: Aldine.

Groenewegen, K. 1989. *Solomon Islands, Report on the census of population 1986.* Report 2.B: Data Analysis. Honiara: Statistics Office, Ministry of Finance.

Howard, A. 1970. *Learning to be Rotuman.* New York: Columbia University Press.

Kaplan, R. B. 1990. Introduction: Language planning in theory and practice. In R. Baldauf, Jr., and A. Luke (Eds.), *Language planning and education in Australasia and the South Pacific.* Clevedon and Philadelphia: Multilingual Matters.

Levy, R. 1973. *Tahitians: Mind and experience in the Society Islands.* Chicago: University of Chicago Press.

McNeil, L. 1986. *Contradictions of control: School structure and school knowledge.* New York: Routledge and Kegan Paul.

Scollon, R., and S. B. K. Scollon. 1979. Thematic abstraction: A Chipewyan two-year-old. In R. Scollon and S. B. K. Scollon (Eds.), *Linguistic convergence: An ethnography of speaking at Fort Chipewyan, Alberta.* New York: Academic Press.

Snow, C. E. 1983. Literacy and language: Relationships during the preschool years. *Harvard Educational Review* 53:165–89.

Solomon Islands Government. 1980. *Solomon Islands national development plan 1980–1984.* Vol. 1. Honiara: GPO.

Tryon, D. T. 1979. Remarks on the language situation in the Solomon Islands. In S. A. Wurm (Ed.), *New Guinea and the neighbouring areas: A sociolinguistic laboratory.* The Hague: Mouton.

Wasuka, M. 1989. Education. In H. Laracy (Ed.), *Ples blong iumi: Solomon Islands, the past four thousand years.* Suva, Fiji: Institute of Pacific Studies, University of the South Pacific.

Watson, K. A. 1975. Transferable communicative routines: Strategies and group identity in two speech events. *Language in Society* 4:53–72.

Watson-Gegeo, K. A. 1987. English in the Solomon Islands. *World Englishes* 6:21–32.

1988. Ethnography in ESL: Defining the essentials. *TESOL Quarterly* 22:575–92.

1990. The social transfer of cognitive skills in Kwara'ae. *Quarterly Newsletter of the Laboratory for Comparative Human Cognition* 12(2): 86–90.

Watson-Gegeo, K. A., and S. T. Boggs. 1977. From verbal play to talk-story: The role of routines in speech events among Hawaiian children. In S. Ervin-Tripp and C. Mitchell-Kernan (Eds.), *Child discourse.* New York: Academic Press.

Watson-Gegeo, K. A., and D. W. Gegeo. 1986a. Calling-out and repeating routines in Kwara'ae children's language socialization. In B. B. Schieffelin and E. Ochs (Eds.), *Language socialization across cultures.* New York: Cambridge University Press.

1986b. The social world of Kwara'ae children: Acquisition of language and values. In J. Cook-Gumperz, W. Corsaro, and J. Streeck (Eds.), *Children's worlds and children's language.* The Hague: Mouton de Gruyter.

1989. Learning to think straight: Language, culture, and cognitive development in Kwara'ae. American Anthropological Association Meetings, 16 November, Washington, D.C.

1992. Schooling, knowledge and power: Social transformation in the Solomon Islands. *Anthropology & Education Quarterly* 23(1): 10–29.

Watson-Gegeo, K. A., and P. Ulichny. 1988. Ethnographic inquiry into second language acquisition and instruction. *University of Hawai'i Working Papers in English as a Second Language* 7(2): 75–92.

Wertsch, J. V. 1985. *Culture, communication, and cognition.* Cambridge: Cambridge University Press.

4 Supporting or containing bilingualism? Policies, power asymmetries, and pedagogic practices in mainstream primary classrooms

Marilyn Martin-Jones and Mukul Saxena

This chapter focuses on a specific form of educational provision that has been developed for bilingual children in primary schools in Britain. It has come to be known in the British context as 'bilingual support'. This form of provision has been developed for bilingual learners from ethnic minority groups, primarily in multilingual urban areas in England. It is the most minimal form of bilingual education provision conceivable, and it is primarily transitional in its goals: That is, the main educational purpose is to facilitate the learner's transition to monolingual English-medium education. Provision is generally organised in the early years of primary education, and an increasingly common pattern from school to school, and from one local education authority (LEA) to another, is that bilingual classroom assistants are appointed to work alongside monolingual class teachers. In this context, then, bilingual support refers to the occasional use of the learner's home and/or community language along with English in classroom settings where the relations between bilingual and monolingual teaching staff are generally characterised by power asymmetries.

During the 1980s, as this particular form of bilingual education provision was being developed in schools in England, there was considerable educational rhetoric about the benefits of "supporting bilingualism" (e.g., Houlton and Wiley 1983) but there was very little discussion among educational practitioners about what the goals of bilingual support should be or about what it should entail in day-to-day practice in the classroom. There was also very little discussion about the dilemmas facing bilingual staff positioned in this way as buffers between local communities and the mainstream education system. A decade later, there is still relatively little debate about the nature and purpose of bilingual support, yet the recruitment of bilingual staff to undertake this kind of work continues apace. Increasing numbers of bilingual adults are being appointed to low-status posts in schools in England as 'bilingual aides' or 'bilingual assistants'. Bilingual teachers already working in local educational services are also being re-deployed into bilingual support work. We still know very little about the nature of the bilingual classroom practice emerging in situations where bilingual support work has been initiated.

Very few classroom-based studies have as yet been conducted (Jupp 1990; Moffat 1991; Thompson 1991; Milroy and Moffat 1992).

We completed two years of ethnographic research in classrooms in the northwest of England where bilingual support work is currently being developed.[1] Our aims in this chapter are as follows: First, we want to present some initial findings from this research, principally from our analyses of the bilingual classroom discourse we observed and video-recorded in this context (primarily Panjabi/English bilingual discourse). Second, we want to illustrate some of the ways in which we feel that a critical approach to ethnographic work can be developed in bilingual classroom settings and in analyses of bilingual classroom discourse. As Martin-Jones (in press) has shown, recent research in bilingual classrooms has been primarily interactionist in nature. We will argue that, unless work of a more critical nature is developed, the contribution made by applied linguists to debates about educational policy will have only minimal impact. We share the view expressed by Rampton (1990) as follows: "The development of microethnographic research was a reflection of a general trend towards the marginalizing of the contribution that researchers can make to debates about policy" (cited in Strubell 1990:112).

In the next section of this chapter, before we present some of the findings from our classroom-based research, we will provide a brief historical account of the development of bilingual support as a form of educational provision. This account will be set in the wider context of educational policy developments in Britain. The focus will be on the shifts that have taken place in educational thinking about provision for learners from ethnic minority groups, the extensive changes that have taken place in the organisation of this provision, and the politics behind the funding of the provision.

Bilingual learners in a monolingual education system: developments in educational policy

There are now a number of detailed analyses of the development of official educational responses to the presence of linguistic minority children in British schools over the last few decades (Linguistic Minorities Project 1985; Tansley 1986; Verma 1987; Reid 1988; Bourne 1989;

---

1 This research was carried out as part of an educational linguistic project based at Lancaster University. The project was funded by the Economic and Social Research Council from 1989 to 1992 as part of a wider research initiative on 'Education for a Multicultural Society'. The members of the research team were: Marilyn Martin-Jones (project coordinator), Mukul Saxena (research associate), David Barton, and Roz Ivanic.

Martin-Jones 1989; Turner 1989; Reid 1990; Bhatt and Martin-Jones 1992). We will focus here on those educational policy developments that paved the way for the development of bilingual support as a specific form of educational provision for ethnic minority children.

Our account is organised chronologically, and different phases of educational policy are outlined. However, up until the late 1980s the educational service in Britain was organised on a decentralised basis. Local educational authorities had considerable autonomy in policy formulation and curriculum development within their areas. The overall picture of policy development with respect to language education is thus a complex and varied one. Although it is possible to identify broad shifts in educational thinking, the nature and timing of the educational response to linguistic diversity was different from one LEA to another.

A predominantly assimilationist ethos

Throughout most of the 1960s and early 1970s, the home languages of bilingual children from ethnic minority groups were excluded from the curriculum. Assimilationist views predominated during this period. The main preoccupation was with the teaching of English as a Second Language (ESL). Special tuition was organised for bilingual children in language centres or withdrawal classes (Ellis 1985). It was during this period that ESL came to be defined as distinct from the teaching of English as a Foreign Language.

The view of the British nation as a unitary whole with a homogeneous culture was implicit in most educational thinking at the time. Children with a different cultural and linguistic heritage were expected to accommodate to 'the British way of life'. In the educational discourse of this period, bilingualism was represented as a problem and minority languages were seen as a source of interference in the learning of English.

A phase of cultural pluralism

In the mid-1970s there was a clear shift in thinking about the home languages of ethnic minority children. The publication of the Bullock Report (DES 1975) marked the turning point. This report was produced by the National Committee of Enquiry set up to look into the use of English and the standards of literacy in the schools. The Bullock Committee interpreted their brief in the widest sense and included in their report a chapter on the language needs of bilingual children. They espoused an explicitly pluralist view and insisted that schools should respect the cultural and linguistic heritage of bilingual children. The report included the following statement of principle:

No child should be expected to cast off the language and culture of the home as he crosses the school threshold and the curriculum should reflect those aspects of his life. (Chapter 20:5)

The late 1970s saw the beginnings of a policy debate about the inclusion of minority languages such as Chinese, Italian, Gujarati, and Panjabi in the school curriculum. Throughout the 1970s, provision for the teaching of minority languages had been organised, for the most part, outside the education system. This provision, including preparation for public examinations, had been steadily growing in response to increasing demand from linguistic minority parents. By the mid-1970s, minority organisations were already beginning to put pressure on LEAs to make provision available for the teaching of their languages within the local schools or, at the very least, to provide free premises for community-run classes.

Local education policy was also influenced in the late 1970s by developments within the European Community context. In 1977, the European Communities directive "On the Education of the Children of Migrant Workers" (77/486) was adopted by all member states. Article 3 of the directive called for the teaching of the 'mother tongue' and culture of the children of migrant workers "in accordance with national circumstances and legal systems" (Council of the European Communities 1977:2).

In the late 1970s and early 1980s, some LEAs began to organise provision for the teaching of minority community languages, primarily in the later years of secondary school. Provision was scattered and was mostly made available in inner-city schools. Those LEAs that moved into this area of curriculum development justified provision in pluralist terms: Minority languages came to be characterised as an educational resource rather than as an impediment to the learning of English.

The mainstreaming of English Language Support

In the majority of LEAs, the main concern was still with ESL teaching. However, during this period, there were significant changes taking place in approaches to ESL teaching. The seventies saw the beginnings of a move, in some LEAs, towards ESL support work in the mainstream classroom, particularly at the primary level. By the end of the 1970s, ESL provision in a number of LEAs had been substantially reorganised. The separate language centres and withdrawal classes set up in the 1960s became LEA 'support services' with a multicultural brief. There was a concomitant redefinition of the role of English Language Support (ELS) teachers. These teachers were generally based at a local support service and worked on a peripatetic basis, regularly visiting one or more schools and developing strategies and materials for mainstreaming. Wherever possible, this was done in collaboration with school-based teaching staff in language-across-the-curriculum work.

The Swann Report

The next major landmark in the development of policy responses to linguistic diversity was the Swann Report (DES 1985). The brief of the National Committee of Enquiry compiling the report was to look into existing educational provision for ethnic minority children. One full chapter (Chapter 7) was devoted to issues in language education policy and practice.

The Swann Committee strongly endorsed the move towards main-streaming of ELS support at both primary and secondary levels. They pointed out that withdrawal systems of provision were "discriminatory in effect" although they might not be "discriminatory in intent" (DES 1985:389). They argued that withdrawal denies access to the full range of educational opportunities offered within the mainstream curriculum of the school. They also argued that children's language development takes place as much in the context of informal spontaneous interaction with their peers at school as it does in the more formal context of the classroom.

The Swann Report was the closest Britain came at that time to having a national policy statement on the language education of ethnic minority children. The discourse of the Swann Report was a rather mixed one, however; the pluralist thinking reflected in some parts of the report was not extended to thinking about bilingualism. The Swann Committee shied away from espousing bilingual education as an option. The ration-ale given for this was that the committee was anxious about recommend-ing special forms of provision that would result in the segregation or marginalisation of black and Asian pupils in a climate of increasing in-stitutional racism.

The report also failed to support the teaching of community languages at primary and early secondary levels. The main burden of responsibility for language maintenance and the development of minority language literacy was placed on the voluntary sector and on classes organised by local community groups in the evenings and at weekends.

The positions adopted by the Swann Committee on bilingual education and community language teaching sparked off considerable controversy. The strongest objections came from bilingual teachers and parents. Re-iterating the Swann Committee's concern with institutional racism, they argued that it was discriminatory to deny a curriculum that could meet the specific needs of bilingual learners from ethnic minority groups. They also drew attention to the fact that separate provision for bilingual educa-tion for Welsh-speaking children was already being organised on a fairly wide scale in Wales and argued that a double standard operated in British educational policies.

The only concession made in the Swann Report with regard to the home languages of bilingual learners was the recommendation that nursery schools and primary schools should endeavour to identify someone who could serve as a 'bilingual resource' "to help with the transitional needs of non-English speaking children starting school" (DES 1985:407). The committee went on to give examples of people who might be called upon to be bilingual resources: The inventory included bilingual staff already appointed to a school (e.g., a bilingual teacher, a nonteaching assistant, or a nursery nurse) and bilingual parents or even older children from local secondary schools who were involved in community service programmes or child care courses. This inventory gives insights into the committee's thinking about bilingual support as a form of educational provision. It was clearly seen as an optional extra that would not have major implications in staffing terms.

The role of someone acting as a bilingual resource was described as follows:

We would see such a resource providing a degree of continuity between the home and school environment by offering psychological and social support for the child, as well as being able to explain simple educational concepts in a child's mother tongue, if the need arises, but always working within the mainstream classroom and alongside the class teacher. (DES 1985:407)

The emphasis was thus on easing the social transition to school. There was also a clear recommendation that the role of the bilingual resource person was primarily to provide support for the class teacher, using the children's home language and acting as an interpreter only from time to time. No guidelines were given as to how bilingual support work might be developed 'alongside' the class teacher in day-to-day classroom practice.

Finally, this minimal form of bilingual provision was clearly distinguished from bilingual education or mother-tongue-medium education along the lines being developed in Wales or Scotland.

We would in no way however see such a situation as meaning that a child's mother tongue should be used as a general medium of instruction or should form a structured part of the curriculum as has traditionally been envisaged in programmes of bilingual education and mother tongue maintenance. (DES 1985:407)

Section 11 funding

From the mid-1980s onwards, LEAs began to formulate their own policy response to the Swann Report. The provision of bilingual support in the early years of primary schooling came to be seen as an increasingly attractive option. Funding for the development of bilingual support was sought from Central Government under Section 11 of the Local Government Act of 1966. Since the 1960s, this has been the main source of funding for special educational provisions for learners from ethnic minority groups. The central government covers 75 percent of the total costs and these are matched by a 25 percent contribution from the LEA seeking support.

Funding has typically been made available to LEAs provided that the posts funded are extra to normal staffing needs and that they are designated to meet the specific needs of "Commonwealth immigrants" and their immediate descendants. Funding was originally made available to LEAs for developing provision for English language support, although, in the 1970s, Section 11 funds also began to be used by some LEAs for developing provision for community language teaching.

The basis of the funding has remained largely unchanged. As Bourne observed in the late 1980s:

Section 11 remains in force today in its original terms of 'immigration', rather than as funding for the development and protection of minority group interests and minority group participation in society. It has therefore been the focus of controversy for many years" (1989: 40).

In the early 1990s, major changes were made in the organisation of Section 11 provision. LEAs applying for Section 11 funding were required to reorganise provision for ethnic minority children so that it would be more school-based, thus bringing it in line with the move to the local management of schools introduced under the Education Reform Act of 1988. Local school-based projects had to be more focused with clearly defined targets and anticipated outcomes. In principle, this restructuring of Section 11 provision could have had beneficial effects: It could, for example, have facilitated joint planning work between language support teachers (monolingual or bilingual) and class teachers, but in practice, movement in this direction was hampered by the fact that teachers were preoccupied with the demands of the National Curriculum.

A further development was that community language teaching could no longer be funded under Section 11 if it was organised within school hours as part of the modern languages curriculum. Since this change was introduced, there has been little evidence of LEAs being able to find resources within their mainstream budget to support community language provision. As a consequence, bilingual teachers in many areas are being re-deployed into bilingual support work.

The funding issue is a crucial one since, as Bourne (1989:11) points out, it is through increasing control over funding that the Central Government has, since the 1980s, been able to influence the nature and extent of language provision for ethnic minority children in Britain without ever having to formulate an explicit policy. Moreover, this control comes from outside the education system: Section 11 funds come from the Home Office, the main government department responsible for immigration matters.

In November 1992, the government finally announced that major reductions would be made in Section 11 funding between 1994 and 1996. These reductions will have a devastating effect on provision for bilingual pupils in England. At this time, it is difficult to estimate the impact in precise terms. Leung (1993) sketches two possible scenarios for initial staff cutbacks. In the best case, two posts in ten would be eliminated in 1994; in the worst case, four posts in ten would be cut.

The impact of the National Curriculum

Since the Education Reform Act of 1988 and the development of the National Curriculum, the question of how best to meet the needs of bilingual learners in schools in England has been sidetracked. From the mid-1980s to the present we have witnessed a retreat to a much more ethnocentric view of the curriculum and, in particular, the English curriculum. The role of Standard English as the emblem of a common national culture was reasserted in the Kingman Report on the Teaching of English (DES 1988) and this continues to be a key feature of current educational policy. It is quite remarkable that, in the model of language presented in the Kingman Report, virtually no reference is made to language variation along the lines of race or class. The main aspects of linguistic variation on the Kingman agenda were historical and geographical variation. As Cameron and Bourne (1988) have noted, the covert effect of the affirmation of the cultural authority of Standard English is the containment of minority community languages and regional forms of English.

In other national curriculum documents, more concessions were made to pluralist views: for example, in the Cox Report (DES 1989) on English learners aged 5–16, in which programmes of study based on the Kingman model of language were outlined in detail; and in the Harris Report (Des 1990) on Modern Foreign Languages in the National Curriculum for learners aged 11–16. The Harris Report endorsed the diversification of the modern languages curriculum and some minority community languages were proposed as Foundation Subjects for the secondary curriculum. However, the strong statements in the Harris Report in favour of the development of community language teaching were undercut by the condition that community languages could be offered in a school timetable only if a national language of one of the countries in the European Union was already on offer.

The trial run of the national curriculum assessment procedures took place in the summer of 1991 (Key Stage One for children aged 7). There was considerable concern among teachers about the impact that this would have on bilingual children. Some schools and LEAs made arrangements for some bilingual input to teacher assessment and to the administration of the SATS: for example, in math and science, where use of the learner's home language is permitted. There has been, however, a good deal of debate about whether arrangements should be made for providing bilingual support during assessment if teaching/learning activities have not been taking place in the child's home or community language. Overall, arrangements for bilingual support in assessment have been made in a rather piecemeal fashion and with little guidance from the Schools Examination and Assessment Council (SEAC). Moreover, there has been very little training for the bilingual staff involved (some of whom are not yet qualified teachers). There has also been very poor communication with bilingual parents about assessment procedures.

The development of bilingual provision

In the immediate post-Swann years, there was considerable interest in the development of bilingual support and community language teaching. A survey carried out by the National Foundation for Education Research (NFER) revealed that, by 1987, 69 out of 108 LEAs in England and Wales were involved in some way in bilingual support work or community language teaching (Bourne 1989:121). Thirty-six percent of all bilingual staff were involved in bilingual support (at primary level for the most part) and 64 percent were involved in community language teaching (mostly at secondary level) (Bourne 1989:118). The proportion of bilingual staff was still quite low as compared with monolingual support teachers: For example, in areas where there were larger concentrations of bilingual children, English language support staff outnumbered bilingual support staff/community language teachers 17 to 1 on average at secondary level and 14 to 1 at primary level.

Eleven languages were reported most often in the survey: They were either taught as subjects or used in bilingual support work. In order of frequency of mention, the languages were: Urdu, Panjabi, Hindi, Bengali, Gujarati, Italian, Chinese, Turkish, Greek, Arabic, and Creoles. Both qualified teachers and instructors without qualifications had been appointed by the LEAs responding to the survey.

The overall picture is likely to have changed considerably since 1987. No reliable statistics are available as yet. But we do know that the most significant trend across LEAs in the late 1980s and early 1990s has been the appointment of bilingual teaching assistants or teacher aides who receive 'on the job' training. It seems that very different arrangements have been made across LEAs for the support and training of bilingual staff and the teachers who are working in partnership with them. Another significant trend has been provision of bilingual support primarily at nursery and primary school level. There is therefore little continuity of support beyond the first few years of schooling.

At the end of the 1980s, we still knew very little about how bilingual support work was being developed in the classroom context. Practice was being worked out school by school with little institutional support and with scarce resources. There was considerable diversity in the ways in which bilingual support was being implemented.

Bourne (1989) reported on visits made to schools in different LEAs as part of her 1987 survey for NFER. She noted that the work of the bilingual support staff she observed fell into three categories:

1. individual support for pupils in mainstream classes
2. written translation work for the school
3. whole class work
   a. with the bilingual practitioner leading the whole class and working bilingually, e.g., in story-telling sessions
   b. with a bilingual and monolingual teacher working in close partnership: involving joint planning, full tandem teaching with pupils engaged in group activities; groups mixed by language and ability. This sort of partnership was only observed in infant classes.

(Bourne 1989:148)

These insights provided the starting point for our study of primary classrooms in the northwest of England, where bilingual support was being developed. We also wanted to take a close look at emerging practices and show how the role of bilingual support staff was being defined. We further aimed to document the ways in which the contributions of bilingual staff to classroom talk were constrained or facilitated in different types of teaching/learning events. In the next section of this paper, we will give a brief account of the local context in which we were working and the approach we adopted for observing and analysing teaching/learning events that were accomplished bilingually.

A close look at classroom practice emerging in one local context

Our focus was on a policy initiative implemented by one LEA in the northwest of England. The LEA opted for a bilingual assistant scheme as part of its overall policy response to the Swann Report. The equivalent of forty full-time posts were created in 1989 with substantial Section 11 funding. There was a very encouraging response from local ethnic minority communities. There was an unexpectedly large number of applicants, many of whom had considerable experience in public sector work such as interpreting in local hospitals and working with playgroup schemes. There were also a number of applicants who had already been acting as bilingual resources in local schools on a voluntary basis. All of the bilingual classroom assistants who were eventually appointed by the authority were women. They were speakers of South Asian languages such as Panjabi and Gujarati. They were appointed to local schools to work in nursery and reception classes alongside monolingual class teachers.

In the autumn of 1989, as the bilingual assistants took up their posts, we began our visits to local schools. Our aim, as researchers, was to provide an account of how this new form of educational provision was being translated into communicative practice in different classrooms and in different types of teaching/learning events. Over a two-year period, we carried out regular classroom observations in local schools where bilingual assistants were working.

In the first year of the project, we visited eight schools on a regular basis. We focused our observations on storytelling events that were conducted bilingually. We chose to focus our observations in this way because storytelling was the one type of teaching/learning event that most bilingual assistants appeared to be involved in during the early days of the scheme.

In the second year of our project, we carried out regular observations in two classrooms. Here, we audio- and video-recorded a wide range of teaching/learning events that were conducted bilingually. These included: artwork; baking activities; computer-assisted learning activities; storytelling; guided play at the water-tray; carrying out a small experiment or going on a small expedition (e.g., around the local neighbourhood); and other small-group activities related to a cross-curricular theme that involved the children in reading, writing, drawing, colouring, or cutting and pasting. There were also news-sharing events at the start of the school day and storytelling sessions that involved the class as a whole towards the end of the school day.

In addition to these classroom observations, we conducted in-depth interviews with the bilingual assistants and the class teachers they were working with, other staff in the school, and local authorities who were involved in implementing the new scheme. Our fieldwork also included participant observation in local training programmes for bilingual classroom assistants and for class teachers.

Our approach to classroom ethnography

During the period in which we were conducting classroom observations, we kept a record of the types of teaching/learning events that were conducted bilingually. The focus on different types of classroom events helped us to get a sense of how monolingual teachers perceived the value and purpose of bilingual support work in their classes. The monolingual teachers made the main decisions day by day as to which events should be conducted bilingually and what role the bilingual assistants should play in those events.

Focusing in on events as a unit of observation and analysis enabled us to identify the different ways in which participant structures were defined across events. Again, the class teachers played a key role in determining the contribution that would be made by the bilingual assistants in different types of teaching/learning events.

We identified four main ways in which bilingual assistants were positioned as participants in different teaching/learning events: (1) leading the event alone; (2) leading the event with a monolingual adult as observer/ silent participant; (3) doing small-group work alongside a monolingual teacher, using the children's home language to introduce a concept with the monolingual teacher following up in English; (4) doing small-group work alongside a monolingual teacher and translating or reformulating the contributions of the teacher in the children's home language(s).

When organisational strategies such as (3) and (4) predominated, turn-allocation was generally controlled by the monolingual teacher. The bilingual assistant took turns when they were assigned to her. Sometimes, overt turn-giving signals were given. These included utterances addressed to the bilingual assistant by the class teacher, such as "Carry on, Miss Khan,"[2] or utterances addressed to the children that made explicit reference to the discourse role of the bilingual assistant. For example, in one primary science activity on electricity, the class teacher introduced a point in English, then turned to the children and said, "Mrs. Anwar will explain. . . ."[3] This served as a cue for the bilingual assistant to take a turn in Panjabi. Thus, the organisation of the bilingual support work in each event shaped the patterns of bilingual talk. When bilingual assistants were positioned as interpreters, they had much less scope for using the children's home or community language and for responding to contributions made by the children.

The focus on events also enabled us to identify and describe the ways in which the constellations of participants varied from one type of teaching/ learning event to another. Sometimes, all the bilingual children taking part in a particular event and the bilingual assistant would share the same language background, for example, a Panjabi-speaking bilingual assistant working with a group of bilingual children who all spoke Panjabi at home. Sometimes, however, the constellation of participants in an event was quite different. The groups sometimes included children whose home language was Gujarati, Urdu, or English. When faced with the communicative challenge of working with groups of mixed home language background, the Panjabi-speaking bilingual assistants usually continued

2 and 3 Fictitious names are given here to preserve confidentiality.

to use Panjabi and English with the group as a whole but code-switched into Urdu and/or Gujarati when addressing individual children.[4]

Focusing on discrete classroom events has become a common feature of observational work in bilingual classrooms (Mehan 1981; Moll 1981; Erikson and Mohatt 1982). This approach to classroom ethnography enabled us to sharpen our focus and to identify the key aspects of variation in classroom practice as outlined here. It also provided us with insights into the teachers' beliefs and pedagogic conventions underpinning the classroom practice we were observing. As Enright (1984) pointed out: "Classroom events are *emic* units of interaction in that they represent the teacher's own conceptualisation of how the flow of interaction in his or her classroom is divided up and conducted" (p. 31).

Through our in-depth interviews and through informal conversations with teachers and bilingual assistants during break times and lunch hours, we were able to check our understanding of the purpose and organisation of classroom events against theirs.

These microethnographic procedures made it possible to provide close descriptions of variation in communicative practices across teaching/learning events and gain detailed insights into some of the ways in which monolingual teachers' views about bilingual support were being translated into practice. However, we wanted to go beyond microlevel descriptions of classroom routines and communicative practices. We also wanted to take account of some of the ways in which the asymmetrical relations between bilingual assistants and class teachers – already created by educational policy decisions – were being reproduced in the communicative cycles of day-to-day life of the schools.

In our observational work, we therefore built up a picture of practices that constituted and reconstituted this working relationship as an asymmetrical one. We documented the way in which the role of the bilingual assistants was defined; the amount of yard duty they were expected to do; the extent to which they were involved in curriculum-planning meetings. When bilingual assistants were involved in staff meetings, we noted how patterns of turn taking and the use of names, titles, and terms of address also served to position the bilingual assistants as low-status staff. In the classroom context, the monolingual class teacher was the main decision maker. She or he took responsibility for assigning a participant role to the bilingual assistant from one teaching/learning event to another.

---

4 The two Panjabi-speaking bilingual assistants in the classes we observed were of Pakistani origin and Urdu was already part of their communicative repertoire. However, they had both made efforts to learn some spoken Gujarati, the home language of some of the children in the class.

A critical approach to bilingual classroom discourse

When we began to look closely at the transcripts of the bilingual talk in some of the teaching/learning events we had observed and recorded, we realised that, in our analysis, we would need to take account of not only the asymmetric social relations of the classroom but also the ways in which the bilingual assistants were positioned as buffers between the bilingual children and the demands of the monolingual mainstream school.

The bilingual assistants were caught in a bind. On the one hand, they were expected to be supportive and nurturing to young children from local minority communities who were making the social and cultural transition from home to school; on the other hand, they were expected to provide them with access to the curriculum. They were expected to use the children's home language to support their learning of English. The transitional nature of provisions for bilingual support was clearly stated in local authority documents and was underpinned by the criteria used in allocating Section 11 funding to support the bilingual assistant scheme.

In examining our transcripts, we found, for example, that the bilingual assistants oscillated between curriculum-oriented and learner-oriented talk. We will exemplify this with reference to a maths activity in which the bilingual assistant was working with a small group of learners. She was reviewing concepts such as *circle, square,* and *triangle.* She began by showing different shapes to the children and asking them what they were. She then asked them, one by one, to pick a shape from the tray on the table. After this, she asked them to place the shapes on coloured paper, to trace around the shapes, and eventually to cut them out and stick them on A4-size white sheets to make geometric designs. Following Heath, we classified the genre of classroom language use in the first part of this teaching/learning event as a "label-quest" (1986:167-68). In this part of the event, the bilingual assistant's main focus was on familiarising the children with the English labels for the geometric concepts she had in mind.

Building on the approach developed by Zentella (1981), we then looked at the pattern of code-switching across initiation–reply–evaluation (IRE) exchanges. One pattern of code-switching predominated in the exchanges that occurred in this label-quest sequence:

INITIATION: Panjabi or Panjabi/English
RESPONSE: English
(FEEDBACK: English)

When there was a code-switch in the utterance used by the bilingual assistant to initiate an exchange, it was most often a switch into English on a key item related to the topic of the teaching/learning event (e.g., shape, colour). This pattern of code-switching into English on single nouns or noun phrases related to the content of the activity recurred in all the label-quests we observed and recorded in this and other classrooms.

The bilingual assistant then went on to explain to the children how to do the tracing, cutting, and pasting activity. She switched back into Panjabi. The children responded in Panjabi and their contributions were more spontaneous. Their utterances were much longer than the one-word utterances in the exchanges previously described. The bilingual assistant's talk was more learner-oriented here. The change of footing from curriculum-oriented to learner-oriented talk was marked by a change in the bilingual discourse. In this and other events, the bilingual assistant clearly used code-switching as a resource for managing conflicting communicative demands; demands stemming from her dual role: as nurturer, or 'auntie', and as a bilingual classroom assistant attempting to ensure access to the curriculum for children in a transitional bilingual teaching/learning situation.

Conclusion

The bilingual classroom practices we have described are local examples of the kind of practices emerging as bilingual support develops in schools and local authorities in Britain. The main beneficiaries of this local bilingual assistant scheme were the schools and the class teachers. From 1989, they had extra members of staff to support them in their work with bilingual learners in nursery and infant classes. When the scheme was first implemented, many schools and teachers were unsure about the benefits accruing from having bilingual staff. But, as the scheme unfolded, attitudes changed significantly. Over the two years we spent visiting local schools, we documented more and more positive accounts of improved communication with parents and fewer difficulties in "settling the children in to school."

The practitioners we interviewed were those most closely involved in the implementation of the scheme, and the views they expressed were inevitably the most positive. They emphasised the importance of valuing the children's home language and culture and building their self-confidence (a broadly pluralist view). This particular group of practitioners put a great deal of energy and commitment into the implementation of the scheme in the classroom context and in local training programmes.

However, the scheme was conceived in primarily transitional terms and this clearly influenced the ways in which the bilingual support work came to be organised in different classroom contexts. As we have shown, the bilingual talk in these contexts was shaped by the ways in which the bilingual assistants were positioned and by the pedagogic conventions operating in the classroom.

Since the bilingual assistants' contributions to teaching/learning events were constrained, learning opportunities for the bilingual children were therefore also constrained. The bilingual assistants were caught in a bind between the children and their families and the mainstream school; hence, the oscillation between curriculum-oriented and learner-oriented discourse.

There needs to be a greater awareness among educational practitioners of the nature of the constraints on the development of bilingual work in the mainstream classroom. Collaborative classroom-based research of the type we have described above offers a way of building a comparative account of emerging practices and of communicative demands currently placed on bilingual practitioners in a range of mainstream classroom contexts. It also offers a way for researchers to engage in a dialogue with practitioners about constraints and also about alternatives for bilingual classroom practice. In the British context, bilingual support is here to stay as a form of educational provision. In schools in England, it is unlikely that there will be any other kind of bilingual provision in the foreseeable future. It is therefore vital to identify the constraints on the provision currently being developed so that alternative ways of working in the classroom can be explored.

References

Bhatt, A., and M. Martin-Jones. 1992. Whose resource? Minority languages, bilingual learners and language awareness. In N. Fairclough (Ed.), *Critical language awareness*. London: Longman.

Bourne, J. 1989. *Moving into the mainstream: LEA provision for bilingual pupils*. Windsor, Berkshire: NFER-Nelson.

Cameron, D., and J. Bourne. 1988. No common ground: Kingman, grammar and nation. *Language and Education* 2(3): 147–60.

Council of the European Communities. 1977. *Directive on the education of children of migrant workers*. Directive 77/486. Brussels: European Communities.

DES (Department of Education and Science). 1975. *A language for life*. The Bullock Report. London: HMSO.

1985. *Education for all*. The Swann Report. London: HMSO.

1988. *Report of the Committee of Inquiry into the teaching of the English language*. The Kingman Report. London: HMSO.

1989. *English from 5-16*. The Cox Report. London: HMSO.

1990. *Modern foreign languages for ages 11–16*. The Harris Report. Department of Education and Science and the Welsh Office. London: HMSO.

Ellis, R. 1985. Policy and provision for ESL in the schools. In C. Brumfit, R. Ellis, and J. Levine (Eds.), *English as a second language in the UK*. ELT Documents 121. Oxford: Pergamon/British Council.

Enright, D. S. 1984. The organisation of interaction in elementary classrooms. In J. Handscombe, R. A. Orem, and B. P. Taylor (Eds.), *On TESOL '83: The question of control*. Washington, D.C.: TESOL.

Erikson, F., and G. Mohatt. 1982. Cultural organization of participant structures in two classrooms of Indian students. In G. D. Spindler (Ed.), *Doing the ethnography of schooling: Educational anthropology in action*. New York: Holt, Rinehart and Winston.

Heath, S. B. 1986. Socio-cultural contexts of language development. In D. Holt (Ed.), *Beyond language: Social and cultural factors in schooling language minority students*. Los Angeles: Evaluation, Dissemination and Assessment Center, California State University.

Houlton, D., and R. Wiley. 1983. *Supporting children's bilingualism*. York: Longman, for the Schools Council.

Jupp, C. 1990. *Bilingual support project: Language service, primary team*. Hounslow: Hounslow Primary Language Service.

Leung, C. 1993. The coming crisis of ESL in the National Curriculum. *Newsletter of the British Association for Applied Linguistics* 45.

Linguistic Minorities Project. 1985. *The other languages of England*. London: Routledge and Kegan Paul.

Martin-Jones, M. 1989. Language education in the context of linguistic diversity: Differing orientations in educational policy-making in Britain. In J. Esling (Ed.), *Multicultural education and policy: ESL in the 1990s*. Toronto: OISE Press.

—— (in press). Code-switching in the classroom: Two decades of research. In L. Milroy and P. Muysken (Eds.), *One speaker, two languages: Cross disciplinary perspectives on code-switching*. Cambridge: Cambridge University Press.

Mehan, H. 1981. Ethnography of bilingual education. In H. T. Trueba, G. P. Guthrie, and K. H. Au (Eds.), *Culture and the bilingual classroom: Studies in classroom ethnography*. Rowley, Mass.: Newbury House.

Milroy, L., and S. Moffat. 1992. Panjabi-English language alternation in the early years. *Multilingua* 11(4): 355–85.

Moffat, S. 1991. Becoming bilingual in the classroom: Code choice in school. *Language and Education* 5(1): 55–71.

Moll, L. E. 1981. The micro-ethnographic study of bilingual schooling. In R. V. Padilla (Ed.), *Ethnoperspectives in bilingual education research*. Vol. 3. Ypsilanti, Mich.: Eastern Michigan University.

Reid, E. 1988. Linguistic minorities and language education: The English experience. *Journal of Multilingual and Multicultural Development* 9(1 and 2): 181–91.

—— 1990. Culture and language teaching: ESL in England. In B. Harrison (Ed.), *Culture and the language classroom*. ELT Documents 132. London: Modern English Publications and the British Council.

Strubell, M. 1990. Code-switching in the classroom: Comments. *European Science Foundation Network on Code-Switching and Language Contact – Papers for the Workshop on "Impact and Consequences: Broader Consequences," Brussels, November 1990*. Strasbourg: European Science Foundation.

Tansley, P. 1986. *Community languages in primary education*. Windsor, Berkshire: NFER-Nelson.

Thompson, A. 1991. *Exploring bilingual support in the secondary school.* Report of the Hounslow Bilingual Support Project. Hounslow: Hounslow Secondary Language Service.

Turner, F. 1989. Community languages: The struggle for survival. In D. Phillips (Ed.), *Which language? Diversification and the national curriculum.* London: Hodder and Stoughton.

Verma, M. 1987. Issues of mother tongue maintenance. In S. Abudarham (Ed.), *Bilingualism and the bilingual.* Windsor, Berkshire: NFER-Nelson.

Zentella, A. C. 1981. *Ta bien,* you could answer me *en cualquier idioma:* Puerto Rican codeswitching in bilingual classrooms. In R. Duran (Ed.), *Latino language and communicative behavior* (pp. 109–32). Norwood, N.J.: Ablex Publishing Corporation.

5 Elite competition and official language movements

Selma K. Sonntag

This chapter explores the politics of official language movements. This is not to deny the cultural and, as some would emphasize, the primordial and emotional dimensions of language movements (see Geertz 1973). By focusing on the political dimension from both a theoretical perspective and through four empirical case studies (Belgium, the United States, India, and the former Soviet Union), the role of competing elites can be underscored.

The politics of language is a relatively sparsely studied field, especially when compared to its terminological inverse, the language of politics (e.g., rhetoric, propaganda, Orwellian manipulations). Political references made by sociolinguists frequently do not extend beyond formal government institutions (see, e.g., O'Barr and O'Barr 1976; Eastman 1983), and the lack of a theoretical framework is frequently evident. Some political scientists have helped to overcome this lacuna found in sociolinguistics. Das Gupta's pioneering work in 1970 emphasized the role of informal politics in language conflict and national development, particularly the role of interest groups and voluntary associations. Weinstein (1983) as well has emphasized the informal, focusing on the role of language strategists, i.e., those individuals both inside and outside government who affect language behavior. Perhaps the most theoretically vigorous work recently has been that of Pool (1991) and Laitin (1988, 1989), both of whom apply formal modeling and game theory to the study of the politics of language.

Laitin (1988, 1989) explicitly focuses on competition among elites. For further treatment of elite competition in arenas such as language politics, one can turn to the literature on ethnicity and politics (given that language is frequently a marker of ethnic identification; see, e.g., Rothschild 1981). There is an ongoing debate in this literature between so-called primordialists and instrumentalists that has ramifications for the study of the role of elites in language movements. Whereas some instrumentalists (e.g., Nagel 1986) analyze ethnic movements resulting from structures

I would like to thank Professors Albert Verdoodt and Jonathan Pool for their comments on an earlier draft.

and policies of an impersonal polity, others (e.g., Covell 1981; Brass 1985) argue that elites manipulate, and in some cases may even create, ethnic identity for political ends. Primordialists, on the other hand, argue that ethnic identification is a cultural given, independent of societal or political structures. According to the primordialists, there is a natural psychological tendency for groups "to cleave and compare" themselves with others, and this, rather than elite manipulation, is the basis of ethnic movements and conflict (Horowitz 1985). Many students of ethnopolitics straddle the line between primordialists and instrumentalists, acknowledging the role of elites but primarily as managers of preexisting societal conflict rather than creators or manipulators (e.g., Rothschild 1981).

My analysis falls within the instrumentalist camp. I hypothesize that official language movements are used in political strategies pursued by emerging elites in multinational states. The goal of the emerging elites is to replace the existing, established elites at the center of political power. The official language movement is perceived by the emerging elites as aiding in the achievement of this goal, by realigning the population along cleavage lines different from the cleavage lines that divide the society under the existing political power structure.

Theoretical framework

An *official language* is a language recognized and sanctioned by a government for use in official business conducted by and in governmental institutions (e.g., administrative and educational institutions). A government may recognize and sanction more than one language as official, and/ or may designate one or more languages as official in particular governmental institutions (e.g., in the administration but not in state schools) or in particular subnational units (e.g., in India where there are fifteen *scheduled*, or constitutionally recognized, languages, with particular ones being official in particular states of the Indian federation). Or, depending on the degree of devolution of power, the relevant sanctioning government may be a subnational one (e.g., in the United States where approximately twenty-two states have declared English as the official state language). Finally, although a language may be designated as official by statutory means, in practice it may not be widely used for government functions, as is the case for Arabic in the Maghreb (Cooper 1989; Souaiaia 1990). Official language is then a technical term that designates language(s) for official government business; it differs from (although in practice may correspond with) *national language*, a term that refers to the language used for the more amorphous purposes of providing national unity and commonality among a people (see Eastman 1983:36–37).

A *language movement* is one in which "individuals and groups . . . can generate a momentum around a linguistic cause among the users of the language" (Annamalai 1979:vii). It is a movement because it is "not tightly organised to the extent of being the programme of a political party nor is so unstructured to be called mob action" (ibid., vii). Movements are not organizations; there is no one-to-one correspondence between the cause and a particular formal organization (Piven and Cloward 1977). A language movement is political when the goal of movement leaders is redistribution and redefinition of power relations in the polity (see McAdam 1982). The focus here is on the role of political elites in these movements. I use the plural of the term *elite*; rarely is a political elite homogeneous and unified (Brass 1985). More likely are competing factions or groups, which are the units of analysis used here. I refer to the competing factions I will analyze as *established* and *emerging* elites. The established elites (who themselves might be characterized by factions) are those who already hold the reigns of power within a national (or subnational) unit. They support the status quo and are threatened by new agendas and new alignments (see Schattschneider 1960).

The emerging elites constitute a group (again, not necessarily homogeneous) that can mount a fairly unified challenge to the monopoly of power of the established elites. They are not without power or power resources themselves (in contrast to McAdam's [1982] assumption that challengers are excluded from power). Indeed, members of the emerging elites may even hold (relatively minor) positions of power in the existing government. Their ability to pool resources and power is what makes their challenge credible. In contrast, there may be other impotent, marginalized groups and spokespersons in society who identify with and even strongly espouse the official language movement in question, but who function as pressure points rather than credible players in the political struggle. For example, in many analyses of Belgian language politics in the early part of the twentieth century, much credence is given to the role of the Flemish nationalists, or Frontists (as many of them were called), in the eventual enactment of language legislation officializing Dutch (see, e.g., Murphy 1988). However, it was the moderate, Flemish Catholics, organizationally and ideologically distinct from the Flemish nationalists, who were the true instigators and power brokers for the official Dutch language movement at that time (see Sonntag 1991).

What distinguishes the emerging from the established elites is who sets the political agenda and who defines the terms of political (and social and economic) discourse. As is well-known in political science, the ability to set the political agenda is a powerful resource. What issues are deemed important and worthwhile influence the allocation and distribution of resources (which is at least one function of government). The established elites wish

to maintain the salience and centrality of the current agenda, not only to pre-serve but also to perpetuate the distribution of power emanating from those salient political conflicts. After all, the exploitation of those issues has resulted precisely in success in the first place. Of course, one way of exploiting is to continue to emphasize the original aligning issues; another is to treat all new issues as logical outgrowths of the original agenda. In both cases the idea is to fight current political battles within the framework of the old. (Carmines and Stimson 1989:6)

Issues that are marginalized often reflect the impotency of those directly affected by those issues (e.g., the issue of homelessness in the United States). Furthermore, it is not only a question of which issues are on the agenda, but of how they are discussed. The established elites define the terms of debate, attempting to marginalize dissent and challenges to their hegemony.

Official language movements, under certain circumstances, have the potential for establishing a new agenda and a new way to talk about political and socioeconomic issues (i.e., new terms of discourse). The emerging elites who espouse the language movement hope to substitute language conflict and its terms of reference for the existing alignment of political (and social and economic) conflict:

The substitution of conflicts is the most devastating kind of political strategy. Alliances are formed and reformed; fortresses, positions, alignments and com-binations are destroyed or abandoned in a tremendous shuffle of forces re-deployed to defend new positions or to take new strong points. In politics the most catastrophic force in the world is the power of irrelevance which trans-mutes one conflict into another and turns all existing alignments inside out. (Schattschneider 1960:74)

To make your rivals' agenda irrelevant is to realign political power in your favor. Official language movements can set a new agenda by trans-muting the linguistic cleavage into a politically salient one.

A preexisting condition to this use of official language movements in the political strategies of emerging elites is that the established elites have their power based on a nonlinguistic alignment or cleavage, such as a religious, socioeconomic, or center-periphery cleavage. The language cleavage is not the most politically salient one (hence the potential for transmuting it *into* the most politically salient one). Of course, the es-pousal of a language movement may be a characteristic of an already politicized language conflict. In such a case, the saliency of the conflict may reflect existent divisions within the established elites (as has been the case in recent decades in Belgium). The conflict would then be over adjustments in the current allocation and distribution of power, rather than an attempt to redefine politics and, in the process, displace the whole group of established elites from power (i.e., the type of case under analysis here).

A second condition of the cases under analysis here is some indication that the established elites are vulnerable to a challenge by emerging elites. The source of this vulnerability is often external, for example, the occurrence of international events or circumstances, such as decolonization, world war, or loss of economic competitiveness (Carmines and Stimson 1989). Third, the emerging elites launching the challenge must be relatively strong competitors; i.e., they cannot be easily susceptible to marginalization by the established elites. If they are susceptible, then it is likely that the movement will remain merely linguistic or cultural rather than being political (i.e., challenging existing power relations). Finally, there must exist some degree of ethnolinguistic discrimination, real or imagined, against some portion of the population. This final condition allows for the emerging elites to make an appeal based on language sentiments to the population, i.e., to make their challenge a movement. The logistics of this elite-mass linkage is an extremely important topic, not least of all because its treatment must synthesize the (primordial?) force for solidarity language serves for the masses with the political (instrumental) interests of the elites. Since the focus here is on elite competition, such a treatment is beyond the scope of this analysis, although I will touch briefly upon the topic in the cases presented here.

I will now apply my theoretical framework to empirical analysis by examining four cases studies: (1) the movement in the 1920s and 1930s to make Dutch the sole official language in administrative matters and education in the northern half of Belgium; (2) the current Official English (or English-Only) movement in the United States; (3) the postindependence movement to make Hindi the official language in India; and (4) movements in various republics of the former Soviet Union to make the language of the republic official, to the exclusion of Russian.

Four cases

The official Dutch language movement in Belgium

Although Flemish is only one of several regional languages, all closely related to Dutch, spoken in the northern half of Belgium, residents of this area are referred to as Flemings, the area as Flanders, and standardized Dutch as the official language. Similarly, Walloon is increasingly used to refer to residents of southern Belgium, where the official language is designated as French, although Walloon is only one of several regional languages related to French (see Aunger 1993). With Flemings successfully barring official census data collection on ethnolinguistic identity, it is estimated that Flemings make up about 57 percent of the population, whereas the French speakers, consisting of Walloons as well as French-speaking residents of Brussels, make up about 42 percent of the population (*The Economist* 2 February 1986). These are relatively the same percentages as at the beginning of the century. There is also a small minority of German speakers primarily in the eastern part of Belgium; for purposes of the analysis presented here, they are inconsequential.

In the second half of the nineteenth century, not long after Belgium's independence in 1830, a Flemish movement developed, concerned mainly with what language planners would call "corpus planning" (as opposed to "status planning"; see Cooper 1989) and led primarily by intellectuals and literary figures. Economic changes around the turn of the century helped to convert it into a (primarily middle-class) mass movement (see Zolberg 1974; Huyse 1981), but it was the events surrounding and immediately following World War I that rendered it political.

The war demonstrated the vulnerability of the existing, established elites. When Germany occupied most of Belgium, the Belgian political leadership exiled itself to Le Havre, leaving younger, less established MPs (Members of Parliament) as the indigenous leaders in the occupied territory. With the exiled leadership losing touch with hardships Belgians encountered under occupation, the new leadership was able to carry out what has been referred to as a palace coup after the war, replacing the old, established leadership (Gerard 1985).

The emergence of this new leadership was not, however, based on any language challenge. In linguistic terms, the new leadership was identical to the old, i.e., Francophone (French-speaking). Belgium had been dominated since independence, in both political and economic terms, by Francophone elites, mostly from Brussels and the provincial cities of Flanders. The new leadership also resembled the old in terms of the cleavage that had been the most politically salient since independence, i.e., the religious cleavage. The parallel system of state (secular) and Catholic (clerical) schools reflected the formula upon which the existing balance of power between Liberals and Catholics within the established elite was based. Although the immediate postwar government in Belgium was a national unity government, and hence included Socialists for the first time, it was the Francophone Liberals and Catholics, albeit younger ones than before the war, who dominated.

As many leaders in Africa must know, a coup is not a strong base for power, even if the ideology or ethnic makeup of the coup leaders is the same as that of those ousted. The palace coup in the final days of the war signified an elite in transition, vulnerable to challenges to its political agenda and to the existing balance of power between Francophone Catholics and Francophone Liberals. Furthermore, the introduction of universal male suffrage immediately after the war (replacing the 1894 plural voting system, in which those with a certain amount of education, as well as property owners and heads of households, had more votes) meant a change in the electorate to which politicians had to appeal. It meant that the Flemings, who tended to be poorer and less educated and to have larger families than the Francophones, could now have representation that reflected their numerical superiority in the population. There was the potential for an emerging Flemish elite.

Young Flemish leaders did increase their political activity after the war through the establishment of political organizations, electoral lists, and political programs espousing the Flemish linguistic cause (see Gerard 1985; Sonntag 1991). By the early 1920s, Flemish MPs were submitting legislative proposals to parliament on the language issue. The result of these proposals was "a weak commitment by the government to advance the equality of Dutch through promoting bilingualism" (Sonntag 1991:62). Although vulnerable, the Francophone elites were not a pushover. Their arsenal for defeating Flemish proposals included rhetorically identifying them with the work of the Flemish collaborators during the war, who had been stigmatized after the war. The emerging Flemish elite had not yet demonstrated that they could not be marginalized through such tactics.

The defeat of the Flemish legislative proposals sharpened rivalry between advocates of the Flemish linguistic cause. Because of the upheaval within the fairly decentralized Catholic party after the war (Gerard 1985), some young Flemish MPs saw the opportunity for advancing their interests within the party while maintaining the legitimacy that an established party could provide (Sonntag 1991:55–56). They began to distance themselves from the increasingly marginalized Flemish nationalists (Sonntag 1991). By the mid-twenties, this emerging Flemish Catholic elite, given the defeat of relatively moderate language proposals at the beginning of the decade, had not yet espoused a movement for making Dutch the sole official language of Flanders as part of their political strategy for challenging the established elites. They instead espoused an economic challenge to the established elites by allying themselves with the Socialists (who were, in power terms, about equal to the Flemish Catholics), resulting in a short-lived Socialist-Christian Democrat government (the latter group being made up predominantly of Flemish Catholics). This government coalition "was strongly opposed by the Francophone established elites. There are some indications that the established elites precipitated a government financial crisis in order to bring the government down . . . It lasted only eleven months. The short-lived government had however demonstrated the competitive strength of the re-emerging Flemish power" (Sonntag 1991:65).

In the late 1920s, the emerging Flemish Catholic elite returned to the language cause, this time in the form of a demand for making Dutch the sole official language of Flanders. Their new allies against the Francophone elites (who were mainly from Brussels and the provincial cities in Flanders) were the Walloons from southern Belgium. The Walloons had felt betrayed by the language laws of the early 1920s because these laws at least nominally promoted bilingualism, which the Walloons saw as a threat to the de facto unilingualism (French-only) that had always existed in Wallonia. It was the Walloons who began advocating publicly a policy of regional unilingualism, which would mean that in government (and local) administration and education only Dutch would be used in Flanders and only French in Wallonia. Indeed, in 1928, the Flemish Catholics stated: "We leave the choice of methods up to the Walloons: unitary bilingualism or separate unilingualism" (quoted in Wils 1973:296).

The new demand by both Flemings and Walloons in the late 1920s for regional unilingualism upped the ante in the political competition between emerging and established elites. Regional unilingualism was potentially much more threatening to the established elites' balance of power than earlier demands for equality of Dutch vis-a-vis French. The latter could be met through promoting bilingualism of both government services and individuals. Bilingualism in government services would not institutionalize the distinctions between Flanders and Wallonia; in individuals, bilingualism blurred the distinction between French-speakers and Dutch-speakers. Regional unilingualism threatened to institutionalize the language cleavage and politicize the [linguistic] identity of individuals. No longer confronted with just a Flemish demand for linguistic equality, but with both Flemings and Walloons demanding regional unilingualism, the established elites were confronted with a different, and decisively more competitive, challenge than the earlier Flemish challenge. (Sonntag 1991:67–68)

In responding to this new challenge, the Liberals among the established Francophone elites attempted to define the new issue, language, in terms of the old agenda, i.e., issues relating to the religious cleavage. They were successful to a significant degree: The final outcome was the language legislation of 1932 that, although recognizing regional unilingualism in principle, provided for serious loopholes, particularly in education. By rekindling the tension between state (secular) and Catholic (clerical) schools, the Liberals were able to weaken the impact of the new language education policy based on the principle of regional unilingualism (see Sonntag 1989).

The alliance between Flemings and Walloons in the early 1930s was tenuous at best, and not the forging of some long-term cooperation. By displacing the religious cleavage in Belgian society with the language cleavage as the most politically salient, the emerging Flemish and Walloon elites hoped to realign the population in political terms, so that constituents' political behavior would be based on linguistic identification (see Nagel 1986). From a long-term perspective at least, this strategy was highly successful; today, in Belgium, "[l]anguage loyalties override all other questions that form part of the body politic of Belgian life" (Baetens Beardsmore 1980:145).

The Official English movement in the United States

The movement to make English the official language in the United States has gained increasing momentum in the past fifteen years. Although it has not met with success in enacting a constitutional amendment officializing English at the national level, it has had numerous victories at the state level: To date, more than twenty states have legislation recognizing English as the official state language.

The movement has organizational backing (Amorose 1989); indeed, "[T]he 'U.S. English' organization provides a model success story for modern entrepreneurial political movements" (Nunberg 1989:579). There is not, however, a one-to-one correspondence between U.S. English or other organizations and each and every attempt to legislate English as official (Nunberg 1989). The term movement is consistently used in the literature and popular press. Its successes "by and large . . . have been achieved without the support of establishment politicians and organizations" (Nunberg 1989:581).

The Official English movement is invariably described in the scholarly literature as a conservative backlash against legislative gains in the areas of bilingual education and bilingual voting in the late 1960s and 1970s (see, e.g., Marshall 1986; Fishman 1989; Citrin et al. 1990). I contend that it is more than this: It is part of an attempt to replace the old liberal, New Deal/Great Society agenda with the right-wing, Reaganite Republican agenda.

It was the issues of poverty and race, not language, that were politicized in the late 1960s under the aegis of the New Deal/Great Society liberal elites. Both bilingual education and bilingual balloting were defined in terms of ameliorating the circumstances of the uneducated poor (who were, and are, predominantly nonwhite). It was what Schneider (1976) refers to as poverty criteria, rather than linguistic criteria, that determined which individuals had access to resources provided by the bilingual legislation. The Bilingual Education Act of 1968 contained a family income ceiling of $3,000 per year to determine which children of limited English-speaking ability should benefit from bilingual education programs. The 1975 extension of the 1965 Voting Rights Act, which provided for bilingual balloting, stipulated that the measure would only be triggered in districts where the illiteracy rate of non- and limited-English speakers "as a group is higher than the national illiteracy rate" (U.S. Code, P.L. 94–73, 1975, p. 403). Those formulating the policies perceived the need to be one of advancing the socioeconomic status of groups that were consistently poor in the United States rather than enhancing the status of languages other than English (see, e.g., U.S. Congress, Senate, 1973, pp. 2587, 2592). The "temporary" nature of bilingual balloting (U.S. Congress, House, 1975, pp. 16246–47) and the "transitional" approach of bilingual education programs point to the lack of language status planning. "In the U.S., bilingual education was instituted as a transitional anti-poverty measure because bilingualism was, and is, largely identified with 'disadvantage'" (Clyne 1986:140). The Liberal elites based their appeal, both to poor constituents and to the middle class and their sense of fairness, on socioeconomic criteria. These were, and have been for some time, the terms of political discourse in the United States.

Ronald Reagan's dramatically successful bid for the presidency in 1980 challenged the liberal political agenda, even more so than earlier attempts of the Nixon administration (on the Nixon administration attempts, see Kilson 1975). Both in 1980 and 1984, there was a lively debate among political scientists over whether these elections were "re-aligning." A realigning election, such as the one in 1932 (reinforced in 1936) that ushered in the New Deal agenda and the liberal elites, is one in which the population begins to identify with, and base their political behavior on, a new cleavage, different from the cleavage that divided the society under the established political structure. If realigning, then the early 1980s elections would clearly indicate the emergence of a new political majority and a new political agenda, that is, prior to the recent momentum of the Official English movement. But as Carmines and Stimson (1989) point out, the whole theory of realigning elections is confused and misleading; the transformation of politics to a new agenda based on a new cleavage alignment is a more subtle and long-term process (as in the Belgian case). And despite the popularity of the Reagan presidency and the capturing of the nation's top office by the Republican right wing, the right wing has been, and has felt, frustrated in their attempts to define the political agenda (see Viguerie and Allen 1990).

The Official English movement has the potential of galvanizing the majority population (i.e., Anglos) into a powerful constituency demanding implementation of a right-wing agenda, because it plays on the "insecurities of anglo-mainstream-oriented American middle class life" (Fishman 1989:647), even if the threat to the de facto status of English in the United States is more imagined than real. "[H]aving discovered that it [Official English/English Only] is an issue that excites the baser instincts, it has been exploited as a fund-raising and voter mobilization ploy for conservative candidates, causes and referenda reaching far beyond the English issue *per se*" (Fishman 1989:647). In the process, it can politicize ethnolinguistic cleavages, especially if English-only legislation entails more than symbolism, as was the case with the Arizona English-only referendum in 1988. When English-only laws start affecting individuals solely because of their language behavior (see, e.g., Barringer 1990 for an instance in connection with the Arizona law), then language becomes salient (Nagel 1986).

Given the loss of U.S. economic and political hegemony since the height of the liberal agenda in the late 1960s, the established liberal elites are clearly vulnerable to such a challenge, as numerous recent treatises on the decline of American liberalism imply (see, e.g., Fraser and Gerstle 1989). The right wing may emerge as the new elite supported by the majority, defined in ethnolinguistic terms (native-English-speaking Anglos), and allied on the English-only issue (and related issues).

The Hindi movement in India

India, "the multilingual 'new state' par excellence" (Pool 1973, 1991), has been replete with language movements (see Annamalai 1979) and language organizations (see Das Gupta 1970), since before it even achieved independence. In India, the role of elites in language movements has been particularly apparent (Annamalai 1979). Upon independence in 1947, when the established elite, the British, finally agreed to depart, competition between emerging elites over the language as well as the religious issue dividing Hindus and Muslims tore the subcontinent in two (Das Gupta 1970; Brass 1974). The partition of India and Pakistan "if anything . . . complicated the language question" (Das Gupta 1970:127) in India. The Indian Congress party, who took the ruling mantle from the British, had adopted the notion of a linguistic basis to Indian federalism as early as 1923 when the party developed into a mass organization (Krishna 1966). But Nehru had second thoughts about a linguistic reorganization of the states for fear that it would foster disintegration rather than unity (Geertz 1973; Laitin 1989). Regional elites bargained hard with center elites over the language issue; the Indian federal system was reorganized on the basis of linguistic states, starting in 1953 with Andhra Pradesh after a close disciple of Mahatma Gandhi fasted to death for the establishment of a Telegu-language state (Akbar 1985).

Nehru not only confronted (and subsequently deferred to) regional elites over the language issue, but also faced, upon independence, a linguistic challenge from within the Congress party at the national level. The Nehru-Gandhian established elite (revered, albeit vulnerable because it had just inherited the status of "established" from the British) advocated Hindustani (the spoken variety of both Hindi and Urdu, popularized by the Mahatma himself) as the national and official language of India. This position was challenged not only by those who advocated the retention of English as the official language, but also by those who wanted Hindi as the national and official language (Das Gupta 1970). The Hindi advocates were purists, even "linguistic extremists" (Austin 1966:266), favoring a Sanskrit-based Hindi as opposed to the Persian-tainted Hindustani. With the removal of most Urdu-speaking Muslim elites from the Congress party through the events leading up to and including the creation of Pakistan, the impetus behind Hindustani as a language that would unite Hindu Hindi speakers and Muslim Urdu speakers weakened. Despite the continued support of the established leaders of the Congress party for Hindustani, the Hindi advocates had the support of much of the party's rank and file (Austin 1966). The result was an "almost equal strength in the [Constituent] Assembly of the rival blocs [Hindi versus Hindustani] in the Congress Party" (Das Gupta 1970:136–37).

Ultimately, a compromise was reached . . . This [compromise] formula did not provide for a national language. It used the term "official language of the Union" and provided that this language would be Hindi written in Deva Nagari script. The acceptance of this provision by the Constituent Assembly of India clearly suggests that in spite of many concessions on details, the Hindi bloc was successful in getting its major demand accepted by the framers of the Indian Constitution. (Das Gupta 1970:137)

The successful adoption of Hindi as the official language of the Union did not lead to the demise of the Hindi movement. Article 351 of the Indian constitution states that "It shall be the duty of the Union to promote the spread of the Hindi language, to develop it so that it may serve as a medium of expression for all the elements of the composite culture of India . . ." (quoted in Srivastava 1979:84). This led the way for numerous volunteer language organizations promoting Hindi to thrive (Das Gupta 1970; Laitin 1989). The Hindi movement could also appeal to the Hindi-speaking masses for support on the basis of perceived discrimination: The Hindi heartland of northern India is the poorest region with the highest illiteracy rate in India (Rudolph and Rudolph 1987:180).

Of course those opposed to the promulgation of Hindi as the official language could also claim discrimination: Non-Hindi speakers would potentially face a reduction in employment and economic opportunities at the all-India (national) level if speaking Hindi were a necessary job skill. The anti-Hindi movement was particularly strong in southern India. Immediately after the constitutionally prescribed deadline of 1965 at which time Hindi was to become the sole official language at the national level at the expense of English, the Tamils in the south rioted, resulting in numerous deaths (Hardgrave and Kochanek 1986). Again a compromise was reached in which English has continued to have the status of an associate official language to Hindi for an indefinite period of time. However, this time competition and compromise did not take place within the confines of the Congress party as it had in the early postindependence period. The new challengers in the south, as well as new challengers in the north, sought and in some cases succeeded at the state-level in the displacement of the Congress party itself.

During the 1960s, the original three-language formula, which gave official status to English, Hindi, and different regional languages in the various states, emerged as a salient issue in secondary education, precisely because the impetus for and debate on the issue reflected the impending power shift away from Congress at the national level to emerging "regional elites" (Harrison 1960) at the state level. The original three-language formula emerged out of a conference of chief ministers, or heads of state governments. As Das Gupta (1970:245) notes in regard to this language-education policy "formula," "[T]he entry of the Chief Ministers' Conference into the national policy-making process indicated a new channel of compromise for the language issue." Chief ministers and other regional elites from the south were opposed to making Hindi mandatory as envisioned in some versions of the formula (Nayar 1969). Given the beginnings of a significant power shift away from Congress in the late 1960s, notably in state governments that had jurisdiction over education, the end result of the three-language formula was a poorly implemented policy, with wide variation among states.

In the 1970s and 1980s, Congress party hegemony declined further, accompanied by mounting political instability (e.g., the suspension of democracy under the Emergency in the mid-seventies, serious secessionist movements in the northeast and northwest of the country, the assassination of Indira Gandhi in 1984). Critical to the changing political scene was the emerging power of backward castes (defined in constitutional terms as backward classes), particularly in the Hindi heartland (Frankel 1988). To a large degree this group overlapped with the "bullock capitalists," that is, small land-owning farmers who benefitted from limited land reform and green revolution technology (Rudolph and Rudolph 1987:340; Frankel 1988:253). The political mobilization of this group in the Hindi heartland by emerging leaders such as Charan Singh and his Lok Dal party represented a challenge to the Congress party, which historically consisted of an alliance of English-educated professionals (i.e., the urban middle class) and upper-caste rural elites in this part of India. The Congress party responded to the challenge by broadening its appeal to include minorities (such as Muslims) and untouchables, both of whom are below the backward castes in the status hierarchy. In electoral terms, the new competition manifested itself in the victory of the Janata party at the national level in 1977, the return of the Congress party to power in 1980, and for the second time since independence, a non-Congress alliance back in power in early 1990 under the prime ministry of V. P. Singh.

The Janata party of the late 1970s was hastily constructed of opposition parties, including not only Charan Singh's Lok Dal based on backward-caste and bullock-capitalist support, but also the upper-caste-dominated Jana Sangh (Frankel 1988). Because of Jana Sangh, Janata's victory in the 1977 national elections "put proponents of Hindu confessional politics in the seats of power in Delhi for the first time" (Rudolph and Rudolph 1987:43). It also again raised the language issue (Hardgrave and Kochanek 1986:132), representing "a government clearly committed to a Hindi vision of India" (Laitin 1989:430). The backward-caste component of the Janata party had its agenda as well: the demand for implementation of a reservations policy (roughly equivalent to a quota-system affirmative action policy) for backward castes. Such a demand did not sit well with the upper castes, and Janata splintered into multiple factions and parties by the 1980 elections, failing to implement either a new language or reservations policy.

The return of a non-Congress coalition to power at the national level in December of 1989 revived the communal pressures that Janata had been under in the late 1970s. In the late summer of 1990, Prime Minister V. P. Singh finally implemented the reservations policy for backward castes/classes, touching off violent protests among the upper-caste urban middle class. In the middle of this crisis, the leader of one of the parties making up V. P. Singh's coalition, Advani of the Bharatiya Janata party (the successor to the Jana Sangh), ignited Hindu religious passions in a controversy over a mosque in the Hindi heartland. The resulting Hindu-Muslim violence, the likes of which had not been seen since partition in 1947, brought down the V. P. Singh government, leading to its replacement by a short-lived, very unstable minority government (with Congress party support). Elections were held in June 1991, resulting in a Congress party minority government that was rocked by riots in late 1992 emanating from the continuing Ayodhya mosque saga.

Although caste and religious cleavages have been most salient in recent Indian politics, through the reservations policy and Ayodhya mosque controversies, it may be the official language issue that will provide the realignment for a successful long-term challenge to Congress party dominance, as opposed to the shot-in-the-arm attempts under the Janata party in the late 1970s and V. P. Singh more recently. Rajiv Gandhi, the leader of the Congress party until his assassination in 1991, was known to be much more comfortable speaking English than Hindi. His religious credentials were not as vulnerable to scrutiny by emerging elites; indeed, it has been suggested that Rajiv was at least partially responsible for the crisis over the Ayodhya mosque by fomenting, for essentially political reasons, Hindu religious fervor in the area in the late 1980s. In contrast to Rajiv, during the waning days of the V. P. Singh government the chief minister of Uttar Pradesh (the state in which the Ayodhya mosque is located), a member of Singh's party, acted to restrain Hindu activists at the mosque by enacting at the state level a reservations policy for backward castes, and yet was considered "an unabashed Hindi-language chauvinist" (Crossette 1990:A6).

It remains to be seen if the Hindi official language movement becomes a major political strategy by emerging elites in India to challenge the established elites best represented in the Congress party. Incidents occur suggesting momentum: On January 10, 1991, a young man in the visitors' gallery of the national parliament shouted, in Hindi, "Use an Indian language!" during a speech in English by a Congress party MP from southern India (*India West*, 18 January 1991, p. 12). In India, a secular state, language demands have much more legitimacy than religious demands. The recent fervor over the Ayodhya mosque may be a flash in the pan compared to the espousal of the language issue by the numerically superior and recently politicized economic/status group, that is, the backward castes/classes of the Hindi heartland.

Official language movements in the former Soviet Union

Gorbachev's Soviet Union exhibited all four conditions identified above as conducive to the use of official language movements in political strategies by emerging elites. Although the multilingualism of the Soviet Union had been an issue since the Bolshevik Revolution (initially with Lenin tolerating multilingualism, replaced later with Stalin's policy of Russification), the dominant cleavage in the Soviet Union was a center-periphery cleavage. The incredible events in the late 1980s in both the Soviet Union and Eastern Europe, ushered in with the advent of glasnost and perestroika, indicated a vulnerable established elite. Because of glasnost, emerging leaders who would have been marginalized under the pre-Gorbachev regimes became significant players in the changing political scene. And, finally, the dominance of Russians and their language in the Soviet Union had fostered over the years a sense of injustice and discrimination among the indigenous populations of the republics.

This sense of discrimination developed especially in the schools, in which Russian was made mandatory in 1938. Although in 1958–59 Russian became "voluntary" in the schools, non-Russian groups, particularly in the Baltics, reacted angrily to this new "freedom of choice" in language education because they knew it would accelerate assimilation to Russian (Karklins 1986:104). In the last years of the Brezhnev regime, rumors were rampant in the Baltics of a new official policy of "extending the use of Russian in the public affairs and the educational systems of non-Russian republics" (Misiunas 1990:208).

There are further complexities that must be added to the above sketch of the final years of the former Soviet Union. The USSR was a federal system dominated by the Communist party. Tension between party leaders in the republics and at the center (in Moscow) defined center-periphery relations. Despite the wishes of center elites, party elites at the republic level were likely to promote the individual republics' self-interests at the expense of some common Soviet good (see Burg 1990; Gleason 1990). This was particularly true if the party elites were native to the area. Under Brezhnev, there had been a significant " 'nativization' of local elite structures, [an] expansion of local autonomy for native elites in the national territories, and . . . growing participation by non-Russians at the center," although the latter seems to have contained a high degree of tokenism (Burg 1990:26). Gorbachev reversed these trends when first coming to office, in effect centralizing control to a larger degree (Burg 1990). Redefining the rules of the center-periphery relationship, to the detriment of the periphery, and at the same time unleashing democratization in the form of glasnost, put party elites at the republic level in the precarious situation of being perceived both as agents of the center by newly emerging popular fronts and as defying central authority by Moscow. As a result, in Lithuania the Communist party of that republic broke from Moscow, declaring its independence, in order to head off even more radical demands for secession by Sajudis. In contrast, in Moldavia, the popular front at times perceived Gorbachev as an ally against a conservative Moldavian Communist party (Fischer 1990).

Recurring in republic after republic in the last years of the Soviet Union, often preceding and becoming part of popular fronts, were movements for officializing the titular language of the republic. These movements were strategic in rallying the masses around a challenge to the established elites. The challenge was initially mounted primarily by intellectuals (see Crowther 1990, for the case in Moldavia), later by the popular front. "[E]thnic elites, intellectuals, and political entrepreneurs throughout the Soviet Union [became aware] of the power available to them by politicizing and mobilizing ethnic identity" (Burg 1990:38). Groups that previously were marginalized, such as (non-Communist) intellectual circles, seized upon the language issue as a crowd mobilizer; in turn the mass demonstrations pressured the existing local party elites to enact legislation officializing the language. As this happened in the Baltics, Moldavia, and other Soviet republics, Russians living in these republics found themselves and their language demoted to subordinate status through legislative means.

The role of local party elites appeared to have been crucial in determining the outcome of the competition between emerging and established elites in the former Soviet Union. In the Baltics, where local party elites in effect joined the emerging popular fronts, the challenge to Moscow was so successful early on that it led to physical suppression by Moscow and the passing of a popular referendum on secession. In contrast, in Moldavia, at approximately the same time, competition remained at the republic level between local party elites and emerging elites. The result was a weakening of legislation officializing Moldavian, and compromise with Moscow (Crowther 1990; Kenny 1990). Linguistic chauvinism and nationalism remained the basis of maintaining the support and mobilization of the Moldavian masses rather than a broader "democratization" appeal (see Crowther 1990). In Moldavia, a challenge based on the language movement remained the preferred political strategy, rather than becoming submerged in a momentous episode of the traditional center-periphery conflict as happened in the Baltics, which of course eventually led to the dissolution of the Soviet Union as a whole.

Conclusion

The four empirical cases presented in this chapter support in general the theoretical premise that official language movements are espoused by emerging elites in their attempt to challenge the existing power alignment. In all four cases the established elites' power was based on a non-linguistic alignment or cleavage. In Belgium, the established elites based their power on the religious cleavage; in the United States, on a socioeconomic cleavage established during the New Deal and Great Society programs; in India, on a colonial political structure; and in the republics of the Soviet Union, on a periphery-center cleavage vis-à-vis Moscow. The vulnerability of the established elites is apparent in each case: in Belgium, the political upheaval of World War I and the immediately subsequent implementation of universal suffrage; in the United States, the decline of U.S. hegemony and the concomitant attack on the liberal vision of the welfare state; in India, independence in 1947 and, later on, the loss of Congress party hegemony; in the USSR, the Gorbachev phenomenon. The emerging elites in all cases proved to be, or are proving to be, strong competitors. In Belgium, the emerging elites were young Flemish and Walloon members of parliament in the traditional parties; in the United States, the Reaganite right has challenged the liberal-dominated political alignment; in India, upon independence, an urban professional middle class redefined politics, and has recently been in turn challenged by an emerging rural elite defined in both economic (bullock capitalists) and status (backward castes) terms; in the waning of the Soviet Union, popular fronts emerged in nearly all republics. Finally, as is the case in nearly all multilingual states, constituent language groups perceive discrimination: the Flemings, until recently, were the numerically superior but socially subordinate group in Belgium; in the United States, fears of reverse discrimination are now common among Anglos; in India, while non-Hindi speakers voice fear of Hindi domination, Hindi speakers perceive their region as economically inferior; in the Soviet Union, years of Russification caused resentment in the republics.

Obviously, important theoretical differences exist between the cases in addition to the similarities. Ideologically, the official language movement in the United States is clearly conservative. In the other cases, the ideological content is not as apparent, with both leftist and rightist components. Even in the U.S. case, there has been surprisingly little vociferous opposition to, and in some cases espousal of, official English by liberals (see Woolard 1989). In all four cases examined here, the middle class has dominated the movement (in the case of Belgium and India, a newly emerging component of the middle class). However, in the United States, the middle class has supported the movement in defense of its status and privileges, whereas in the other cases the middle class has been on the offensive. Despite these differences, these movements have all been espoused by emerging elites in their bid for power; and it is this competition for power that has been the focus here.

A final comparison: The arena for conflict between competing elites has often been language policy in education, although the parameters of contention have differed among the cases studied here. In Belgium, a policy of regional unilingualism implemented in the schools was crucial in stopping the flow of assimilation to French, a situation paralleled in the former Soviet Union. In these two cases, emerging elites espoused rigid, nationalistic language policies, whereas the established elites preferred voluntary freedom of choice. In the United States, proponents of English-only are often criticized for not realizing that freedom of choice has been accomplishing quite successfully what they wish to do by legislative mandate – most third-generation Mexican-Americans are monolingual English speakers (see, e.g., Veltman 1990). Indeed, it has been suggested that the U.S. English organization spend its money on expanding the availability of English language classes for immigrants, most of which have long waiting lists, rather than attacking bilingual education. Finally, in India, where Hindi would not spread by voluntary means (compared to the dominant language in the other three cases), the status of Hindi in education is a result of compromise among elites.

References

Akbar, M. J. 1985. *India: The siege within.* New York: Penguin.
Amorose, Thomas. 1989. The Official-Language movement in the United States: Contexts, issues, and activities. *Language Problems and Language Planning* 13(3): 264–79.
Annamalai, E. (Ed.). 1979. *Language movements in India.* Mysore: Central Institute of Indian Languages.
    1979. Introduction. In E. Annamalai (Ed.), *Language movements in India* (pp. vii–viii). Mysore: Central Institute of Indian Languages.
Aunger, Edmund A. 1993. Regional, national and official languages in Belgium.

International Journal of the Sociology of Language (A. Verdoodt and S. K. Sonntag, Guest Eds.) 104:31–48.

Austin, Granville. 1966. *The Indian Constitution: Cornerstone of a nation.* Oxford: Claredon Press.

Baetens Beardsmore, Hugo. 1980. Bilingualism in Belgium. *Journal of Multilingual and Multicultural Development* 1(2): 145–54.

Barringer, Felicity. 1990. Judge nullifies law mandating use of English. *New York Times,* 8 February, p. A1.

Brass, Paul R. 1974. *Language, religion and politics in north India.* New York: Cambridge University Press.

    1985. Ethnic groups and the state. In Paul R. Brass (Ed.), *Ethnic groups and the state* (pp. 1–56). Totowa, N.J.: Barnes and Noble.

Burg, Steven L. 1990. Nationality elites and political change in the Soviet Union. In Lubomyr Hajda and Mark Beissinger (Eds.), *The nationalities factor in Soviet politics and society* (pp. 24–42). Boulder, Colo.: Westview Press.

Carmines, Edward G., and James A. Stimson. 1989. *Issue evolution: Race and the transformation of American politics.* Princeton: Princeton University Press.

Citrin, Jack, Beth Reinhold, Evelyn Walters, and Donald P. Green. 1990. The 'Official English' movement and the symbolic politics of language in the United States. *The Western Political Quarterly* 43(3): 535–59.

Clyne, Michael. 1986. Comment. *International Journal of the Sociology of Language: Language Rights and the English Language Amendment* 60:139–43.

Cooper, Robert L. 1989. *Language planning and social change.* Cambridge: Cambridge University Press.

Covell, Maureen. 1981. Ethnic conflict and elite bargaining: The case of Belgium. *West European Politics* 4(3): 197–218.

Crossette, Barbara. 1990. A campaign to supplant English with Hindi is renewed in India. *New York Times,* 28 May, p. A6.

Crowther, William. 1990. The politics of mobilization: Nationalism and reform in Soviet Moldavia. Paper presented at the 1990 Annual Meeting of the American Political Science Association, 30 August-2 September, San Francisco.

Das Gupta, Jyotirindra. 1970. *Language conflict and national development.* Berkeley: University of California Press.

Eastman, Carol M. 1983. *Language planning: An introduction.* San Francisco: Chandler and Sharp.

The Economist. 1986. It's Hard Going: A Survey of Belgium, 2 February, pp. 50 ff.

Fischer, Mary Ellen. 1990. Nationalism as catalyst or obstacle to political reform: The cases of Romania and Soviet Moldavia. Paper presented at the 1990 Annual Meeting of the American Political Science Association, 30 August-2 September, San Francisco.

Fishman, Joshua A. 1989. *Language and ethnicity in minority sociolinguistic perspective.* Clevedon, Eng.: Multilingual Matters.

Frankel, Francine R. 1988. Middle classes and castes in India's politics: Prospects for political accommodation. In Atul Kohli (Ed.), *India's democracy* (pp. 225–61). Princeton: Princeton University Press.

Fraser, Steve, and Gary Gerstle. 1989. *The rise and fall of the New Deal order, 1930–1980.* Princeton: Princeton University Press.

110   *Selma K. Sonntag*

Geertz, Clifford. 1973. *The interpretation of cultures.* New York: Basic Books.
Gerard, Emmanuel. 1985. *De katholieke partij in crisis.* Leuven, Belgium: Kritak.
Gleason, Gregory. 1990. *Federalism and nationalism: The struggle for republican rights in the USSR.* Boulder, Colo.: Westview Press.
Hardgrave, Robert L., Jr., and Stanley A. Kochanek. 1986. *India.* New York: Harcourt Brace Jovanovich.
Harrison, Selig S. 1960. *India: The most dangerous decades.* Princeton: Princeton University Press.
Horowitz, Donald L. 1985. *Ethnic groups in conflict.* Berkeley: University of California Press.
Huyse, Luc. 1981. Political conflict in bicultural Belgium. In Arend Lijphart (Ed.), *Conflict and coexistence in Belgium* (pp. 107–26). Berkeley: Institute of International Studies.
India West. 1991. Youth jumps into Lok Sabha. 18 January, p. 12.
Karklins, Rasma. 1986. *Ethnic relations in the USSR.* Boston: Allen and Unwin.
Kenny, Tim. 1990. Soviets raze protesters' 'tent city'. *USA Today,* 31 December, p. 1.
Kilson, Martin. 1975. Blacks and neo-ethnicity in American political life. In Nathan Glazer and Daniel P. Moynihan (Eds.), *Ethnicity: Theory and experience* (pp. 236–66). Cambridge, Mass.: Harvard University Press.
Krishna, Gopal. 1966. The development of the Indian National Congress as a mass organization, 1918–1923. *The Journal of Asian Studies* 25(3): 413–30.
Laitin, David D. 1988. Language games. *Comparative Politics* 20(3): 289–302.
    1989. Language policy and political strategy in India. *Policy Studies* 22:415–36.
Marshall, David F. 1986. The question of an official language: Language rights and the English Language amendment. *International Journal of the Sociology of Language: Language Rights and the English Language Amendment* 60:7–75.
McAdam, Doug. 1982. *Political process and the development of black insurgency 1930–1970.* Chicago: The University of Chicago Press.
Misiunas, Romuald J. 1990. Baltic nationalism and Soviet language policy: From Russification to constitutional amendment. In Henry R. Huttenbach (Ed.), *Soviet nationality policies* (pp. 206–20). London: Mansell.
Murphy, Alexander B. 1988. *The regional dynamics of language differentiation in Belgium.* Geography Research Paper No. 227. Chicago: University of Chicago.
Nagel, Joane. 1986. The political construction of ethnicity. In Susan Olzak and Joane Nagel (Eds.), *Competitive ethnic relations* (pp. 93–112). New York: Academic Press.
Nayar, Baldev Raj. 1969. *National communication and language policy in India.* New York: Praeger.
Nunberg, Geoffrey. 1989. Linguists and the Official Language movement. *Language* 65(3): 579–87.
O'Barr, William M., and Jean F. O'Barr. 1976. *Language and politics.* The Hague: Mouton.
Piven, Frances Fox, and Richard A. Cloward. 1977. *Poor people's movements.* New York: Vintage Books.

Pool, Jonathan. 1973. Review of *Language conflict and national development* and *National communication and language policy in India. American Journal of Sociology* 78(6): 1590–93.
    1991. The official language problem. *American Political Science Review* 85: 495–514.
Rothschild, Joseph. 1981. *Ethnopolitics.* New York: Columbia University Press.
Rudolph, Lloyd I., and Susanne Hoeber Rudolph. 1987. *In pursuit of Lakshmi.* Chicago: University of Chicago Press.
Schattschneider, E. E. 1960. *The semi-sovereign people.* New York: Holt, Rinehart and Winston.
Schneider, Susan Gilbert. 1976. *Revolution, reaction, or reform: The 1974 bilingual education act.* New York: Las Americas.
Sonntag, Selma K. 1989. The school as a bargaining point in language politics: The Belgian Language Law of 1932. *Language, Culture and Curriculum* 2(1): 17–29.
    1991. *Competition and compromise amongst elites in Belgian language politics.* Plurilingua XII. Brussels: Plurilingua Series, Research Centre on Multilingualism, and Bonn: Dummler.
Souaiaia, Mohamed. 1990. Language, education and politics in the Maghreb. *Language, Culture and Curriculum* (special issue on "Language legislation and the schools," Selma K. Sonntag, Guest Ed.) 3(2).
Srivastava, R. N. 1979. Language movements against Hindi as an official language. In E. Annamalai (Ed.), *Language movements in India* (pp. 80–90). Mysore: Central Institute of Indian Languages.
U.S. Code, P.L. 94–73. 1975. Voting Rights Act of 1965 – Extension. *Congressional and Administrative News* 1(August 6): 400–406. 94th Cong. 1st sess. Washington, D.C.: GPO.
U.S. Congress. House. 1975. *Congressional Record* 121. 94th Cong., 1st sess. Washington, D.C.: GPO.
U.S. Congress. Senate. 1973. Committee on Labor and Public Welfare. *Education Legislation, 1973, Hearings on S. 1539.* 93rd Cong. 1st sess. Washington, D.C.: GPO.
Veltman, Calvin. 1990. The status of the Spanish language in the United States at the beginning of the 21st century. *International Migration Review* 24(1): 108–23.
Viguerie, Richard A., and Steve Allen. 1990. Bush loses the right wing. *New York Times,* 18 December, p. A23.
Weinstein, Brian. 1983. *The civic tongue: Political consequences of language choices.* New York: Longman.
Wils, Lode. 1973. Bormsverkiezingen en compromis des Belges. *Tijdschrift voor Hedendaagse Geschiedenis* 4:265–330.
Woolard, Kathryn A. 1989. Sentences in the language prison: The rhetorical structuring of an American language policy debate. *American Ethnologist* 16(2): 268–78.
Zolberg, Aristide R. 1974. The making of Flemings and Walloons: Belgium: 1830–1914. *The Journal of Interdisciplinary History* 5:179–235.

6 American language policy and compensatory opinion

Thomas S. Donahue

In this chapter I propose to discuss the public susceptibilities, the underlying social forces, and the range of probable motives behind the current political activity that is shaping the English as an official language movement. The discussion will begin with some pertinent facts in the state and national drives toward establishing English as an official language in the United States. I will then review and characterize the research published so far on the issue of recent national susceptibilities of the American public on this topic, and on the probable motivations of the local and national leadership of U.S. English, the major group directing the English as an official language drive. I will then reexamine the official language issue with a fresh look at the significance of the stresses and strains that have materialized in our political system along with the emerging English as an official language issue. First, I will show that the two major sides in the controversy are actually at the edges of the mainstream of political science thinking – namely, in either the group pluralist (a right-wing emphasis) or the core-periphery (on the left wing) models of analysis. Next, I will discuss an alternative closer to the political center, a more descriptive and Weberian approach that emerges after a careful scrutiny of the level of political tension that is cultivated at various scenes of the official language controversy. To do this, I will offer in the central portion of this chapter an account of the political thrusts and counterthrusts concerning the official language issue in certain states during the 1988 election. The analysis concludes with a new perspective on the reasons why this issue is coming to the forefront of political concern in this particularly vulnerable time in the formation of American public opinion.

The facts concerning the origin of the English Language Amendment, as recounted by Judd (1987) and Dyste (1989) are as follows. On April 27, 1981, Senator S. I. Hayakawa (R, California) proposed as a constitutional amendment Senate Joint Resolution 72. Senator Hayakawa intended that English be declared the official language of the United States, and in addition that it be unlawful for the "federal government or any state [to make or enforce] 'any law which requires the use of any language other than English'" (Judd 1987:116). Further, the resolution applied this prohibition to "laws, ordinances, regulations, orders, programs, and policies" by both state and federal governing bodies as well as to "orders and decrees by any court of the United States or any State." The amendment would have allowed languages other than English in "educational instruction" as a "transitional method of making students who use a language other than English proficient in English." (Judd 1987:116)

At the time, it was perceived that the language in this bill would have an influence beyond the prohibition of bilingual ballots and maintenance (as opposed to transitional) bilingual education; it would have possibly forbidden "both foreign language instruction in general and the use of languages other than English for reasons of health and public safety" (Judd 1987:117). In its first version, this bill died before it reached any congressional committees.

Before long, when Senator Hayakawa's views on English as an official language first became well-known, he was approached by activists of a rather different stripe. John Tanton, the organizer of the Federation for American Immigration Reform (FAIR), saw in Senator Hayakawa's efforts an opportunity to give his group a new sort of legitimacy. Tanton, an ophthalmologist from Petoskey, Michigan, had long been active in a variety of public action concerns, including interests in "conservation, nature, wilderness, Planned Parenthood, bees, combating political gerrymandering, essays, letter writing, and a string orchestra at Petoskey High School" (*Detroit Free Press*, 14 February 1989). In recent years, Tanton has been reported to think on an intellectually respectable plane. In an interview, he remarked that "Immanuel Kant wrote that language and religion were the ultimate dividers of mankind" (*Detroit Free Press*, 14 February 1989). But in the late 1970s and early 1980s, Tanton's personal anti-Catholic beliefs and his worries about Hispanic fecundity were not well-known. In reaching out to Senator Hayakawa, he formed the basis for a new national respectability for his group. The new entity that was formed through the combination of FAIR with those who were interested in Senator Hayakawa's ideas called itself U.S. English.[1] In subsequent years, this organization has had an extremely strong influence on language policy on both the state and federal levels in the United States.

Between 1984 and 1990, the leaders of U.S. English developed a successful campaign to mobilize opinion along two political fronts: They sold the American public on the idea that English should be the official language of the United States, and without distinguishing between the transitional and the maintenance varieties, they mounted a strong attack against bilingual education. On the state level, they have had outstanding

---

1 It is only in later years that the true character of this mesalliance was brought to light. Geoffrey Pullum quotes the highly respected sociolinguist John Baugh as saying that "the support for the English language issue started right there – a marketing decision by a P. R. man for a group of bigots" (Pullum 1987:607).

success. Since 1984, and in most instances through the influence of U.S. English, each of the following states has declared English to be the official language: North Carolina, Georgia, Florida, Kentucky, Tennessee, Mississippi, Illinois, Arkansas, North Dakota, South Dakota, Colorado, Arizona (a result since suspended and now under litigation), and California (results through mid-1990; cf. Baron 1990). There is a large array of possible reasons behind the success of U.S. English over the last decade. To begin our investigation, let us now turn to a larger and more academically informed perspective on these issues.

Scholarly views: group pluralist and core-periphery

Scholarly reaction to the sorts of power manipulations underlying the official language controversy in the United States follows one of three lines of analysis. The first, termed the "group pluralists" by Brass (1985), holds that in a given polity groups with dissimilar languages or patterns of belief, or groups that claim different ethnic heritages, are inherently destabilizing in that polity. A state or a federation that has a policy of maintaining neutrality among its dissimilar groups is always at risk from the leadership elite of the ethnic groups; elites seeking power will work to exaggerate ethnic differences and to mobilize their followers in ways that cause unrest and ultimately division and power sharing in the polity. Brass analyzes the work of Furnivall (1939, 1956) and Smith (1969, 1974) and positions them among the theorists of group pluralism. For our purposes, the most accessible expression of this line of thought in recent language policy is to be found in the information packets mailed out for recruitment by U. S. English. To illustrate this point, I will turn to a brief discussion of some of these documents.

Materials mailed by U.S. English in 1991 include a flyer entitled "A Common Language Benefits Our Nation and Its People." In this, which is probably the group's most influential handout, it is noted that:

A common language benefits a country and its people. In our country this common bond is more important than in most because Americans continue to be diverse in origin, ethnicity, religion and native culture. (U.S. English 1990)

Ex-U.S. Senator Hayakawa is quoted as saying that "a common language unifies, multiple languages divide"; he believes that the solution to potential divisions is the English Language Amendment, which "is a measure to strengthen the ties that bind together all of us, of whatever national origin or race, through the magical bond of a common language" (U.S. English 1990). Also included is a copy of Senator Hayakawa's 1985 monograph, "One Nation . . . Indivisible?" in which he alleges that in the future "a division perhaps more ominous in the long run than the division between blacks and whites" is currently being threatened by "the ethnic chauvinism of the present Hispanic leadership" (p. 11). An accompanying newsletter (*U.S. English Update,* January-February 1990) offers such post hoc assertions as "The USSR, currently torn by linguistic separatism, consists of 15 republics, 114 languages, and 300 dialects" (p. 2); and current bilingual legislation should in fact be called "The Bilingual Dropout Law" (p. 2; quoting Boston University president, John Silber).[2] A later issue of the newsletter (May-June 1990) raises the question of the venality of ethnic elites. Chairman Stanley Diamond writes that:

[T]hese self-appointed leaders are out of step with the public they ostensibly serve. I never cease to wonder: Where do these "leaders" get their authority? Who decides what the minorities need and want?

Harry Lujan, writing in the *Greeley Tribune,* seems to have put his hand on the answer, "Many Hispanics make their livings perpetuating the problems Hispanics face, by insisting on special programs, special treatment and special handouts." (p. 3)

Donahue (1985) attempts to show that most of the positions taken by U.S. English showed a suspicious thrust toward disinformation; in the group's current mailings, with Hugh Graham's arguments that speaking Spanish *causes* racial tensions and low economic achievement, little has changed (Graham 1990). Documentation for this analysis could be given at great length; the point remains that when all misdirection is cleared aside, U.S. English remains the prisoner of the group pluralist perspective, and as will be seen below, nearly all of those in support of their position are under the same spell.

A second line of scholarly analysis commonly found in response to the official language controversy follows an adapted core-periphery analytical approach. This perspective, best articulated in recent times by Hechter (1975) and Wallerstein (1979), holds that any attempt to divide subject populations along lines of class, language or ethnicity, occupation, or geographical region, is in fact an attempt to create a cultural division of labor in which a marginalized minority is held subservient to the economic and political interests of a core majority. In the official language issue, core-periphery arguments allege that a central elite that owns property and the means of production purposely restricts the political, social, and economic power of minority-language-speaking groups on the periphery of society in order to sustain and expand their own core wealth and power. Baron (1990) gives a detailed account of the history of American nativist sentiments and the consequent exclusionary policies in law and in the schools. Donahue (1985) argues that a cultural division of

2 There is an interesting term for those who persist with extreme rigidity in a desystematized and watered-down form of the group pluralist perspective in a strongly stable government. C. Wright Mills called such individuals "crackpot realists" (1959:356).

labor and related exclusionary policies in language use derive from a natural development of the collective wisdom in bourgeois societies. Others describe and analyze core-periphery conflicts in more tactical terms. After a review of the possible effect of a national English Language Amendment on voting rights, bilingual education, employment access for members of minority groups, and court interpretation services, Duenas Gonzales concludes that "understanding the motivations and strategies of U.S. English makes clear the intentions of this powerful group: to deprive one group of Americans [of] their rights" (1988:58). Sledd envisions as the political results of the language movement a rising proportion of segregated populations, rising rates of poverty, high school dropouts, unemployment, and the consequent "creation of a permanent underclass in the land of opportunity" (1988:92). Davis predicts quite plainly the inevitable results of core-periphery tensions underlying official language policy in America:

Such a policy would accomplish everything violence and oppression were once used to achieve – and all legally. Obviously most current immigrants are not now literate in English and likely will not be in the immediate future. How handy to have these new laws which make them illegal, non-citizens, disenfranchised. How convenient, in the name of offering them a chance of assimilation, to actually prevent it. Then these new immigrants will not be able to develop or assert political power and will lack the ability to defend themselves against those groups or laws that would oppress them. They will be unable to compete in the marketplace; thus they will always be a ready pool of laborers for the dead-end, risky, low-paying jobs that "true Americans" do not want. (1990:76)

As we will see when we review the battles of opinion reported in the nation's newspapers, most ethnic leadership elites speak from this viewpoint as they oppose the official language position.

An alternative view: Weberian stresses and strains

In those polities with stable governments and with political systems that are flexible enough to respond to minority groups and the demands of their leadership elites, there is a Weberian descriptive alternative to the cultural pluralist analysis. To begin with, we may assume that individuals on both sides of an issue are moved by what Weber called a "calculative spirit" (1978:375), and that they voluntarily begin a social action, or join an ongoing social action, with a desire to achieve their ends with rational means. In the case at hand, however, we may see evidence that many of the people involved are acting from what may be charitably described as a lower-level morality. Let us then proceed in our assumption as follows: As a central characteristic of a flexible political system, individuals may seek to exert political leadership *even when the very act of mobilizing opinion on an issue is itself an empty exercise.* Given the nature of wide publicity and exposure in modern mass communication, ambitious individuals may wish merely to achieve notoriety for a given cause, without regard to the fairness, justice, ultimate tests of constitutionality, or even the immediate success of that cause. What matters is that to achieve leadership, one must first become widely known. In what seems to be an utterly cynical value, problems of truth and falsity can be dealt with not at the outset, but later, as a matter of process; indeed, truth may simply be a matter of what one can get the public to believe.

It is crucially important to ponder such an alternative possibility, for it is entirely likely that those seeking to establish political leadership in a flexible system may indeed take advantage of the very flexibility of that system by taking positions that have a low-level destabilizing effect. As will be obvious in what follows, many of the leaders in the English as an official language movement are primarily attempting to exert leadership (in a quite opportunistic fashion), and only secondarily trying to establish and follow an ideological line.

We must begin by noting that there are several respectable (and hardly ideologically driven) descriptions and analyses of the circumstances underlying the politics of English as an official language. Two important contributions consider the legality of any proposed constitutional amendment that would establish an official language. Hornberger (1990) shows that in a language-planning context there is no certain outcome at this stage of the English as an official language movement; there is no predicting what the outcome may be from legal challenges to the reduction of support for bilingual education, and there is evidence that the Fourteenth Amendment to the Constitution may not offer legal protection to the rights of minorities (p. 19). Weinstein, on the other hand, believes that if any amendment

disempowers the state legislature and all state agencies from responding to the needs of linguistic minorities then . . . there is a fair presumption that what has motivated that provision is a desire to disempower the minority groups themselves. In that case, the official English provision may well be unconstitutional. (1990:278)

MacKaye (1990) shows in an analysis of letters to the editors of major California newspapers that people on either side of the controversy share in differing proportions the *same beliefs* about the role of language in a society: Language is a common bond uniting diverse elements of a society, language shows a primordial connection to one's ethnicity, and one may choose a language for social mobility and access in a society. In an analysis of the success of Proposition O, which asked city officials in San Francisco in 1983 to urge that voting materials be made available in English only, Woolard (1990) found that the public disapproved of certain ethnic leadership elites in that city: "A main issue was limiting the influence that minority politicians have over bilingual ballots and voters" (p. 136). But in a comparison with language policy in Ireland, Hudson-Edwards (1990) agrees with Fishman (1988) and concludes that in the United States

[I]t is difficult, in the final analysis, not to see this phenomenon as a re-surgence of nativist sentiment, a backlash against legislative and judicial toler-ance toward linguistic minorities in the areas of civil rights, voting rights, and educational opportunity . . . The cyclic rise and fall of nativism, in turn, tends to follow the rise and fall of national self-esteem, and if, for a whole variety of reasons, national self-esteem is now at its lowest ebb in forty years, then this may well account for the enthusiasm with which the concept of official En-glish has been embraced in four of the most heavily Spanish-speaking states in the whole United States.

In two publications (1989 and 1990), Dyste demonstrates that voters had two primary belief systems on the issue. Many believed that it was impor-tant to "strengthen the position of English in California" (1990:147), but to a great extent "voter ignorance and overt and symbolic racism" – the latter defined as adult behavior that "results from symbolic predisposi-tions acquired in childhood" (1990:146) – had a large influence. Zentella, who studied two versions of a *New York Times*/CBS News English-only poll, found that people with the highest levels of education were more sensitive to authoritarian connotations in the language used to describe official English sentiments: Highly educated people opposed the more "restrictive" wording of the second version of the poll in 1987, whereas most other people did not notice the change (1990:171).

The scholarship analyzing the significance of the official language con-troversy should allow us to center our thinking before we proceed with the next section. Such dispassionate analyses serve to highlight the con-trast between scholarly thought on this issue and the usual *zwischenzug* of public debate on language policy. The account that follows, which is taken from the *Newsbank* service, is instructive for the perspective it gives on the American capacity for building, and then adjusting to, politi-cal tensions.

An account of politics and public tensions

Arizona

The development of pro-English as an official language sentiment in Arizona in the period 1987–90 shows a remarkable case history of the kind of divisiveness that has characterized the issue from the very begin-ning. At the outset, Arizona state lawmakers, eager to follow the example of California's Proposition 63, the 1986 initiative declaring English to be California's official language, started in 1987 to lay the groundwork for a similar initiative by alleging that past encouragements in the use of Spanish had slowed the assimilation of Hispanics into the Anglo mainstream, and that in forming language ghettos, "we are also forming economic ghettos" (State Representative Dave Carson, quoted in the *Arizona Republic*, 2 February 1987). In mid-January 1987, Representative Carson sponsored House Bill 2031, which proposed a referendum that would declare English to be the official language of Arizona. The immediate response on the part of Hispanic leaders to this attempt to exert political leadership was to interpret it as a message "to the world that we have to be white to be all right in Arizona" (State Senator Pete Rios, quoted in the *Arizona Republic*, 2 February 1987). At the same time the Arizona Senate held hearings on Senate Concurrent Resolution 1005, which proposed to call for a public vote in 1988 on the question of amending the state constitution to declare English the official language. When the State Senate Judiciary Committee met to consider the proposal on February 2, 1987, over 250 persons appeared in the meeting to support testimony against the resolution. At this point, the senate resolution failed and was put on indefinite hold, and the house measure was referred to a subcommittee of the House Government Operations Committee. Republican State Senator Tony West was quoted as saying that "I don't think this Legislature needs to deal with issues that polarize the community" (*Arizona Republic*, 4 February 1987).

At this stage, the Arizona executive for U.S. English began to exert a significant amount of pressure. Robert Park, who is a retired Immigration and Naturalization Service criminal investigator, announced that the state politicians "are responding to a high level of intimidation, and it's really regrettable" (*Arizona Republic*, 4 February 1987). Throughout the month of February 1987, the issues aligned themselves in the following triangle: The groups U.S. English and English First undertook a cultural pluralist approach; the opponents followed the cultural division of labor view, insisting that official language measures would cause disorder and that they threatened the constitutional rights of individuals; and members of the state legislature were in retreat, abdicating their responsibilities. U.S. English pushed the argument that biculturalism disunites: Spanish language advertising, bilingual ballots, and bilingual education are signs of disunion. Opponents insisted that the initiatives were racist and unjust: "Before a person waives his basic constitutional rights, before we deprive a parent of custody . . . we have an obligation to ensure he understands the proceedings" (Judge B. Michael Dann, quoted in the *Arizona Republic*, 4 February 1987). State legislators were reeling from this episode of confrontational politics: State Senator Jacque Steiner remarked that "listening to deep, emotional feelings of people for a three-hour period certainly has an impact" (quoted in the *Arizona Republic*, 4 February 1987).

Something had to give among these forces in such a political triangulation during the next month, and there were two significant events: On March 10, 1987, the Senate Judiciary Committee moved to send the concurrent resolution forward to the full Senate for a vote (after a rancorous exchange between the Committee Chairman Peter Kay and a Phoenix developer named Tom Espinoza), and on March 26, Senator Kay withdrew the resolution in the face of a promised filibuster by state Democrats. In April, two thousand Spanish-speaking citizens marched to the state Capitol to protest the English-only sentiments held by some in the state legislature and to state their resentment at having their constitutional rights threatened. At the same time, Robert Park announced a U.S. English-sponsored drive for an initiative to put the English language issue on the ballot for 1988. State Representative Armando Ruiz planned a counter initiative that would "recognize English as the official language but also recognize other languages and protect bilingual education" (*Arizona Republic*, 24 May 1987); but at the very end of the month news came that U.S. English had filed a statement of organization as a campaign committee in the Secretary of State's office, and that the group's proposal would qualify for the November ballot if they could collect 130,048 signatures for the initiative drive. With this, one might say not that a battle was joined, but instead that a one-sided assault was formed.

As U.S. English mobilized during the initiative drive, spokespeople for the group selected as the major issues bilingual ballots and bilingual education – implying, as they had in the past, that redress was available by state, rather than by federal, action. U.S. English chose to persist with the criticism that bilingual ballots were expensive and interfered with the assimilation of minorities, and that bilingual education causes a high dropout rate and low economic achievement among Hispanics. The best solution to the problems of bilingual education is immersion in English, the group maintained, because immersion "offers a better opportunity to learn the language than bilingual education" (*Tucson Daily Star*, 29 March 1987). Thus U.S. English chose, again, to persist quite cynically in its successful "crackpot realist" approach, rather than acknowledge the results of scholarly research by the combined American and European academy. Over the summer, the group announced that it had chosen former U.S. senator Barry Goldwater as its honorary chairman. The selection of this popular individual proved to typify the U.S. English approach, which followed a method of playing to the public's emotional predispositions rather than to their capacity for rational thought.

Predictably, when there appeared early that fall Arizona English, a rival group that intended to place an alternative initiative on the ballot that "would push for the teaching of English but continue to allow the publication of some documents and ballots in Spanish" (*Arizona Republic*, 10 October 1987), the group made no emotional connection with the public and met with little popular success. The Arizona House passed with a vote of 47 to 8 a resolution by Arizona English that would require that the state's official policy be to "promote proficiency in English, the common language of the United States, while recognizing this state's unique history, languages and diversity" (*Tucson Daily Star*, 10 May 1988). The House resolution did not make it through the Senate Judiciary Committee because Senator Peter Kay demanded that an additional resolution making English the official language of Arizona also be passed by the Arizona House.

During the spring and summer of 1988, U.S. English circulated its petition for the November ballot. It asked for an amendment to the Arizona Constitution that would:

1. Make English the official language of the state and all its political subdivisions, including public schools and local governments;
2. Require the state to preserve and protect the English language and enhance its role in the state;
3. Prohibit the state from using languages other than English, making invalid any governmental document unless it is in English.

(*Tucson Daily Star*, 8 July 1988)

By the first week in July, the group submitted a total of 209,154 signatures to the Secretary of State; Robert Park admitted that his group had enlisted the help of a company called American Petition Consultants of Sacramento, California, in this task, and that the company was paid up to $1.00 a signature and its signature collectors up to 55 cents a name (*Tucson Daily Star*, 8 July 1988).

As election day approached, there were reports of corporate hostility to the speaking of Spanish on the job. The Payless Cashways company forbade its employees to speak Spanish to its customers in Yuma, Arizona; a man was fired after 16 years with the Pepsi-Cola company in Tucson because the company decided he had insufficient English to do the job well. According to the *Tucson Citizen* of 31 August 1988:

Civil rights advocates say employers are becoming more intolerant of workers who can't speak English. And they say the blame is easy to place: national and state campaigns to make English the official language. The movement to make English the official language of state government has created an "atmosphere of intolerance," in their opinion.

"All of a sudden we are starting to hear about these kinds of cases," said Louis Rhodes, the director of the Arizona Civil Liberties Union. "I believe the English-only movement has to be fueling it."

Whether this was true or not, it was apparent that U.S. English had sounded the right emotional pitch because it proved to be impervious to a potentially damaging scandal in the month leading up to election day.

John Tanton, who was still the chairman of the board of directors of U.S. English, had prepared in October 1986 a seven-page presentation for a discussion group named WITAN (Anglo-Saxon for "wise men"). The language of this memo was intentionally provocative and high-spirited. The content of the memo, however, was quite impolitic and highly offensive to some groups. Tanton wrote of his concerns about the impending reproportioning of the Hispanic and white mix in the population of the United States. In his discussion for the Mesa, Arizona, *Tribune* for Friday, 21 October 1988, James Crawford reported of Tanton's worries over a "Latin onslaught" that will overpower the "assimilative capacity of the country." Tanton asked, "Will the present majority peaceably hand over its political power to a group that is simply more fertile? . . . Can homo contraceptivus compete with homo progenitiva if borders aren't controlled?" Looking ahead to the foreseeable future, Tanton wrote:

Is Apartheid in southern California's future? The demographic picture in South Africa now is startlingly similar to what we'll see in California in 2030. In southern Africa, a white minority owns the property, has the best jobs and education and speaks one language. A non-white majority has poor education, jobs and income, owns little property, is on its way to political power and speaks a different language . . . In the California of 2030, the non-Hispanic whites and Asians will own the property, have the good jobs and education, speak one language and be mostly Protestant and 'other.' The blacks and Hispanics will have the poor jobs, will lack education, own little property, speak another language and be mostly Catholic. Will there be strength in this diversity: Or will this prove a social and political San Andreas Fault? (excerpted in the *Arizona Republic*, 9 October 1988)

Tanton warned in addition that with more Spanish speakers here, we will be at risk of "the tradition of *mordida* (bribe) [sic] the lack of involvement in public affairs"; in addition, the dominance of Roman Catholicism threatens to "pitch out the separation of church and state." Further, America will be overwhelmed by people with "low 'educability' and high school-dropout rates; limited concern for the environment; and of course high fertility." Elsewhere in the memo, Tanton's vivid remarks promised even more trouble:

Perhaps this is the first instance in which those with their pants up are going to get caught by those with their pants down . . . As Whites see the power and control over their lives declining, will they simply go quietly into the night? Or will there be an explosion? . . . We are building a deadly disunity. (*Arizona Republic*, 9 October 1988)

When this memo surfaced in October, 1988, reaction took two forms: First, damage control was undertaken by U.S. English. Certain celebrities (Walter Cronkite and Linda Chavez, a Republican politician who had been the president of U.S. English) resigned their connections with the group. Tanton resented that the memo had surfaced in the first place, and announced that all attacks on him were like McCarthyism (*Arizona Republic*, 9 October 1988); within the week he resigned as head of U.S. English. The new acting chairman of the group, Stanley Diamond, insisted that for Arizonans, John Tanton is not the issue; "the issue is Proposition 106" (*Arizona Republic*, 18 October 1988). In an attempt to take a high road in the debate, Diamond challenged "our opponents to get this issue out of the gutter, out of the big lies, out of the character assassinations . . . and move it to a debate where both sides can be heard with their arguments in depth" (*Arizona Republic*, 21 October 1988). The form of the second reaction, the immediate response in October of the voting public, was not recorded right away. Polls taken near election day showed a favorable sentiment for the proposition; positive support varied between 57, 61, and 66 percent (*Tucson Citizen*, 27 October 1988). For the most part, there was a vast silence, much as if the memo by John Tanton had helped to articulate certain fears and suspicions held by many members of the general public for quite some time.

In the two weeks before election day, a variety of influential groups sought to introduce a more sophisticated perspective on the meaning and possible consequences of Proposition 106. At a news conference on October 26 in Phoenix, Christian and Jewish leaders urged a "no" vote because the measure was "racist"; Bishop Thomas O'Brien of the Catholic Diocese of Phoenix was quoted as calling Proposition 106 "regressive, divisive, and unnecessary" (*Arizona Republic*, 27 October 1988). State Attorney General Robert Corbin questioned the constitutionality of the proposition, and remarked that he would be forced to use English when he conducted state business in Mexico (he also alleged a personal constraint: "I'll have to use an interpreter to order a beer for me, I guess") (*Arizona Republic*, 29 October 1988). Officials dealing with the state's Indian tribes worried whether speakers of Navajo and Apache would be able to seek assistance in courthouses if it were permissible to speak only English (*Arizona Republic*, 6 November 1988). Such last-minute efforts were to no avail, however; on November 8, Proposition 106 passed with a vote of 584,459 for and 572,800 opposed – a 1 percent margin out of the votes cast.

In a way out of proportion to the narrow margin of victory, Proposition 106 had a larger impact than either supporters or opponents had expected. Government officials came to realize that the state lottery could no longer be advertised in Spanish; the state Office of Tourism found that promotional brochures published in French, German, Spanish, and Japanese were now forbidden; the use of Spanish was now outlawed in the offices responsible for the distribution of food stamps; there were possible restrictions on notes and announcements to parents in Spanish-speaking school districts (*Phoenix Gazette*, 10 November 1988); questions arose over the printing of motor-vehicle pamphlets in non-English languages and over the use of non-English languages to answer queries by applicants for driver's licenses; issues of accurate translatability came up in connection with the use of English to speakers of Indian languages; there was confusion over whether or not non-English names could be given to towns, highways, streets, or bridges; and there was a fear that the state's trade office in Taiwan might have to be shut down over the use of Chinese instead of English (*Arizona Republic,* 7 December 1988 and 21 January 1989). In one significant case there was an instance of personal outrage: On November 10 Ms. Marie-Kelly Yniguez, an employee of the Risk Management Division of the State Department of Administration, sued in the U.S. District Court in Phoenix, alleging that her First Amendment rights guaranteeing freedom of speech had been violated, and that Proposition 106 was thus unconstitutional.

In the midst of considerable confusion and anguish over this issue in many segments of the state's population during the weeks and months after election day, State Attorney General Robert Corbin chose to move slowly in implementing the proposition. While the *Yniguez* case was in litigation, Mr. Corbin appointed a separate task force to research the constitutionality of the amendment (*Arizona Republic,* 1 December 1988). In the meantime, while various offices awaited an interpretation from the attorney general, government employees felt at liberty to use "whatever language is most effective" in dealing with their constituents (*Arizona Republic,* 21 January 1989). When the attorney general's analysis was released early in 1989, it interpreted the proposition to apply "only to official acts of the government" but "not prohibiting the use of languages other than English" (*Phoenix Gazette,* 7 February 1990). This deftly nonconfrontational opinion seemed to give state officials a welcome amount of maneuvering room for nearly a year.

On February 6, 1990, after a year of tension, conflict, and divisiveness throughout the state, U.S. District Judge Rosenblatt ruled in the *Yniguez* case: He found that Proposition 106 was unconstitutional. Judge Rosenblatt remarked that the law was "invalid on its face" and that it was "in violation of the First Amendment of the Constitution of the United States" (*Arizona Republic,* 7 February 1990). The judge wrote that:

Yniguez's self-imposed decision to refrain from speaking Spanish while performing her job . . . is but a product of her legitimate sensitivity to the perils posed by the article's language and her desire to restrict her conduct to that which is unquestionably safe.

A law which reasonably results in such restrictions is substantially overbroad. (*Tucson Citizen,* 7 February 1990)

Robert Park, the U.S. English representative in Arizona, vowed to appeal Judge Rosenblatt's decision to the Ninth Circuit Court; the results of this action have not yet been reported.

Florida

In Florida the story was rather different. On November 4, 1980, Dade County voters had approved a referendum that outlawed "the spending of county money to conduct business in any language other than English" (*Miami Herald*, 3 June 1987). County Commissioner Jorge Valdes believed that throughout the decade of the 1980s "that piece of paper, that ordinance, hurts the feelings of a large segment of this community" even after he worked for changes in the law in 1984 that permitted county money to be spent "to promote public health and safety in languages other than English" (*Miami Herald*, 3 June 1987). The ordinance had originally been enacted as a result of public sentiment against certain issues of the late 1970s: Haitian immigrants, riots in Miami, and the criminal element among those arriving in the Mariel boat lift. But Commissioner Valdes believed that in 1987 it was time to mobilize opinion for the repeal of that law. As it happened, however, 1987 was the year that U.S. English decided to move into Florida in order to propose the following language for Amendment 11 to the Florida Constitution:

Article II, Section 9. English is the Official Language of Florida.
(a) English is the official language of the state of Florida.
(b) The Legislature shall have the power to enforce this section by appropriate legislation.

Furthermore, there was a confrontational segment among Florida voters who were spoiling for a fight over official English as a symbolic issue: Terry Robbins, the leader of a group called Dade Americans United, urged that a public forum be held "because it was time for a 'bloodletting' on the issue" (*Miami Herald*, 8 March 1987). It appears that Commissioner Valdes could not have chosen a worse time than spring 1987 to move for a repeal of the anti-bilingual ordinance.

As U.S. English organized its Florida campaign, it seemed determined to take a softer line in its appeal and in the wording of its usual arguments. Ms. Pat Fulton, the forthright and vocal leader of Florida English in Tampa, was in time supplanted in overall visibility by Dr. Mark La Porta, a Miami Beach physician who was named the campaign chairman for Florida. Throughout the voters' petition drive, Dr. La Porta persisted with an understated and quiet approach:

We're pro-English, not anti-anything. We are not rabid rednecks. Our intentions are good . . . No fights, or we leave. Respect is very important. We hope to keep it nice and peaceable and quiet. What we're aiming for here is an amiable process. (*Miami Herald*, 6 March 1988)

However this strategy was contrived, it had the remarkable practical effect of *disturbing nothing* in the Florida public opinion polls on the official language question. In the fall of 1987, it was reported that 86 percent of the population was for the amendment (including 64 percent of the Hispanic voters); a year later, the amendment passed with a positive vote of 83 percent. In the intervening year, U.S. English persisted in its arguments about forming a linguistic and cultural unity and avoiding a potential "Tower of Babel" divisiveness in the state. In March 1988, Commissioner Valdes attempted for the second time to have the bilingual ordinance of 1980 overturned, but he received no support from influential Hispanic leaders, who wanted to avoid antagonizing others in the electorate (*Miami Herald,* 9 August 1988). In its Florida efforts, English Plus called attention to the facts that the U.S. English stance masked negative attitudes toward foreign tourists, and that the proposed amendment did not spell out exceptions for non-English speakers in cases of health, safety, welfare, and justice (*Orlando Sentinel,* 27 June 1988). A group called SUN (Speak Up Now) warned that the amendment "would create havoc in commerce, tourism, and the judicial system and eventually would cost state taxpayers millions of dollars" (*Palm Beach Post,* 15 August 1988). It appeared that the voting public listened to such objections, but chose to disregard them. Studies showing that an official language policy was unnecessary because over 90 percent of the foreign born become proficient in English in the first generation (*Miami Herald,* 31 July 1988) had no effect. Reports of educators who were afraid that the amendment would cause youngsters to be ashamed of a non-English mother tongue (*Miami Herald,* 31 October 1988) were received without alarm. When the scandal about John Tanton's memo surfaced in October 1988, the news was received with a quiet imperturbability. Opinion research showed that the movement was an outlet for those with xenophobic or racist feelings: An article in the *St. Petersburg Times* found a person who "is just the kind of person backers of the "English Only" campaign were looking for – white, middle-class and irritated with changes in her hometown":

There are parts of this city where I can't even communicate because no one speaks English. . . . I hope [the amendment] passes. You shouldn't have to speak Spanish just to survive. (9 March 1988)

Yet journalistic revelations such as these proved not to be revelations at all and made no difference in public opinion.

The approach of election day was marked by a last-minute legal maneuver and, in response, a classic example of doublespeak. In October, four Spanish-speaking citizens sued to remove the proposed amendment from the ballot because no petitions for gathering signatures on the issue had been provided in the Spanish language. As the suit progressed rapidly in the court system, it was at first turned down because it was alleged that the Federal Voting Rights Act did not apply in the private petitioning effort by U.S. English; but then five days before the election, U.S. attorneys filed papers repeating the allegations of the original plaintiffs.

During this time, Pat Fulton of U.S. English remarked that voters would not endure such machinations: "I think voters are going to be outraged at the prospect of being disenfranchised. This could bring on a backlash. One puny lawsuit is not going to stop this issue" (*Miami Herald,* 12 October 1988). In the end, the U.S. Supreme Court agreed in July 1989 that the Federal Voting Rights Act did not apply in this instance.

Quite predictably, after the victory on November 8, many people felt that acting with certain aggressions was part of their new entitlement. A cashier at a supermarket in Coral Gables was suspended for speaking Spanish while she worked. A customer at the catalog order window at a Sears, Roebuck store was told she would have to speak English to place an order. At Mount Sinai Medical Center in Miami Beach, an 18-year-old clause in the employee handbook that required everyone to speak English during the day was invoked once more. In general the concept that an "official language" applies only to government business was redefined to pertain to the private sector, and Miami lawyer Jon Weber was quoted as saying that "many employers believe it is a license to repress foreign languages" (*Orlando Sentinel,* 11 December 1988). As more difficulties, confusions, and hostilities emerged after election day, Tom Ferguson, president of an economic development corporation of Dade County, re- marked that "I'd be happy if the Legislature does nothing with the amendment. I'd be happier if we didn't have the stupid thing in the first place" (*Orlando Sentinel,* 11 December 1988).

Colorado

In Colorado, the push for English as an official language was begun by State Representative Barbara Philips, a former elementary school teacher whose experience with bilingual education was negative. Her teaching site in Colorado Springs had been designated a bilingual school, with unproductive results:

There was no need for teaching in a foreign language but that's what they said we had to do. The children didn't want it, the teachers didn't want it and the program was a failure. The students' scores fell dramatically. (*Rocky Mountain News,* 10 July 1988)

Serving in the Colorado legislature in 1987, Ms. Philips sponsored legis- lation for an English-only bill, but then withdrew her initiative; instead, with her Colorado Official English committee she gathered nearly seventy thousand signatures for a proposed constitutional amendment (Amend- ment 1), which would be worded as follows on the November 1988 ballot: "Should English be designated the official language of the state of Colorado?" By November 1987 the measure had qualified for the ballot and Glen Philips, her husband, remarked that "The big job is completed.

Now we look to next year for our educational phase" (*Denver Post*, 14 November 1987).

The Philipses' efforts to convince the broader electorate that official English was a good idea were far from smooth. Powerful individuals took a stand against the issue. During the signature-gathering process in 1987, Bishop Richard Hanifen of Barbara Philips's home district in Colorado Springs remarked that he "cannot support a bill which has the appearance of excluding other languages from the dignity they deserve" (Colorado Springs *Gazette Telegraph*, 3 October 1987). He criticized the proposed law as a

pointlessly provocative initiative that has the potential of creating an atmosphere of hostility and resentment. Good law requires clear intent and demonstrated need. Neither has been apparent in the history of this measure. I personally dislike, even resent any actions taken officially which could be construed as showing prejudice against (Hispanics), or fear of these beautiful citizens of our state. (*Gazette Telegraph*, 3 October 1987)

Richard Castro, the executive director of the Denver Human Rights and Community Relations Agency, remarked that most of the electorate does not "understand the hidden agenda" behind the initiative, and the legislation would only "divide the people"; further, it is "narrow vision and a twisted kind of logic to suggest that to speak only one language is better than people who speak two or three" (*Rocky Mountain News*, 30 October 1987). Marilyn Braveman, a national director of education for the American Jewish Committee, was convinced that the legislation would divide people "along economic, sociological, racial and religious lines"; she remarked that "opposing a group's language is the first step to suppressing a people" (*Denver Post*, 11 November 1987).

The Philipses felt free to disregard such criticisms from their opponents during the year-long "educational phase" on the issue beginning in November 1987. If a meeting would get testy, Mrs. Philips would simply excuse herself and leave early: A meeting in June in Colorado Springs drew angry shouts from Spanish speakers, and as denunciations accumulated, she "brought the debate to an abrupt end by announcing she had to leave because of other appointments" (*Colorado Springs Gazette Telegraph*, 25 June 1988). Mrs. Philips persisted in her loyalty to her perceived constituency, remarking at the outset that "Coloradans don't want two languages, side by side, with equal status" (*Rocky Mountain News*, 19 November 1987). Opinion research early in 1988 found that "the biggest reservoirs of support for the amendment appear to be among older Coloradans, people with annual incomes between $20,000 and $50,000, and people with less than a college education" (*Denver Post*, 4 February 1988). Dolores Conte, of the Colorado Civil Rights Commission, remarked that "the less people are educated about the issue, the more likely they are to vote for it" (*Pueblo Chieftain,* 8 May 1988). However the supporters might be characterized, projections showed that 63 percent of the voting public remained in favor of the amendment.

Tension over the proposed amendment escalated in the summer of 1988. Barbara Philips was accused of violating state laws "by using taxpayer-paid telephones and state workers as an answering service for the constitutional amendment" (*Denver Post,* 17 August 1988). While the use of state resources was being questioned, a group of lawyers who belonged to the National Lawyer's Guild sued to remove the amendment from the ballot because Mrs. Philips' petitions had not been written in Spanish as well as English, a violation of the Federal Voting Rights Act of 1965 (also tested at this time in Florida). Former California senator Hayakawa was pressed for a contribution to the debate, and he volunteered the opinion that the National Lawyer's Guild could be linked to the International Association of Democratic Lawyers, which he termed a "Soviet front group" (*Pueblo Chieftain,* 24 August 1988). The possible presence of Soviet influence notwithstanding, the U.S. District Court ruled that "the initiative cannot go to a vote" (*Denver Post,* 17 September 1988); the secretary of state for Colorado decided that the initiative could remain on the ballot but the votes it gathered on election day would not be counted. At this juncture U.S. English entered the picture with plans to spend "about $100,000" in Colorado in order to collect by October 3 enough signatures to "offset the 61,000" thrown out in the district court ruling (*Rocky Mountain News,* 23 September 1988). On October 12, the previous month's ruling was overturned in the Tenth U.S. Circuit Court of Appeals, and Amendment 1 was reinstated on the ballot.

It is difficult to say whether or not the delayed entrance of U.S. English into Colorado had any effect one way or the other. When the November 8 vote was counted, the amendment passed with 828,883 votes for to 528,762 against – a victory by 61 percent of the vote. As was the case in Florida, there were instances soon after election day of individuals acting out previously repressed feelings: At a fast-food restaurant in Denver the manager forbade an employee from helping a South American visitor with the menu, saying "I don't want anyone speaking Spanish here" (*Denver Post,* 19 November 1988). Stories were told of schoolchildren "telling Hispanic playmates the law somehow made them 'unconstitutional'" (*Denver Post,* 27 November 1989). In Grand Junction, "a school bus driver reportedly told students they could not speak Spanish on the bus" (*Denver Post,* 28 December 1988). The mayor of Denver decided to restore calm by issuing an executive order that prohibited "city officials from discriminating against citizens or employees for speaking a language other than English" (*Denver Post,* 28 December 1988).

Other states

The elections of November 1988 in Arizona and Florida were targeted by
U.S. English as the most significant in mobilizing future opinion on the
English as an official language issue; the group decided only at the last
minute to come to the rescue in Colorado by registering voters there. But
certain politicians in other states attempted to form bases for political
leadership by putting their fellow citizens through similar sorts of *Sturm
und Drang* on this question. In Texas, State Representative L. P. Peterson
announced early in March 1987 that official English was an "educational" and a "jobs" issue (*Houston Chronicle,* 3 March 1987); but
shortly after he proposed a constitutional amendment that English be
named the official language of Texas, a poll conducted by the Public
Policy Resources Laboratory at Texas A&M University showed a widespread fragmentation of opinion. Altogether, 74 percent of the state population supported such an amendment; but 14 percent said it would have
"no consequence," another 12 percent believed that it would "force
people to learn to speak English," and 2 percent believed the amendment
"would help 'rid Texas of foreigners'" (*Austin American-Statesman,* 14
May 1987). The progress of this proposal in Texas went through an
extraordinary set of twists and turns in the following months. Initially, it
was shelved for lack of support in the Texas House. Then presidential
candidate George Bush distanced himself from the divisiveness in the
issue by opposing the amendment in May 1987, and GOP leaders began
to worry that "the party's out-front position in favor of the movement
could harm Republicans' efforts to woo Hispanics" (*Dallas Morning
News,* 24 May 1987). In November, the Republicans voted to place the
issue on their March 8 primary ballot, despite warnings from George
Strake, their state chairman, that Democrats would seize the advantage
to "demagogue against us," and despite the urging of Republican Governor Bill Clements to "just forget it" (*Dallas Morning News,* 22 November 1987). Surveys taken as the primary approached showed that 83
percent of Dallasites approved the measure (*Dallas Times Herald,* 29
February 1988). But later in the year, when the measure came up in the
Texas Senate, Hispanic legislators organized to block the official English
movement, comparing it to the "Know-Nothing Party and the anti-
immigration movements of the 19th Century" (*San Antonio Express
News,* 23 November 1988).

Attempts to mobilize opinion on the official language issue in other
states show the same kind of push-me pull-you character. Proponents in
New Jersey argued that the use of other languages causes "separatism
and divisiveness" and cautioned that without English as an official language, New Jersey could become like Canada; opponents found the issue
"discriminatory," "dumb," and "insulting" (*Asbury Park Press* of Nep-

tune, New Jersey, 15 June 1987). Citizens of Nevada in 1987 fought Assembly Joint Resolution 11, which would declare English to be the official language of the state, by saying that it was "pure racism," and that it "would not allow Latin people their culture"; the resolution's sponsor, Assemblyman Virgil Getto, stated that "this is a very simple measure and I can't understand all the wild interpretations" (*Las Vegas Review Journal*, 22 February 1987). Proponents of official language legislation in Rhode Island hoped that such legislation would unite the state's citizens while at the same time "eliminating such services as bilingual election ballots and driver's license exams"; opponents insisted that the movement "will rob people of their civil rights, hurt bilingual education programs, and breed racism," and in a more general sense "encourage bigotry" (*Providence Journal*, 22 March 1987). In Massachusetts, pro-official language forces worried that both the state and the nation were "becoming fragmented into pockets of ethnicity." Francis Doris, the state legislator sponsoring an official language proposal, declared further that his measure was "an expression of frustration by many people. I filed this bill because of comments from a lot of constituents . . . who have expressed concerns over the years." Doris' opposition contended that the issue was likely to "encourage bigotry, divisiveness and resentment" (*Fall River Herald News*, 5 March 1987). Representative Charles E. Silvia, another state political leader taking up the issue in Massachusetts, declared that his support derived from his "patriotism and love of country"; his colleague, Representative Robert Correia, interpreted that sentiment as "a lot of hogwash" (*New Bedford Standard Times*, 22 November 1987).

In comparison with the agonizing debate in Arizona, Florida, and Colorado, the decision about official English in New Mexico was sudden and swift. On February 4, 1987, State Representative Marty Lambert announced her sponsorship of a state constitutional amendment establishing English as the official language of the state because it would "help immigrants fulfill the American dream" (*Santa Fe New Mexican*, 4 February 1987). Peter Gomez, the head of the Santa Fe chapter of the League of United Latin American Citizens, responded with this statement:

By forcing people to speak only English, it makes the Spanish language and culture second best. It makes those people feel inferior and feel that their language and culture are second best. (*Santa Fe New Mexican*, 4 February 1987)

On the next day, Governor Garrey Carruthers said of the proposal: "I don't think it's productive. I don't understand what it would do for the state. It's offensive to Native Americans and Hispanic people" (*Santa Fe New Mexican*, 5 February 1987). On February 6, 1987, the proposed amendment was voted down unanimously in the New Mexico House of Representatives.

In still other states, the issue took on the character of *opera buffa:* Joe Rizzo, a legislator for Suffolk County on New York's Long Island, proposed that English be named the official language of Suffolk County. In a public meeting one woman responded as follows:

I came here from Puerto Rico in 1959. I've worked here all these years and now they want me to move out of this country. We should put Rizzo in a boat and send him to Cuba. Let him boss the people around down there – he can be the second Fidel Castro! (*New York Daily News,* 26 February 1989)

In North Carolina, the sponsor of official language legislation successfully moved his bill through the State House, and announced his victory by addressing his startled colleagues in French (*Charlotte Observer,* 25 June 1987). In Ohio, State Representative Richard E. Rench carved out a position showing that he did not want to be mistaken for just any public servant: In a newpaper interview, he remarked that "If people don't want to learn our English, they can go to a country that speaks whatever language they want" (*Cleveland Plain Dealer,* 14 May 1987).

In one important instance, official English sentiments have had a significant result: In California, the original legislative provisions allowing for state direction of bilingual education were allowed to expire in 1988. But for the most part, after the posturing, the attacks, and the counter denunciations, there is little question that once official English legislation takes hold, there comes a flood of instances of petty tyrannies. Since 1990, four years after English was declared the official language in Proposition 63, the American Civil Liberties Union has become involved in continuing legislation showing that a nominal "official" language does not apply to behavior in the private sector. Supervisors have sought to spy on, and to reprimand, nurses speaking Tagalog in the Pomona Valley Hospital Medical Center near Los Angeles. In nearby Monterey Park, the mayor opposed a gift of Chinese books to the city library because "if people want foreign-language [books], they can go [buy them] on their own" (from an account in the *Los Angeles Times,* 10 June 1990). Also in Monterey Park, a person hired because she had bilingual skills was told not to speak Spanish at work in private conversations. Certain activist private citizens in that city pushed for a resolution against Korean and Chinese grocers, demanding that all market signs be in English; similar sentiments against Koreans are reported from the Orange County city of Garden Grove (*Los Angeles Times,* 10 April 1987). For a time in Pomona, there was an ordinance requiring that store signs be "at least 50% English" (the *Los Angeles Times,* 10 June 1990). A former chef at the University of California Medical Center in San Francisco spoke of moving around as quietly as possible in order to catch people who violated the center's English-only rule (*Los Angeles Times,* 10 June 1990). In numerous instances, it seems that English-only policies, as the *Los Angeles Times* concluded, "provide an outlet for expressing negative attitudes toward newcomers" (10 June 1990).

A summing up and two hypotheses

In the first place, it is obvious that on the local and state levels, ambitious politicians are exploiting the official language issue in order to exert political leadership. It seems that a variety of entry-level politicians who wish to expand their influence in a way that brings a great deal of mass communications exposure do not hesitate to make use of the methods and resources of U.S. English. At the strategic center, the policies of U.S. English seem designed to move along a middle way between the mobilizing of opinion on the state level and avoiding contact with the present legal provisions on the federal level. According to Daniels (1990:8), "the overall strategy seems to be to get some official-English law on the books of a majority of states and to continually fan public resentment over schooling policies that 'degrade English' and 'cater' to immigrants." Part of the cynicism of this approach is evident in the group's apparent lack of concern for the extremes of feeling that it stirs up; indeed, there is an apparent ethic that among the venues for beginning political activity it is acceptable to foster a climate "that perpetuates anti-immigrant attitudes and behavior in our society" (Judd 1990:45). The group attracts would-be leaders who simply do not mind the fact that, as Frick stated it, "when a climate of hatred is created, real people get discriminated against, deprived, devalued, and hurt" (1990:33).[3]

At this stage in the official English movement, it seems that one can pull from the group pluralist theory only an inadequate explanation for the behavior of American groups in conflict. Instead of the predicted destabilization and near-chaos, we have small-minded grudges and petty fumings and fussings between native-born Americans and immigrant groups.[4] On

---

3 In her article, "Official English and the Urge to Legislate," Betty Dubois remarks that "the study of law as power brings the realization that law does not lead away from conflict, as is sometimes assumed, but toward it" (1990:233). In the case of U.S. English, it is important to realize that at the outset, the very proposing of legal changes is undertaken with an intent to provoke conflict, and establishing a campaign for legal changes involves the orchestrating of conflict over a period of months and years.

4 Notice, however, that a high level of distracted activity in the political system actually delays action in the legal system. Motives and possible results are in such a confused disarray that the legal system will provide no guarantee of an appropriate form of justice. As Judge Noel Fidel writes:

If the political culture cannot determine the goal, if it does not understand the goal, if it does not know itself what it is trying to wall in or wall out, and if instead it simply conducts an emotionally charged battle over symbols, and if it does so by posturing over orthodoxies, then do not expect the legal system to sort it all out in a consistent, coherent, and cohesive way. (1990:305)

the other side of the critical scale, analysis according to the core-periphery model *also* serves principally to highlight the struggle of U.S. English to mobilize (and perhaps misdirect) sentiment on the *state* level against the protections guaranteed by *federal* law for bilingual ballots and bilingual education. During this stage, political leaders following the strategy of U.S. English know that they cannot produce a fixed result; indeed, they know that the only thing they can do at present is to divide the American public along the lines of long-standing ethnic antagonisms, and to keep the citizenry heated up to a boiling hostility. Thus, when we look more intensely through our mediating Weberian perspective, we find that the debate has been tainted by misrepresentation and illogicality: Individuals for the official language movement may have a hidden agenda, and they do not choose to argue with complete rationality (and in fact in many instances they do not mind descending to buffoonery); but on the other hand those defending ethnic interests are forced to base their count-erarguments on heavily emotional premises.

Thus, a scrutiny of the political forces at work in the English as an official language issue shows that hardly anything is as it seems, that emotions among the general public are inflamed, and that thinking among the citizenry is at a stage of high vulnerability and susceptibility. We must address this issue on different terms: What is really going on as individuals and language interest groups attempt to mobilize opinion for installing English as an official language? By taking a larger view, and by pushing the core-periphery model toward a more provocative direction, one may proceed with a hypothesis that is long overdue in the discussion of this issue. I propose the following levels of analysis and interpretation.

The first hypothesis: compensatory opinion during recapitalization

We must consider at the outset that the most significant political fact of the last two decades in the United States is the upward redistribution of private wealth in the American economy since the 1974 resignation of Richard Nixon from the presidency. We are in the midst of an era of *recapitalization:* Largely through tax reductions and through market and real-estate speculation, a select class of property and resource owners has rapidly accumulated a larger proportion of wealth for private use and for investment purposes. In a report released in 1986 by the Survey Research Center of the University of Michigan, there were interesting results for 1983, a survey year directly in the middle of the recapitalization era: 1 percent of all American families owned 41.7 percent of all the country's wealth, and one half of 1 percent of American families owned 35 percent of the available wealth. Phillips (1990) shows that in 1987 dollars the top 5 percent of income-earners enjoyed an increase of 23.4 percent between

1977 and 1988, and the top 1 percent saw an increase of 49.8 percent (p. 17). Robert Reich (1991) describes a "fortunate fifth" among the wealthiest of the population who are withdrawing from public participation; they enjoy the most favorable tax rates, whereas at the highest level (those with incomes over $500,000 a year) the charitable donations have dropped from an average of $47,432 in 1980 to $16,062 in 1988 (p. 43). Phillips's figures show that the fortunate fifth have had an average increase of income of 17.5 percent during the years of recapitalization (p. 17).

For certain segments of our society, such information is *prima facie* destabilizing. For the third through the seventh of Philips's income deciles, who lost an average of $1,346 in income from 1977 to 1988 (1990:17), there was a setback that strikes at the heart of all the middle-class mythologies about working hard to get ahead in life. At the same time that the redistribution of wealth was being carried forward, the political party platforms have filled the public mind with topics and issues that have diverted the attention of the citizenry to other subjects: abortion, the Equal Rights Amendment, the agenda of the religious right-wing, and abuses in the public welfare system, among others. An emphasis upon English as an official language is itself one of these diversionary ploys. The political strategy behind such moves seems to be a continuously applied "divide and rule" tactic; a government can establish stability through building conflicts, and then managing and manipulating them. The immediate result of encouraging such cleavages is to realign allegiances from former splinter groups and to attract new members to the more conservative of the two political parties in a two-party system.

Of absorbing interest is the fact that in the classical Marxist sense, this is a matter of the dissemination of false consciousness, an attempt to keep the public in a form of stabilized and prerevolutionary opinion. In a neo-Marxist sense, Marcuse's concept of repressive desublimation (1966) has come full circle: In a return to the arena of political debate, public opinion is forced into a level of ultimately harmless and unproductive thrust and counterthrust. By any measure in a core-periphery perspective, the public sensibility has been redirected to concerns far from the center of wealth and power, and social antagonisms are manipulated in order to indefinitely postpone the meeting of citizens' economic needs by authorities in the state or federal governments.

Perhaps the least inflammatory perspective (but one with an irreducible irony) on this issue has something to teach us at the present time. In a Weberian sense, in which one pays rigorous analytical attention to the stresses and strains in a given instant in a society, the language issue comes along as a form of *compensatory opinion*. Those who do not benefit from the transfer of wealth and power in the past two decades at least have in compensation a kind of emotional and intellectual recreation through their political opinions and any related activities. Of course, the long-term result is still a matter of misdirection and deception, and of masking or disguising what is going on in the upper reaches of American wealth. We are currently witnessing a deeply cynical leadership method in political debate, in which leadership elites take on the role of performing magicians: Through illusion and distraction, and through the manipulation of opinion, public attention is being turned away from the real issues of the redistribution of wealth and the restructuring of the American class system.

A second hypothesis: the control of charismatic appeal

It may not be sufficient, however, only to claim that the moves for re-capitalization have proceeded through distraction, misdirection, and disguise and through the centering of public attention on compensatory opinion in the past decade and a half. A rigorous line of political science inquiry insists that we judge intentions by results. The most obvious result has been the reallocation of wealth, resources, and property to individuals in the higher stratification levels – a figurative strip-mining of wealth away from the middle class. Yet there is another intention, another purpose, manifest in the nature of the debased and degraded discussion surrounding the English as an official language issue. To understand this particular motive, we must examine briefly the current thinking about the nature of charismatic leadership in modern political life.

Since the time of Max Weber, it has been understood that in times of instability and change there may emerge a leader with special characteristics of personal grace – one who is attractive, engaging, and appealing to male and female voters, a person who has new or nontraditional political constituencies, and one who has a forceful action agenda that moves at the very borderline of current legal norms. Such a person may gather sudden power in a democracy in a way that threatens the conventional modes for appropriation and ownership. Much of the traditional research on charisma has focused on the nature of individual leadership and personalities; but the most recent research argues that charisma may not be definable in a rigorous way, and instead shifts attention to the changing patterns of need and personal susceptibility among members of the electorate (see Madsen and Snow 1991). Voters are quite vulnerable to charisma in times of inequitable distribution of wealth. When the national economy weakens, people lose their sense of personal control over events, and the crucially important feel of self-efficacy is compromised. At such times, the average person becomes willing to pass along "proxy control" over events that impact on one's personal life if one can find a way of bonding with a leader (Madsen and Snow 1991:9–17). Thus, on an individual level, a vulnerability to charisma is at its strongest when voters come to identify with intimate characteristics of the personality of the candidates: Voters attach themselves emotionally to the would-be leader, and then as they surrender proxy-control they come to invest the leader with those qualities of wisdom, integrity, compassion, efficacy, and altruistic energy that they themselves find lacking as they attempt to cope in their personal lives.

We may assume that the current "division" on political issues stems from the fact that the level of debate during this time of recapitalization has been degraded on purpose. I claim in addition that the intentionally degraded debate over the English as an official language issue, together with similar treatment of allied issues of potential difference, is part of a strategy to prevent the emergence of charismatic leadership in the political opposition. Constant division, disputation, insults to ethnic heritage, charges and countercharges, imputations of and demonstrations of stupidity – such moves prevent the initial emotional identification and bonding from forming with any potential charismatic leader. The overall strategy is carried on in an attempt to establish stresses and strains in the Weberian sense, and then by persisting, to paralyze debate and to cripple the possibility of political change.

I conclude by suggesting this extension of the Weberian perspective: English as an official language may be a phony issue. So is all the excitement managed over abortion, a cash-poor foreign policy directed toward Eastern Europe and the former Soviet Union, the vacillations over defense spending, the orchestrated sentiments over family values, and the mannered attention paid to the agenda of the religious right wing. We are witnessing a purposeful attempt to paralyze debate and to prevent the formation of alternative leadership in a democracy at a time when a two-decade-old policy of resource reallocation proceeds unabated.

Implications for educational policy

A crucial portion of the manipulation of opinion on the official English issue concerns the continuous attacks on bilingual education policy in the United States. The issues as defined, for example, in Donahue (1982, 1983) and Edwards (1981, 1982, 1984) have been discussed widely in both scholarly treatments and in the public media. Proponents of either transitional or maintenance bilingual education (as reported by Donahue) argue that the primary effort in current bilingual education policies rests on promoting the general welfare: Education to literacy in the mother tongue is indispensable for forming the early emotional and intellectual health of children, and the bicultural population that results is destined for an emotionally centered, stable, and productive adult life. Opponents of bilingual education (see the work of Edwards) argue that present educational policies foster an elite, that most children are ill-served because they form mixed allegiances to socially dominant groups, and that the public expense is too high. It is of profound interest to note that most of the objections to bilingual education policies rest on the group pluralist school of analysis, and lately these ideas have been articulated in such a way that they serve as the divisive "wedge issues" that have surfaced in the English as an official language campaign.

   Those whose responsibility it is to formulate educational policy for bilingual populations doubtless will find the line of analysis suggested in this essay most provocative. As one possible alternative, policy makers may conclude that the critics of bilingual education have in most instances allowed themselves to be victimized by compensatory opinion. The next stage of analysis is, of course, more extreme: All interested parties may wish to consider the possibility that the manipulations and misdirection that underlie compensatory opinion are carried on for the purpose of postponing action and buying time while recapitalization continues. As public opinion is diverted and distracted during such a process, one may ponder the ways in which state capitalism is still served:

1. The present division of labor is sustained.
2. The increased rate of the accumulation of capital by certain segments continues.
3. No appropriate increases in public spending are committed.
4. Social mobility is slowed to a rate that more closely approximates a caste system than a class system.

When we do in fact judge a policy's intentions by its results, we see that most people holding anti-bilingual education views have been cooperating in a massive delusion.

   A healing strategy in educational policy most properly would return to values articulated by Weber. Policy for education generally, and for bilingual education specifically, should be directed toward mobility in the class system. An optimal educational system must provide more options and choices, so that upward mobility may be promoted, and individuals simply can have more chances in life. In our current political system, there is opposition to providing such options and choices, and that opposition uses instruments that can be subtle but at times bludgeoning. But in any analysis, it would seem that the opposition is not interested in promoting the general welfare.

References

Adams, Karen L., and Daniel T. Brink (Eds.). 1990. *Perspectives on Official English: The campaign for English as the official language of the USA.* New York: Mouton de Gruyter.

Baron, Dennis. 1990. *The English-only question: An official language for Americans?* New Haven: Yale University Press.

Brass, Paul. 1985. Ethnic groups and the state. In Paul Brass (Ed.), *Ethnic groups and the state* (pp. 1–56). London: Croom Helm.

Castro, Max J., Margaret Haun, and Ana Roca. 1990. The Official English movement in Florida. In Karen L. Adams and Daniel T. Brink (Eds.), *Perspectives on Official English* (pp. 151–60). New York: Mouton de Gruyter.

Cazden, Courtney B., and Catherine E. Snow (Eds.). 1990. English Plus: Issues in bilingual education. *The Annals of the American Academy of Political and Social Science,* vol. 508. Newbury Park: Sage Publications.

Daniels, Harvey A. (Ed.). 1990. *Not only English: Affirming America's multilingual heritage.* Urbana: National Council of the Teachers of English.

   1990. The roots of language protectionism. In Harvey A. Daniels (Ed.), *Not only English: Affirming America's multilingual heritage* (pp. 3–12). Urbana: National Council of the Teachers of English.

Davis, Vivian J. 1990. Paranoia in language politics. In Harvey A. Daniels (Ed.), *Not only English: Affirming America's multilingual heritage* (pp. 71–76). Urbana: National Council of the Teachers of English.

Donahue, Thomas S. 1982. Toward a broadened context for modern bilingual education. *Journal of Multilingual and Multicultural Development* 3(2): 77–87.

   1983. On certain basic flaws in the criticism of modern bilingual education. In John Morreal (Ed.), *Proceedings of the Ninth LACUS Forum* (pp. 445–56). Columbia, S.C.: Hornbeam Press.

   1985. 'U.S. English': Its life and works. *The International Journal of the Sociology of Language* 56:99–112.

DuBois, Betty. 1990. Official English and the urge to legislate. In Karen L. Adams and Daniel T. Brink (Eds.), *Perspectives on Official English* (pp. 229–36). New York: Mouton de Gruyter.

Duenas Gonzales, Roseann, Alice A. Scott, and Victoria F. Vasquez. 1988. The English language amendment: Examining myths. *The English Journal* 77:24–30.

Dyste, Connie. 1989. Proposition 63, the California English language amendment. *Applied Linguistics* 10:313–30.

   1990. The popularity of California's Proposition 63: An analysis. In Karen L. Adams and Daniel T. Brink (Eds.), *Perspectives on Official English* (pp. 139–50). New York: Mouton de Gruyter.

Edwards, John R. 1981. The context of bilingual education. *Journal of Multilingual and Multicultural Development* 2:25–44.

   1982. Bilingual education revisited: A reply to Donahue. *Journal of Multilingual and Multicultural Development* 3:89–101.

   1984. Language, diversity, and identity. In John R. Edwards (Ed.), *Linguistic minorities, policies, and pluralism* (pp. 277–320). New York: Mouton.

Fidel, Noel. 1990. On walling in and walling out. In Karen L. Adams and Daniel T. Brink (Eds.), *Perspectives on Official English* (pp. 301–306). New York: Mouton de Gruyter.

Fishman, Joshua A. 1988. "English Only": Its ghosts, myths, and dangers. *International Journal of the Sociology of Language* 77:125–40.

Frick, Elizabeth. 1990. Metaphors and motives of language restriction movements. In Harvey A. Daniels (Ed.), *Not only English: Affirming America's multilingual heritage* (pp. 27–35). Urbana: National Council of the Teachers of English.

Furnivall, John Sydenham. 1939. *Netherlands India: A study of plural economy.* Cambridge: The University Press.

1956. *Colonial policy and practice: A comparative study of Burma and Netherlands India.* New York: New York University Press.

Graham, Hugh Davis. 1990. American liberalism and language policy: Should liberals support Official English? *A U.S. English Discussion Paper* (pp. 1–30). Washington, D.C.: U.S. English.

Hayakawa, S. I. 1985. One nation . . . indivisible? (pp. 1–19). Washington, D.C.: Washington Institute for Values in Public Policy.

Hechter, Michael. 1975. *Internal colonialism: The Celtic fringe in British national development.* London: Routledge and Kegan Paul.

Hornberger, Nancy H. 1990. Bilingual education and English-Only: A language planning framework. In Courtney B. Cazden and Catherine E. Snow (Eds.), English Plus: Issues in bilingual education (pp. 12–26). *The Annals of the American Academy of Political and Social Science,* vol. 508. Newbury Park: Sage Publications.

Hudson-Edwards, Alan. 1990. Language policy and linguistic tolerance in Ireland. In Karen L. Adams and Daniel T. Brink (Eds.), *Perspectives on Official English* (pp. 63–82). New York: Mouton de Gruyter.

Imhoff, Gary. 1990. The position of U.S. English on bilingual education. In Courtney B. Cazden and Catherine E. Snow (Eds.), *English Plus: Issues in bilingual education* (pp. 48–61). *The Annals of the American Academy of Political and Social Science,* vol. 508. Newbury Park: Sage Publications.

Judd, Elliott L. 1987. The English language amendment: A case study on language and politics. *TESOL Quarterly* 21:113–35.

1990. The federal language amendment. In Harvey A. Daniels (Ed.), *Not only English: Affirming America's multilingual heritage* (pp. 37–46). Urbana: National Council of the Teachers of English.

MacKaye, Susannah D. A. 1990. California Proposition 63: Language attitudes reflected in public debate. In Courtney B. Cazden and Catherine E. Snow (Eds.), *English Plus: Issues in bilingual education* (pp. 135–46). *The Annals of the American Academy of Political and Social Science.* Vol. 508. Newbury Park: Sage Publications.

Madrid, Arturo. 1990. Official English: A false policy issue. In Courtney B. Cazden and Catherine E. Snow (Eds.), *English Plus: Issues in bilingual education* (pp. 62–65). *The Annals of the American Academy of Political and Social Science,* vol. 508. Newbury Park: Sage Publications.

Madsen, Douglas, and Peter G. Snow. 1991. *The charismatic bond.* Cambridge: Harvard University Press.

Marcuse, Herbert. 1966. *One-dimensional man.* Boston: Beacon Press.

Marshall, David F. 1986. The question of an Official Language: Language rights and the English Language movement. *International Journal of the Sociology of Language* 60:7–75.

Mills, C. Wright. 1959. *The power elite.* Oxford: Oxford University Press.

Nunberg, Geoffrey. 1989. Linguists and the Official Language movement. *Language* 65:579–87.

Phillips, Kevin. 1990. *The politics of rich and poor.* New York: Random House.

Pullum, Geoffrey K. 1987. Here come the linguistic fascists. *Natural Language and Linguistic Theory* 5:603–609.

Reich, Robert. 1991. Secession of the successful. *New York Times Magazine,* 20 January.

Sledd, James. 1990. Anglo conformity: Folk remedy for lost hegemony. In Harvey A. Daniels (Ed.), *Not only English: Affirming America's multilingual heritage* (pp. 87–95). Urbana: National Council of the Teachers of English.

Smith, M. G. 1974. *The plural society in the British West Indies.* Berkeley: University of California Press.

Smith, M. G., and Leo Kuper (Eds.). 1969. *Pluralism in Africa.* Berkeley: University of California Press.

Survey Research Center, University of Michigan. 1986. *Report to the Joint Economic Committee of Congress.*

U.S. English. 1990. A common language benefits our nation and its people. Washington, D.C.: U.S. English.

U.S. English Update. 1990. (January-February) vol. 8, no. 1.

1990. (May-June) vol. 8, no. 3.

Wallerstein, Immanuel. 1979. *The capitalist world-economy.* Cambridge: Cambridge University Press.

Weber, Max. 1978. *Economy and society.* (Guenther Roth and Claus Wittich, Eds.). Two volumes. Berkeley: University of California Press.

Weinstein, James. 1990. Is language choice a constitutional right? Outline of a constitutional analysis. In Karen L. Adams and Daniel T. Brink (Eds.), *Perspectives on Official English* (pp. 273–80). New York: Mouton de Gruyter.

Woolard, Kathryn A. 1990. Voting rights, liberal voters and the Official English movement: An analysis of campaign rhetoric in San Francisco's Proposition "O." In Karen L. Adams and Daniel T. Brink (Eds.), *Perspectives on Official English* (pp. 125–39). New York: Mouton de Gruyter.

Zentella, Ana Celia. 1990. Who supports Official English, and why? The influence of social variables and questionnaire methodology. In Karen L. Adams and Daniel T. Brink (Eds.), *Perspectives on Official English* (pp. 161–77). New York: Mouton de Gruyter.

7 Spanish language loss as a determinant of income among Latinos in the United States: Implications for language policy in schools

Ofelia García

One of the major functions of U.S. public schools has been to assimilate culturally and linguistically the children of the different ethnolinguistic groups that make up the country. It is widely believed that success will come only to those who are English monolinguals, and that bilingualism and biculturism are obstacles to achieving economic prosperity. Given these beliefs, U.S. educators often measure their success in educating the children of immigrants by evaluating how quickly they have given up their ethnic language and shifted to English.

In the last 25 years, as a result of the civil rights movement, U.S. public schools have relaxed their English-only policies and made room for the limited use of ethnic languages in the education of language minorities. Bilingual education programs have proliferated in the last two decades, and the debate about their merit has been arduous. However, the view that English monolingualism holds the key to economic success has continued to be widely accepted in schools, even in many bilingual education programs.

At the center of the public debate about language policy in public schools are Spanish speakers. The argument is often made that the education of Latinos must focus on teaching English so that they can progress in U.S. society. Spanish-speaking ability is widely seen as a major cause of Latino poverty and educational failure, and educators evaluate their success according to the rate at which their Latino students shift from Spanish to English.

The statistical analyses presented in this chapter were done while the author was a Fellow of the Inter-University Consortium for Political and Social Science Research at the University of Michigan, Summer 1990. I am grateful to Jorge Chapa for his assistance in the Latino Research Issues Seminar, and especially to Katherine Baisden who made the HHANES tape available to me and encouraged me to use it. Thanks also to Elyce Rotella at the ICPSR for her guidance with multiple regression. But most of all, I am grateful to Ricardo Otheguy who took our family to Ann Arbor so that I could be near the children and the computer at the same time.

How this shift from Spanish to English is to be achieved is the subject of much debate. Some argue that Latino teachers should speak Spanish in transitional bilingual programs. Others oppose even this limited use of Spanish, arguing for English as a second language and for structured-immersion classes, in which instruction is entirely in English. Rarely, however, is the value of English monolingualism for educational and economic success questioned. Yet, my experience in the education of Latinos leads me to believe that the value of English may be limited. Therefore this chapter poses the following question: For Latinos in the United States, what role, if any, does English monolingualism play in their struggle to achieve economic prosperity?

This chapter first provides a sociohistorical framework for analyzing Spanish-language loss among Latinos in the United States. Next a multiple regression analysis examines whether Spanish-language loss is a determinant of income among Latinos from three major U.S. Latino groups. The major findings are then used to examine language policy in public schools.

Sociohistorical framework

Language shift or language loss? The difference between linguistic choice and restraint

The most essential characteristic of language is that it involves *choice*. Speakers constantly need to choose one feature over another in order to appropriately communicate a message. Sign-based analyses of language (Diver 1975; Reid 1991) focus precisely on why speakers select one microlinguistic feature over another. The sociology of language has made the reasons for the choice of macrolinguistic features its major object of study. The central question of the field – Who speaks what, to whom, and for what purposes? – assumes that in selecting some features over others speakers have choices (Fishman 1972). Although it is true that all speakers are to some extent involved in this "choosing game," the options for speakers of prestigious languages (and especially for those who are wealthy and educated) are clearly greater than those offered to language minority speakers (and especially to the poor and illiterate). Sociopolitical oppression of a language minority group often involves some form of *linguistic restraint*.

In the United States intergenerational *language maintenance* has seldom been an option, since bilingualism is regarded with suspicion and given little public societal support (Fishman 1966, 1985). *Language shift*, however, and the resulting monolingualism does not operate equally for all language groups. For some groups (mostly white, skilled, and with values congruous with those of mainstream U.S. society), complete shift to English is often accompanied by socioeconomic success. For others (mostly nonwhite, unskilled, and colonized), however, the loss of the native language often sinks them even further into the silence of the oppressed. We will reserve the term language shift to refer to the real choice given to language minority groups when the majority wishes them to integrate not only linguistically, but also socially and economically. But we will refer to the linguistic restraint imposed on language minorities who are not given social and economic access as *language loss.*

Spanish language loss: stages of linguistic restraint

Spanish has a long history in the United States. Kloss (1977:18) identifies Spaniards in the Southwest as "solitary original settlers" since they settled there even before the Anglo-Saxons. Kloss points out that accordingly, Spanish speakers in the Southwest might be expected to enjoy greater linguistic rights than more recently arrived groups. But as Kloss himself reminds us, minority rights in the United States have never encompassed the racially different. As we will see, the restraint of Spanish has taken many forms, depending on its sociohistorical context.

After the United States provoked a war with Mexico and took one half of Mexico's national territory in 1846, Mexicans were granted U.S. citizenship status but were not given any cultural or linguistic rights. In the late nineteenth century, for instance, an editorial in the *New York Evening Post* said: "The Mexicans are Aboriginal Indians, and they must share the destiny of their race" (Steinfield 1970:74). As such, the policy that was pursued, especially in schools, was that of cultural and linguistic eradication. The same harsh linguistic policy was pursued in Puerto Rico where English was made the medium of instruction in all upper grades until 1934 (Cebollero 1945).

During the 1960s and 1970s, great strides were made in the relaxation of such policies. Educational programs that used the native language were expanded and the U.S. policy clearly became one of greater cultural and linguistic tolerance. Nevertheless, bilingual programs have been mostly assimilationist and have had a language-shift orientation.

The 1980s saw the growth of organized linguistic restrictionist movements such as U.S. English and English First. No longer able to openly express racist attitudes and under the threat of a shrinking U.S. economy, nativists opposed the structural incorporation of nonwhites and immigrants by seizing language as a category for discrimination. Linguicism has grown as more and more states have embraced English language amendments. (For a complete treatment of this topic, see Marshall 1986; Adams and Brink 1990. For a fuller treatment of linguicism, see Phillipson and Skutnabb-Kangas 1986).

That the Latino population in the United States has been historically involved in a process of language loss can hardly be argued. Studies on Spanish language maintenance/shift agree that the rate of Spanish language loss has been and continues to be alarming. Whether in Texas (Skrabanek 1970; Thompson 1974), New Mexico (Ortiz 1975; Gutiérrez 1980; Hudson-Edwards and Bills 1980), California (López 1978), Colorado (Floyd 1985), New York (Pedraza 1985; Otheguy, García, and Fernández 1989), Miami (Solé 1982; Otheguy and García 1988), or nationally (López 1982; Veltman 1983; Fishman 1984; Veltman 1988; Bills 1989; Hart-González 1988) researchers have found strong evidence of Spanish language loss.

Tying language to income as a mechanism of language restriction

Sociolinguistic studies of Spanish language maintenance and/or shift also reflect the sociohistorical stages of Spanish language restraint. The field of language maintenance/shift was not developed as a field of inquiry until Fishman (1966) acknowledged the possibility of stable bilingualism. Thus studies were nonexistent during the stage of linguistic eradication. But they proliferated during the era of linguistic tolerance and continue to do so under the linguistic restrictionist movement of today. But whereas during the period of linguistic tolerance, studies merely described the patterns of language maintenance/shift, during the current linguistic restrictionist period, many studies are intent on linking degrees of Spanish language maintenance/shift to economic attainment.

The reason for this new focus of research is that as the U.S. economy has shrunk, the need to show that it is Spanish that is the cause of the economic failure of Latinos has been greater than ever. Victims (in this case poor Latinos) are blamed for what is seen as their obstinate refusal to relinguify.

Since 1980 the National Commission for Employment Policy (NCEP) has been sponsoring economic research that focuses on the relationship between English language ability and income differentials (Gould, McManus, and Welch 1982; Stolzenberg 1982). All NCEP studies support the conclusion of the 1982 NCEP Report: "A lack of fluency in English is the major source of the labor market difficulties of all [Hispanic] subgroups. It directly *affects* their labor market position, their educational attainment, and is one facet of labor market discrimination" (p. 2, emphasis added).

These results, which are often interpreted as equating English language ability to Spanish language loss, reflect the linguistic restrictionist era of today. Bean and Tienda (1988:44), for example, say:

Presumably, people of Hispanic origin who are *more structurally assimilated* – that is, integrated into the social and economic institutions of the mainstream English-speaking society, should *use Spanish less* (if at all) than those who are less well integrated. (Emphasis added.)

Yet, none of the NCEP studies differentiate between Latino-English monolingual speakers and Latino bilinguals, and so say nothing about the relationship between Spanish language loss (or English monolingualism) to income.

Although studies by sociolinguists (López 1982; Veltman 1983; Fishman 1984; Hart-González 1988; Veltman 1988; Bills 1989) have suggested that Spanish language maintenance significantly correlates with low income, they have been quick to point out that correlational studies do not support cause and effect, and they do not take into account all possible variables. As Hart-González (1988:33) insists for her study: "It is not clear whether the generally lower income and education levels of the Mexicans are associated simply with Spanish maintenance or *with some other*, perhaps more potent variable." (Emphasis added.)

The multiple regression study reported in this chapter intends to overcome the problems posed by NCEP-sponsored research, as well as by traditional sociolinguistic research. Like some of the NCEP-sponsored research, and unlike traditional sociolinguistic research, the present study identifies *income* as the *dependent* variable. But unlike the NCEP-sponsored research, this study takes into account only *Spanish language loss* (and not English language ability) as one of many *independent* variables. It also attempts to go beyond correlational sociolinguistic studies in an effort to identify the independent variables that contribute most to the income level of English-speaking Latinos, whether monolinguals or bilinguals. In doing so, it specifically addresses the mythical nature of the proposition that English monolingualism leads to the economic success of Latinos.

But before turning to the quantitative study, it is important to provide sociohistorical and sociolinguistic evidence to debunk the sociolinguistic myth that *cultural and linguistic assimilation* translates for everyone into *structural incorporation*. (For a discussion of the distinction between cultural factors and economic-structural ones, see Skutnabb-Kangas 1979).

Qualitative observations

The sociolinguistic myth that English-only implies economic success has been part of U.S. society since its inception. The beliefs that the United States had the resources to structurally incorporate its citizenry and that economic success would be linked to a natural shift to English led the founding fathers to reject the imposition of English as the official language. But although the myth became reality for millions of white immigrants during the era of physical and economic expansion, it has remained a myth for Native-Americans, African-Americans, and Latinos.

There are two reasons for the rejection of the myth, based on qualitative evidence. First, despite the high rates of linguistic assimilation achieved by African-Americans and by most Latinos in the United States, they have had little economic success. Second, despite the low rates of linguistic assimilation achieved by one Latino group (Cuban-Americans), this group has had the greatest economic success.

Linguistic assimilation does not equal structural incorporation

There is a great deal of historical evidence that linguistic assimilation has not resulted in the structural incorporation of racial minorities. It is well-known, for example, that although African-Americans have completely shifted to English, they remain excluded from the socioeconomic mainstream of the United States. Even affirmative action programs have done little to redress this situation.

Although the eradication of Spanish among Latinos has been less successful than the shift to English among African-Americans (because of the continuous immigration of Spanish speakers), Latinos have, as we have noted, experienced tremendous Spanish language loss and yet do not partake of many economic benefits. Out of the eleven million Spanish-origin respondents identified in the Current Population Survey in 1975, only 11 percent of the population identified were Spanish monolingual (Veltman 1988:12). Yet, based on 1988 income, 24 percent of Latino families fell below the poverty level, compared with 9 percent of non-Latino families (U.S. Bureau of the Census 1990). It is clear that despite high rates of linguistic assimilation, the Latino group as a whole has achieved low levels of economic success.

Structural incorporation does not equal linguistic assimilation

Structural incorporation into U.S. society has generally depended more on the racial and social group to which the minority belongs, as well as its economic opportunities, than on linguistic assimilation (for a fuller discussion of this topic, see Greer 1972 and Otheguy 1982). That the Latino group has been subjected to unequal treatment is evident in the higher level of income and education achieved by the Cuban-American community. For example, in 1988, the median household income was $19,839 for Mexican-Americans and $15,447 for Puerto Ricans. Yet, the median household income of Cuban-Americans was $21,793 (U.S. Bureau of the Census 1990). The advantage of Cuban-Americans is also evident when comparing percentages of people over age 25 who have completed 4 years of high school or more. Whereas 43 percent of the Mexican-American population and 54 percent of the Puerto Rican population were at least high school graduates, 63 percent of the Cuban-American population had completed at least 4 years of high school (U.S. Bureau of the Census 1990). Yet, the linguistic profile of the Cuban-American community reveals it to be the most Spanish monolingual Latino group. The 1976 Survey of Income and Education shows that whereas 22 percent of Mexican-Americans and 20 percent of Puerto Ricans claimed to be Spanish monolinguals, 27 percent of Cuban-Americans claimed to speak Spanish only (Veltman 1988:78). (For a discussion, see García and Otheguy 1985, 1988; Hart-González 1988.)

But beyond these observations, the question still remains whether loyalty to Spanish, even after acquisition of English, is a problem or a resource, and whether it functions differently for diverse Latino groups. It is to these questions that we now turn.

Spanish language loss as a determinant of income: a multiple regression analysis

The main question addressed in the multiple linear regression study that is presented here is whether Spanish language loss for Latinos who speak English is an important determinant of their income levels, as the popular literature and media presume. The study attempts to determine whether linguistic assimilation causes structural incorporation. Since the poverty of Latinos is of major concern, this study seeks to specify the real determinants of their income.

Method, model, and hypotheses

Multiple linear regression is a statistical method for measuring the effects of *several* independent variables simultaneously on a dependent variable (Berry and Feldman 1985; Schroeder, Sjoquist, and Stephan 1986; Lewis-Beck 1990). Thus it is the best statistical method to overcome the shortcomings of correlational sociolinguistic studies as identified by Hart-González (1988).

Regression analysis as a statistical technique does not prove causation, but the regression model, if based on a carefully constructed theory, contains causation. Any study of the determinants of *income* (the *dependent* variable) for the general population includes level of education, age, and sex as important *independent* variables. Thus our model includes those variables, which we call *unmarked,* following Fishman (1972), because they are not different for the minority population. But our model adds immigration generation and Spanish language loss as *independent* variables, since these have been generally identified in the ethnicity and assimilation literature as important determiners of income. We call these two variables our *marked* independent variables, since they are specific to a minority population. Our model includes, then, the following variables:

Dependent variable	*Independent variables*	
Income	Level of education	
	Age	} Unmarked
	Sex	
	Immigration generation	} Marked
	Spanish loss	

The model for analysis is thus the following:

$$y = a + b1x1 + b2x2 + b3x3 + b4x4 + b5x5 + b6x6$$

where y = income (continuous variable)
      a = intercept or constant
      b = slope or regression coefficient
      x1 = level of education (continuous variable)
      x2 = age (continuous variable)
      x3 = male (dummy variable for sex)
      x4 = generation 2 (dummy variable for generation)
      x5 = generation 3 (dummy variable for generation)
      x6 = English monolingual (dummy variable for Spanish loss)

The reader is reminded that multiple regression analysis is mostly concerned with *b, the regression coefficient of any independent variable*. It is this regression coefficient that shows how much the dependent variable changes in response to a change in that independent variable while holding the other independent variables constant. In the model above, for example, the regression coefficient of level of education (bx1) would tell us how much income changes when level of education changes by one unit.

The reader is also reminded that categorical data in a regression model must be entered as dummy variables taking the value of zero or one. When dummy variables are entered into the model, one group is always excluded and serves as a reference group against which comparisons can be made. Thus, in the model provided, the regression coefficient of males (bx3) tells us how much income changes for males when compared to females (the excluded group).

We know language functions differently in speech communities that are defined not only through ethnic identity but also through regional and geographic boundaries. Thus, our analysis of the determinants of income among Latinos, and specifically of how Spanish language loss affects economic success, must consider each Latino group separately within its own ethnic enclave. Therefore three different regression analyses were run, one for Mexican-Americans living in selected counties of Texas, Colorado, New Mexico, Arizona, and California, one for Puerto Ricans in the New York area, and finally one for Cuban-Americans residing in Dade County, Florida.

Based on the qualitative evidence presented previously, it was hypothesized that the unmarked variables would have a positive effect on income, whereas the marked variables would not have the very large negative effect on income that restrictionist movements have led us to believe. Furthermore, because of the economic vitality of the Dade County Cuban-American community (Portes and Bach 1985), we hypothesized that the marked variables would have the least effect on income among Cuban-Americans.

Since the regression model assumes not only a right model, but also appropriate data, a word must be said about the data before we turn to our results.

The data

The most recent large-scale survey containing data not only on socioeconomic characteristics of Latinos, but also on their linguistic experience is the Hispanic Health and Nutrition Examination Survey (HHANES) conducted from July 1982 to December 1984. The most recently published U.S. Bureau of the Census survey with the same information is the Current Population Survey of November 1979. HHANES is an appropriate data base for a sociolinguistic study not only on account of its recency, but also because it is a survey of the three Latino subgroups in selected areas of the United States rather than a national probability sample. This enables us to generalize results for the three separate groups in the specified geographic areas, and to treat ethnolinguistic characteristics within the context of the speech community.

One limitation of the data was that although we used the characteristics of head of household as independent variables, household income was used as the dependent variable, since the income of individual household members was not reported. The assumption was made that household income most often reflects that of the head of household. Another limitation is that the analysis includes mostly males, since heads of households, except in the Puerto Rican community, are predominantly male. In fact, 81 percent of the Mexican-American respondents and 78 percent of the Cuban-American respondents were males, in contrast to the Puerto Rican community in which only 54 percent of the heads of household were males.

The multiple regression analysis that we will present is based on Hispanic heads of household between the ages of 25 and 65 that were proficient in English. Table 1 summarizes the descriptive data for the 3,716 cases included in the study.

The results

The results of the three separately run multiple regression analyses appear in Table 2.

The regression coefficients for the three unmarked variables (age, education, and sex) show that, as expected, income of the three groups changes greatly when changes occur in the unmarked variables. Being a year older increases income by $117.15 for Mexican-Americans and $139.25 for Puerto Ricans. However, the effect of age was not significant for Cuban-Americans, signaling the difference of this community that will become evident when we discuss the marked variables. An additional year of education produces an approximate increase of $1,000 in income, with this difference being less felt in the Mexican-American community ($881.95) and most felt in the Cuban-American community ($1,281.66). For Puerto Ricans, an additional year of education increases their income by $1,117.15 on the average. As with years of education, sex makes the most difference in the Cuban-American community, with males earning $9,422.34 more than women on average. However, sex has the least impact on income in the Puerto Rican community (although the difference continues to be great and significant), where males make on average $8,912.74 more than females. Except for age, then, the Cuban-American community seems to profit the most from differences in unmarked characteristics that generally impact *positively* on income. As we will see, this greater profitability of the Cuban-American community is also reflected in its being the least affected by differences in marked characteristics that generally impact *negatively* on income.

A surprising result of our regressions is that the effect of generation on income is not statistically discernible except for second-generation Puerto Ricans. Puerto Ricans born in the United States of foreign-born parents make on average $3149.62 more than those born on the island (first-generation). But the same cannot be said of native-born Mexican-Americans and Cuban-Americans when compared to their foreign-born compatriots.

The literature on assimilation and immigration often points to the economic achievement of native-born Latinos when compared to immigrants (Chiswick 1978; Neidert and Farley 1985; Chavez 1989). However, Chapa (1988) has shown that despite the assimilation that accompanies being a third-generation Mexican-American, the education, earnings, and occupational distribution of these Mexican-Americans is

TABLE I. MEANS AND STANDARD DEVIATIONS FOR THREE LATINO GROUPS

	Mexican-Americans N = 2295		Puerto Ricans N = 946		Cuban-Americans N = 475	
	Mean	S.D.	Mean	S.D.	Mean	S.D.
Income	$20,193.86	(12,080.40)	$16,477.31	(12,432.94)	$24,592.61	(14,313.71)
Age	43	(10.60)	43	(9.87)	47	(9.49)
Education	9.50	(4.17)	9.80	(3.71)	11.30	(4.00)
Sex[a]	.81	(.39)	.54	(.50)	.78	(.42)
Gen2[a]	.19	(.39)	.14	(.35)	.015	(.12)
Gen3[a]	.52	(.50)	.03	(.16)	.01	(.05)
Spanish loss[a]	.96	(.20)	.95	(.23)	.98	(.15)

[a]These were all dummy variables with values of 1 and 0.
Sex: males = 1; females = 0
Gen2: if yes = 1; if no = 0
Gen3: if yes = 1; if no = 0
Spanish loss: if Spanish ability = 1; if English monolingual = 0

TABLE 2. REGRESSION COEFFICIENTS OF DETERMINANTS OF INCOME BY LATINO
SUBGROUP

	Mexican-Americans N = 2295 b coeff	Puerto Ricans N = 475 b coeff	Cuban-Americans N = 946 b coeff
Age	117.15[a]	139.25[a]	.94 (n.s)[b]
Education	881.95[a]	1117.15[a]	1281.66[a]
Sex	9240.50[a]	8912.74[a]	9422.34[a]
GEN2	816.13 (n.s)	3149.62[a]	1092.76 (n.s)
GEN3	818.46 (n.s)	1299.02 (n.s)	25384.09 (n.s)
Spanish loss	−3928.07[a]	−3217.18[a]	988.03 (n.s)
(Constant)	2539.08	1682.32	−2701.22
Note:	Adj R Sq = .20	Adj R Sq = .20	Adj R Sq = .28

not similar to that of Anglo-Americans. Our findings confirm that second- and third-generation Mexican-Americans and Cuban-Americans are not earning more than their first-generation compatriots who speak English. The reader should remember that our sample consists only of people who claimed to be speakers of English, and that differences in income between immigrant and native-born Latinos are often the result of their English ability. Among first-generation Latinos who are speakers of English, one often finds those who had middle-class status in their countries of origin since they often learned English in school. This factor may account for our finding that generation is not a determinant of income for either Cuban-Americans or Mexican-Americans.

The difference with the Puerto Rican community may be the result of the shrinking New York economy of the last twenty years. Unable to incorporate new arrivals at the fast rate it once did, New York City marginalizes first-generation Latinos much more than the less urbanized areas of the Southwest or Dade County and much more than it did during the influx of Puerto Ricans to New York City in the period prior to 1970. Another reason for the difference that generation makes on income between Puerto Ricans and the other two groups may be that for Puerto Ricans English language ability may not be as strong a determiner of income as for the other two groups.

In order to test this assumption, another set of regressions were run, this time including also those who spoke only Spanish, increasing our total number of cases to 5,188. Although the income of those who claim to speak English only or mostly when compared with those who claim to speak Spanish only or mostly is $6,197 more for Cuban-Americans and $5,761 more for Mexican-Americans, it is only $3,768 more for Puerto Ricans. This finding confirms our assumption that English language ability is not as strong a determinant of income among Puerto Ricans as it is among the other two groups.

Going back to our original regressions and focusing now on the important question about Spanish language loss that is the main focus of this paper, we see that being bilingual (rather than English monolingual) has a different effect on Mexican-Americans and Puerto Ricans than on Cuban-Americans. Mexican-Americans and Puerto Ricans who are bilingual earn on average $3,928.07 and $3,217.18 *less* respectively than those who are monolingual English speakers. This finding seems to confirm the belief that poverty among Latinos is a direct result of their inability to relinguify. But it is the finding for the Cuban-American community that leads us to reject the effect that has been ascribed to English monolingualism in the economic success of Latinos.

The impact of Spanish language loss on income among the Cuban-American community is not statistically discernible. That is, there is no statistically discernible difference in earning between Cuban-Americans who are English monolingual and those who are bilingual. Thus we can conclude that a minority language is not always a static characteristic that affects income in exactly the same way under all circumstances. We turn now to the different role that Spanish has negotiated for itself in Dade County, compared to other ethnic communities.

Negotiating a role for Spanish: the case of Dade County

Spanish in Dade County has negotiated for itself a very different role than that to which it has been relegated in other ethnic communities. There are four factors associated with the Spanish of Dade County that have made it possible for its speakers to gain advantages for themselves:

1. Less markedness (congruence)
2. Less foreignness (absent homeland)
3. More socioeconomic power (economic value)
4. More density (instrumentality for communication)

Because of the history of their immigration, Cuban-Americans have socioeconomic characteristics that are more similar to those of Anglo-Americans than to those of other Latino groups (for a discussion of the waves of Cuban migration to the United States, see Llanes 1982; Boswell and Curtis 1983; Portes and Bach 1985; García and Otheguy 1988). In Dade County, Spanish is less marked than in other areas of the United States because it is mostly spoken by speakers who have a higher level of income and a higher level of education, and who are more often considered white than other Latino groups in the United States. This makes it possible for its speakers to push for equality of treatment.

The advantage gained by the greater congruence of the social characteristics of Cuban-Americans with Anglos in Dade County is multiplied by the weaker homeland-language link that exists for Cuban-Americans. Many Cuban-Americans in Dade County came to the United States fleeing Fidel Castro's regime, and most have not returned to their homeland. This differs greatly from the continuous migration cycle and visits to the homeland of Mexican-Americans and Puerto Ricans. Furthermore, by allying themselves with the United States as enemies of Castro's Cuba, many Cuban-Americans are seen as political allies. Thus, the Anglo majority views these speakers of Spanish with less suspicion than those who still hold political allegiances to their homelands. This makes it possible for the Anglo majority to enter negotiation for equality of treatment of these Spanish speakers.

But besides being less marked and less foreign than in other Spanish-speaking communities, Spanish in Dade County has more socioeconomic power than it does in other less affluent communities. Spanish in Dade County is the language of a powerful business community. The largest business firms owned by Spanish speakers in the United States are found in Dade County. In the last two decades, Spanish in Dade County has become an important resource in trade with Latin America, with many major U.S. corporations moving their Latin-American divisions to the area. This factor makes it possible for the minority to negotiate the use of Spanish as a gainful resource from which the majority can also profit.

Finally, Spanish in Dade County is not only a resource for negotiation with the majority, but it is also a resource for negotiation with the minority itself. That is, it has greater density, guaranteeing its value as an instrument for communication among Spanish speakers. Cuban-Americans in Dade County have a higher rate of Spanish monolingualism than Mexican-Americans in the Southwest and Puerto Ricans in the Northeast. There are also more foreign-born first-generation Cuban-Americans than Mexican-Americans and Puerto Ricans. Finally, there has been a large influx of Latinos, not only from Latin America but also from other areas of the United States, into the Dade County area in the last decade. This further adds to the density of Spanish and to its value as an instrument for communication, guaranteeing also intergenerational maintenance. This factor makes it possible for the minority to continue to claim Spanish as their own resource in negotiating with the majority.

The factors impacting on Spanish in Dade County have made it possible to abandon the majority description of Spanish as a *static characteristic* of a minority with a *problem*. Instead, the language minority has been able to engage the majority in viewing Spanish as a *negotiable* factor in a *relationship* that could be a *resource* for all. (The difference between ethnicity as characteristic and as negotiable is suggested by Skutnabb-Kangas 1991.) This has been done by entering into a dynamic cycle in which the language minority pushes for equality of treatment by emphasizing the decreased markedness of Spanish, the majority responds by entering the negotiation accepting the decreased foreignness of Spanish, the minority engages the majority in negotiation by focusing on the socio-economic power of Spanish, and finally the minority continues to define Spanish as a resource for intraethnic communication. However, this negotiating cycle has not been carried out without interethnic conflict. In November 1980, voters in Dade County reversed a policy of official bilingualism and biculturism that had been passed in 1973. And in November 1988 the Florida English Language Amendment was passed (Castro, Haun, and Roca 1990).

In the United States, English monolingualism does not always result in greater economic success. When the minority language is not viewed as a suspicious characteristic that must be eradicated, but as a resource with which to negotiate, English monolingualism has no effect whatsoever on income. This has been the role of Spanish in Dade County since the 1960s. With the renewed strength of linguistic restrictionism in the 1990s and the changing profile of the Spanish-speaking community in Dade County, it remains to be seen whether Spanish will continue to be seen as a resource.

The question that must be asked, then, when studying the effect of minority language maintenance on structural incorporation of a minority into majority society is whether the speakers of the minority language are oppressed minorities categorized by others through their language characteristics, or whether they are capable of self-categorization and of negotiating a resourceful role for their language. (For a fuller treatment of the processes of categorization by others and self-categorization in boundary maintenance, see Allardt 1979). The danger of linguistic restrictionist movements such as English-only is precisely that they take away the possibility of using the non-English language as a resource, reducing it to a problem that cannot be silenced in a shrinking U.S. economy.

Conclusion: implications for language policy in schools

Policy makers for public schools in the United States are often monolingual members of the majority group. It is not surprising, then, that they understand neither bilingualism nor the minority language experience. But increasingly, children who attend public schools are racially and linguistically different from the majority. Eager to keep their powerful influence, school administrators and policy makers may feverishly hold on to the myth that English-only is the key to economic prosperity, and so they impose English-only as a major educational goal. The education of language minorities is thus reduced to an intensive English language acquisition campaign that focuses narrowly on English language skills. Absent from many classrooms with language minorities – whether English-only or bilingual education classes – is a rigorous academic curriculum that increases knowledge about the world.

But our findings demonstrate that speaking only English does not always make a difference in the achievement of economic prosperity, and that bilingualism, rather than monolingualism, is a useful commodity in some communities, including the Latino one. This conclusion suggests that school administrators and policy makers should change the goal of education for Latinos from one of relinguification to one of truly increasing students' knowledge through academic programs that present educational challenges rather than linguistic obstacles.

But in order for this to occur, the myth of the link between English monolingualism and economic success must be rejected. Indeed, a successful and educated Latino may not always be a speaker of English only. A bilingual educational policy could thus be adopted that ensures rigorous academic programs in Spanish for Latinos who speak little English, and that brings the rich content, information, and literature of Spanish to English-speaking Latinos (cf. Cummins 1981). By focusing on opening up the world of knowledge to all students, regardless of their language, U.S. public schools could add to the greater understanding and knowledge that are crucial to personal, social, and economic success.

References

Adams, K. L., and D. T. Brink. 1990. *Perspectives on Official English: The campaign for English as the official language of the USA*. New York: Mouton de Gruyter.

Allardt, E. 1979. Implications of the ethnic revival in modern industrialized society: A comparative study of the linguistic minorities in Western Europe. *Commentationes Scientiarum Socialium* (Helsinki) 12.

Alvarez, C. 1989. Code-switching in narrative performance: A Puerto Rican speech community in New York. In O. García and R. Otheguy (Eds.), *English across cultures: Cultures across English* (pp. 373–86). Berlin: Mouton de Gruyter.

Bean, F. D., and M. Tienda. 1988. *The Hispanic population of the United States*. New York: Russell Sage Foundation.

Berry, W. D., and S. Feldman. 1985. *Multiple regression in practice*. Newbury Park: Sage.

Bills, Garland. 1989. The U.S. Census of 1980 and Spanish in the Southwest. *International Journal of the Sociology of Language* 79:11–28.

Boswell, T., and J. Curtis. 1983. *The Cuban American Experience: Culture, images and perspectives*. New Jersey: Rowman and Allanheld.

158   *Ofelia García*

Castro, M. J., M. Haun, and A. Roca. 1990. The Official English movement in Florida. In K. L. Adams and D. T. Brink (Eds.), *Perspectives on Official English* (pp. 151–60). New York: Mouton de Gruyter.

Cebollero, P. 1945. *A school language policy for Puerto Rico.* San Juan: Educational Publications, series II, no. 1.

Chapa, J. 1988. The myth of Hispanic progress: Trends in the educational and economic attainment of Mexican Americans. *Harvard Journal of Hispanic Policy* 9.

Chavez, L. 1989. Tequila sunrise: The slow but steady progress of Hispanic immigrants. *Policy Review* (Spring).

Chiswick, B. R. 1978. The effect of Americanization on the earnings of foreign-born men. *Journal of Political Economy* 86:897–921.

Cummins, J. 1981. *Bilingualism and minority–language children.* Toronto: OISE.

Diver, W. 1975. Introduction. *Columbia University Working Papers in Linguistics (CUWPL)* 2:1–26.

Edwards, V. 1989. Patois and the politics of protest: Black English in British classrooms. In O. García and R. Otheguy (Eds.), *English across cultures: Cultures across English* (pp. 359–72). Berlin: Mouton de Gruyter.

Fishman, J. 1966. *Language loyalty in the United States.* The Hague: Mouton.
  1972. *The sociology of language: An interdisciplinary social science approach to the study of language in society.* Rowley, Mass.: Newbury House.
  1984. Mother tongue claiming in the United States since 1960: Trends and correlates related to the "revival of ethnicity." *International Journal of the Sociology of Language* 50:21–99.
  1985. *The rise and fall of the ethnic revival.* Berlin: Mouton de Gruyter.

Floyd, Mary Beth. 1985. Spanish in the Southwest: Language maintenance or shift? In Lucía Elías-Olivares (Ed.), *Spanish language use and public life* (pp. 13–25). Berlin: Mouton de Gruyter.

Gal, S. 1989. Lexical innovation and loss: The use and value of restricted Hungarian. In N. C. Dorian (Ed.), *Investigating obsolescence: Studies in language contraction and death* (pp. 313–31). Cambridge: Cambridge University Press.

García, O., and R. Otheguy. 1985. The masters of survival send their children to school: Bilingual education in the ethnic schools of Miami. *Bilingual Review/Revista Bilingüe* 12:3–19.
  1988. The language situation of Cuban Americans. In S. L. McKay and S. C. Wong (Eds.), *Language diversity. Problem or resource?* (pp. 166–92). Cambridge, Mass.: Newbury.

Gilles, G. 1981. An analysis of the effect of language characteristics on the wages of Hispanic-American males. Paper presented at the meeting of the Societe Canadienne de Science Economique, 13–14 May, Sherbrook, Quebec.

Gould, William, Walter McManus, and Finis Welch. 1982. Hispanics' earning differentials: The role of English language proficiency. NCEP-sponsored research. Spring.

Greer, C. 1972. *The great school legend.* New York: Basic Books.

Gutiérrez, J. R. 1980. Language use in Martineztown. In F. Barkin and E. Brandt (Eds.), *Speaking, singing and teaching: A multidisciplinary approach to language variation* (pp. 454–59). Anthropological Research Papers, no. 20. Tempe: Arizona State University.

Hart-González, Lucinda. 1990. Current population survey and household Spanish maintenance among Mexican Americans. In J. L. Ornstein-Galicia, G. K. Green, and D. J. Bixler-Márquez (Eds.), *Research issues and problems in United States Spanish* (pp. 25–39). Brownsville, Texas: Pan American University at Brownsville.

Hart-González, Lucinda, and Marcia Feingold. 1988. Retention of Spanish in the home. *International Journal of the Sociology of Language* 84:5–34.

Hudson-Edwards, A., and G. D. Bills. 1980. Intergenerational language shift in an Albuquerque barrio. In E. L. Blansitt, Jr., and R. V. Teschner (Eds.), *A Festschrift for Jacob Ornstein* (pp. 139–58). Rowley, Mass.: Newbury House.

Kloss, H. 1977. *The American bilingual tradition.* Rowley, Mass.: Newbury House.

Lewis-Beck, S. 1990. *Applied regression: An introduction.* Newbury Park: Sage.

Llanes, J. 1982. *Cuban-Americans: Masters of survival.* Cambridge, Mass.: ABT Books.

López, D. E. 1978. Chicano language loyalty in an urban setting. *Sociology and Social Research* 65:311–22.

1982. The maintenance of Spanish over three generations in the United States. Report R-7. Los Alamitos, Calif.: National Center for Bilingual Research.

Marshall, D. F. 1986. The question of an official language: Language rights and the English language amendment; Rebuttal. *International Journal of the Sociology of Language* 60:7–75; 201–11.

National Commission for Employment Policy. 1982. *Hispanics and jobs: Barriers to progress.* Report no. 14, September 1982. Washington, D.C.

Neidert, L. J., and R. Farley. 1985. Assimilation in the United States. *American Sociological Review* 50:840–50.

Ortiz, L. I. 1975. A sociolinguistic study of language maintenance in the northern New Mexico community of Arroyo Seco. Ph.D. diss., University of New Mexico.

Otheguy, R. 1982. Thinking about bilingual education: A critical appraisal. *Harvard Educational Review* 52:301–14.

Otheguy, R., and O. García. 1988. Diffusion of lexical innovations in the Spanish of Cuban Americans. In J. Ornstein-Galicia, G. K. Green, and D. Bixler-Márquez (Eds.), *Research issues and problems in United States Spanish* (pp. 203–41). Brownsville, Tex.: Pan American University.

Otheguy, R., O. García, and M. Fernández. 1989. Transferring, switching, and modeling in west New York Spanish: An intergenerational study. *International Journal of the Sociology of Language* 79:41–52.

Pedraza, P. 1985. Language maintenance among New York Puerto Ricans. In L. Elías-Olivares, E. A. Leone, R. Cisneros, and J. Gutiérrez (Eds.), *Spanish language use and public life in the USA* (pp. 59–72). Berlin: Walter de Gruyter.

Phillipson, R., and T. Skutnabb-Kangas. 1986. *Linguicism rules in education.* Roskilde: Roskilde University Center, Institute VI.

Portes, A., and R. Bach. 1985. *Latin journey. Cuban and Mexican immigrants in the United States.* Berkeley, Calif.: University of Caifornia Press.

Reid, W. 1991. *English verb and noun number: A functional explanation.* London and New York: Longman.

Schroeder, L. D., D. Sjoquist, and P. E. Stephan. 1986. *Understanding regression analysis. An introductory guide.* Newbury Park: Sage.

Skrabanek, R. I. 1970. Language maintenance among Mexican-Americans. *International Journal of Comparative Sociology* 11:272–82.

Skutnabb-Kangas, T. 1979. *Language in the process of cultural assimilation and structural incorporation of linguistic minorities.* Rosslyn, Virg.: National Clearinghouse for Bilingual Education.

———. 1991. Swedish strategies to prevent integration and national ethnic minorities. In O. García (Ed.), *Bilingual education: Focuschrift in honor of Joshua A. Fishman.* Amsterdam: John Benjamins.

Solé, C. 1982. Language attitudes among Cuban-Americans. In J. A. Fishman and G. D. Keller (Eds.), *Bilingual education for Hispanics in the United States* (pp. 254–68). New York: Teachers College Press.

Steinfield, M. (Ed.). 1970. *Cracks in the melting pot.* Beverly Hills, Calif.: Glencoe Press.

Stolzenberg, Ross M. 1982. Occupational differences between Hispanics and non-Hispanics. Report prepared for the National Commission for Employment Policy. Santa Monica, Calif.: Rand Publications Series.

Thompson, R. M. 1974. The 1970 Census and Mexican-American language loyalty: A case study. In G. Bills (Ed.), *Southwest Areal Linguistics* (pp. 65–78). San Diego: Institute for Cultural Pluralism.

U.S. Bureau of the Census. 1990. The Hispanic population in the United States: March 1989. *Current Population Reports,* ser. P-20, no. 444. Washington, D.C.: GPO.

Veltman, Calvin. 1983. *Language shift in the United States.* Berlin: Mouton.

———. 1988. *The future of the Spanish language in the United States.* New York and Washington, D.C.: Hispanic Policy Development Project.

8 Ideological influences on linguistic and cultural empowerment: An Australian example

Brian M. Bullivant

The emergence of the ideology of "empowerment" in the last twenty years has owed not a little to the new sociology of education (e.g., Young 1971) and the influence of the New Left in general. The work of Apple (1982), Bernstein (1977), Bourdieu and Passeron (1977), Willis (1977), and Young (1971), among others, has focused on the power of the school curriculum and the educational system to reproduce the interests of the ruling or dominant class. The outcome is that students from the "ruled" working class obtain lesser life chances in the form of low-paid, repetitive, and unrewarding jobs. Various proposals for ameliorating such a situation through educational programs to produce greater equality of opportunity for students have been part of the foregoing discourse. Some analyses incorporate a Marxist view of the role of education vis-à-vis the state (e.g., Gramsci 1971). This view ultimately came into Australia through the work of Connell et al. (1982), among other neo-Marxist theorists, and has been adopted as a framework for the analysis of immigrant education by such theorists as Jakubowicz (1984), Kalantzis and Cope (1988), and Rizvi (1986).

Another more culturalist approach to analyzing inequality in schools has extended thinking into the domain of schools and educational systems in which there are significant numbers of children from ethnocultural backgrounds. Multicultural education and the role of languages have taken center stage in this culturalist discourse; their influence on student equality of opportunity and empowerment has been increasingly debated, along with consideration of the evolution of the multicultural ideology itself.

Examples of significant contributions in this area are Banks (1986), who has focused mainly on the problems of minority group children in the United States, Bagley and Verma (1983), Cashmore and Troyna (1990), James and Jeffcoate (1981), Jeffcoate (1984), Lynch (1983), Mullard (1982), Tomlinson (1983, 1984), and Verma (1989), among others in Britain; and Bullivant (1973, 1981a, 1981b, 1984, 1986a,

161

1986b, 1986c, 1987a, 1989a), Foster (1988), Foster and Stockley (1984), Martin (1976, 1978), contributors to de Lacey and Poole (1979), Poole, de Lacey, and Randhawa (1985), and Smolicz (1979) in Australia. Specific problems of ethnic and migrant language maintenance in several Western pluralist societies have been discussed by authors in Edwards's edited book (1984) and as part of the wider issue of language policy across the curriculum by Corson (1990).

In the Australian case, both these approaches have played their part in determining the direction of the debates about and policies for making educational provisions for immigrants. Historically, the class-focused approach was the first and continues to exert a powerful influence over thinking. The other, more recent, is culture-focused, stemming from a belated response to the post-Second World War waves of immigrant settlers. First one, then the other has been the dominant discourse. Australian experience thus provides an instructive example of the way pluralist ideologies have evolved, but always within the parameters of an egalitarian metaideology that has dominated the Australian ethos and mass culture virtually since first settlement in the early 1800s.

Ideologies of pluralism

Although the ideology of empowerment usually takes much of its direction from a Marxist class-based view of power relations, I am using the term ideology in a more general sense, following Gould's definition: "A pattern of beliefs and concepts, both factual and normative, which purport to explain complex social phenomena with a view to simplifying socio-political choices facing individuals and groups" (1964:315–16).

It is important to distinguish between normative and factual patterns of beliefs and concepts. For example, prima facie, the statement "Australia is a multicultural society" is a factual one, claiming to be an accurate, descriptive truth-claim about the pluralist composition of the society. When the claim is subjected to empirical analysis that reveals that nearly 80 percent of the population of the society is still of Anglo-Celtic origin, the accuracy of the claim and its ideological status must be examined.

Empirical verification of a truth-claim is not possible with an ideology that is normative. A normative ideology is one that advocates prescriptions for a future state of affairs, usually based on a utopian view of the world in which idealistic wishing for a state of events prevails over more sober assessment of what is possible. Normative statements cannot be challenged by fact – unless the statements are so bizarre as to be self-discrediting – but by more appealing normative claims.

The ideology and rhetoric of empowerment

It is difficult to pin down exactly what is meant by educational empowerment; the amount of rhetoric with which the term is clouded makes precise definition even more difficult. This difficulty is compounded by the shifts in emphasis that have occurred over several decades. In the post-Second World War period, largely as a result of the 1944 Education Act in Britain, a general educational philosophy evolved in some Western democracies that supported the broad principle of making schooling and its outcomes more responsive to the needs of disadvantaged pupils, especially those from the working-class and minority groups. A succession of educational reform movements attempted to conceptualize the reasons for their lack of achievement in terms of educational deficit theory: They were educationally disadvantaged, educationally deprived, culturally deprived (in respect of ethnic minorities), and culturally different.

Equality of educational opportunity became a central discourse in this philosophy, with argument between those who favored equality of opportunity per se and those who favored equality of outcomes through differential inputs into the educational system. Empowerment appears to be the latest in this evolutionary sequence and is closely related to the concept of affirmative action. Both have the underlying rationale of enabling disadvantaged minorities and women to obtain fairer shares of economic and social rewards in such institutions as the workforce and education.

Like the debate between equality of opportunity versus equality of outcomes, two types of empowerment qua affirmative action have been advocated. "Soft" affirmative action programs aim to achieve greater equality of opportunity for those who are disadvantaged by encouraging employers to achieve a more equitable balance in the proportions of minorities and women who are employed in key or senior positions. "Hard" affirmative action programs go further in forcing employers to reach mandatory quotas in their workforces, that is, to achieve equality of outcomes rather than of opportunity.

It is not always apparent which of the two emphases is being advocated, and this difficulty is exacerbated by the rhetoric that invariably accompanies statements about achieving empowerment for minorities. The term too easily becomes a catchall phrase encapsulating various discourses such as "equity and access," "equality," "equality of outcomes," "social justice," "individualism and personal freedom," and "parity of esteem." These both obfuscate the real purpose of the empowerment policy and simultaneously reveal its ideological status in a welter of unclear, banal aims and objectives (Edelman 1977).

In Australia, affirmative action/empowerment ideas have found fertile ground in a general Anglo-Celtic-Australian metaideology of antielitism and egalitarianism. Left-wing ideologues who support such ideas propagate them especially through the various ideological state apparatuses (Althusser 1971; Gramsci 1971) over which they can exert influence. The apparatus relevant to this chapter is the state education system and those educational organizations over which the federal government can exercise some control.

To keep my discussion within manageable length, I will restrict it to empowerment through linguistic and cultural means. That is, I am mainly concerned with tracing the evolution in Australia of language and cultural programs that have been planned with the objective of empowering ethnocultural minorities and Anglo-Celtic citizens. The sense in which I use empowerment follows Dahrendorf (1979) and LeVine and White (1986), who analyze the improvement of educational development in terms of Dahrendorf's concept of "life chances."

Life chances are "the joint product of the options (choices) and ligatures (social attachments) made available by the social structure" (LeVine and White 1986:18). Within the structure, the educational system in particular is initially influential in providing the means to form both ligatures and options. Foundations for the former are more likely to be laid down in the period of primary enculturation or socialization (Berger and Luckmann 1971). Options in terms of available future career and social roles are likely to be thought about in secondary and anticipatory occupational socialization of young people (Bullivant 1986b, 1987a). The language and cultural needs for all students, indigenes and immigrants alike, thus extend through both primary and secondary education.

The evolution of pluralist ideologies and language programs

Pluralist ideologies are subject to evolution and modification according to social and demographic changes, political expediency, and other forces. The history of pluralist ideologies in Australia is an instructive illustration of this process. It is possible to distinguish several phases through which the various pluralist ideologies have evolved since the major waves of immigrants became such a feature of Australian development in the period following the Second World War. Each phase can be matched with a particular view of empowerment in which language has played a greater or lesser role.

Assimilation and Anglo-conformism

Prior to 1973, the dominant pluralist ideology was that of assimilation and Anglo-conformism. Immigrants, the majority of whom were initially from northern and eastern Europe, were expected to abandon their own cultures and assimilate into that of the Anglo-Celtic-Australian majority. In the 1960s, this still constituted some 90 percent of the total Australian population. The overwhelming problem of migrant children – New Australians, as they were called – was seen in educational, especially linguistic, deprivation terms. Educators and official surveys during this period established that such children lacked knowledge of the English language and claimed that their inability to conform to teachers' expectations disrupted normal class teaching and contributed to discipline problems – a classic "blame the victim" reaction typical of the prevailing educational deficit ideology.

Until the mid-1960s, little was done to remedy this situation. As Martin (1976:42–43) explained, citing the official views of one education department officer: "The general philosophy has been that they 'pick it [English] up'; so it's a 'sitting next to Nelly' idea; you pick it up and that's that." Even by the time of the influential 1974 Inquiry into Schools of High Migrant Density in the States of New South Wales and Victoria (where the great majority of migrant children were located), it was found that the response to the presence of migrant children in schools had been minimal.

However, from the mid-1960s onwards, some of the ideas of the progressive child-centered philosophy of education had begun to percolate from Britain and the United States, coupled with an increase in teacher autonomy in the classroom. A very few enlightened teachers began to demand special assistance to cope with the growing numbers of migrant children in their classes, which by then were starting to include more from southern Europe and a variety of Middle Eastern and Near East source countries.

In 1967, the Department of Education in the State of Victoria was the first to introduce a series of short (one-month) in-service training courses for teachers of English as a second language. The aim was to assist with the training of teachers to cope with the numbers of immigrant children invariably in withdrawal classes for English as a second language. This withdrawal strategy for ESL was to become the major approach to assisting newly arrived immigrant children.

An attempt was made in 1968 to reformulate the official federal government ideology to that of integration rather than assimilation, and to encourage ethnic minorities to retain and take pride in their cultures, while assimilating into the Anglo-Celtic structural components of the society. But this ideology had little impact on the mass of Anglo-Celtic-Australian public in general and educators in particular.

Two developments at the beginning of the 1970s heralded the dawning of a new phase in official government reactions to Australia's burgeoning and by then obvious ethnocultural pluralism. The first was the introduction of the Commonwealth Child Migrant Education Programme

(CMEP) in 1970; the second was the Immigration (Education) Act in 1971.

Predictably, however, solutions to the increasing problems of immigrant children were still seen in language terms. Both the new measures gave increased federal financial support to making ESL provisions for migrants, although the latter put more emphasis on adults than children. In the outcome, the demands on teachers and schools were increasing so greatly that the period 1970–75 saw an expansion of the CMEP. This occurred gradually, despite many deficiencies in teaching materials, lack of accurate statistics about the numbers of migrant children in schools and classrooms (due to teacher and departmental opposition to officially recognizing the existence of immigrant children), and apathy among the majority of teachers.

Informing the demands of caring teachers and underlying the official reports on the needs of migrants that had been published was an ideology of migrant disadvantage coupled with narrowly focused compensatory education to overcome it. In Lo Bianco's assessment (1988:26):

These reports overwhelmingly used the "discourse of disadvantage." They characterized the migrant situation as having several key and seemingly permanent elements: inequality equalling lack of English, equalling ethnicity, equalling urban inner city life, equalling manufacturing industry. Inequality through linguistic mismatch between the population and the governing and dominant institutions of the society was the overwhelming image communicated about the place of migrants in Australia. The programs which were proposed targeted immigrants or Aborigines only, the means for changing or ameliorating "the situation" was to be a linguistic one, i.e. the provision of ESL teaching to children and to adults.

LEVELS OF STUDENT EMPOWERMENT

Despite these developments, there was still considerable indifference towards the needs of immigrant children among the great majority of teachers. The effects on children's empowerment during this first phase of Australian pluralism were predictable. In terms of structural empowerment, the life chances of immigrant children were scarcely enhanced, especially as the majority of innovative ESL teaching was applied to the primary rather than the secondary level in which decisions about future careers are made.

There were minimal developments in ESL teaching carried out by a few pioneering teachers, but with little or no concomitant cultural enrichment in either the Anglo-Celtic culture or that of the children's own ethnic communities. However, to what extent this empowered students is problematical. It is true that knowledge of the English language might be regarded as an essential prerequisite for later occupational socialization and the ability to cope with Australian institutions that were dominated by the medium of the English language. But as Mullard (1982) in the United Kingdom, Polesel (1990) in Australia, and Banks (1986) in the United States, among many others, have suggested, concentration on ESL as the exclusive method of assisting immigrant children is inherently limiting and might even be unconsciously racist (in the British context). Suffice it to say, there is now a considerable backlash against the exclusive ESL approach in all these and other pluralist countries. As Banks has commented about the situation in the United States: "An exclusive language approach is doomed to fail" (Banks 1986:15).

One result of this exclusive approach in Australia's case was that immigrants' cultural ligatures, the second component in life chances, were devalued by most teachers and by the dominant Anglo-conformist and assimilationist ideology. Very little intercultural understanding pervaded the classrooms. Immigrant children were actively discouraged from using their home languages and expressing ideas about their home cultures, at least in public places such as schools, classrooms, and even on the public transport, where it was quite common for migrants speaking their own language to be abused by "dinkum" Aussies.

It was left to the immigrant child's home and community to provide the cultural ligatures; it could be argued that, by being thrown back on this resource, the ligature component of life chances might have been strengthened. However, even in those early days, the insidious influence of the Anglo-Celtic-Australian culture, then taking on elements of the American chromium-plated culture, was starting to erode the migrant child's subjective culture (Fiedler et al. 1971; Bullivant 1973). The home culture was beginning to be supplanted and the home language corrupted into a "kitchen dialect."

Utopian and pragmatic multiculturalism

As it is difficult to separate the next phases of utopian and pragmatic multiculturalism; I bracket them together in the following discussion. Both shared the underlying ideology of multiculturalism, and many of the ideas that I term utopian were the foundation for the more pragmatic recommendations that quickly followed.

Analysis of the migrant problem in culturalist terms had its origins in the ideas of some academics in the late 1960s (see details in Bullivant 1981a, 1984; Foster and Stockley 1984; Foster 1988), but was to gain greater exposure through the activity of A. J. (Al) Grassby, then minister for immigration in the new Labor government that had swept into power in 1972 and immediately embarked on an ambitious program of social reform.

An astute and energetic publicist, Grassby assiduously pushed his ideas about a multicultural Australia. This was despite the fact that few of them were novel, having been adopted from the few writings of academics on the topic and from developments in Canada and the United States. For the Australian situation, they were couched in equally utopian and rhetorical terms with the dominant metaphor being the "Family of the Nation" (e.g., Grassby 1973, 1974). Gradually a wave of academic and educational enthusiasm developed for what became a virtual bandwagon.

One of its outcomes – and a further sign of the changing times – was the Committee on the Teaching of Migrant Languages in Schools (CTMLS). This was set up in 1974 by the Labor Government to "bring together up-to-date information about the extent of the teaching of languages of migrant groups in government and non-government schools . . . to seek to collate views about desirable courses; . . . to make suggestions about possible lines of action" (Committee on the Teaching of Migrant Languages in Schools 1976:11).

Although the assumptions it made about the multicultural nature of Australia were naive and clearly in line with the nascent multicultural ideology, the committee's ideas about language education were well in advance of their time. Moreover, they constituted a clear move away from justifications for language policy that were focused on class, structural inequality, and equality of economic opportunity towards ones that favored a broader eclectic view of language plus culture learning for all. Thus the recommendations bracketed teaching migrant languages with recognition of the importance of culture learning, intercultural studies as a part of every child's education, bilingual education programs (despite their recognized and acknowledged difficulties), and greater cooperation between day schools and part-time ethnic schools.

There was considerable stress on community languages despite the fact that little empirical justification was adduced for such an approach. As Lo Bianco has commented (1988:26):

Social reasons for widely teaching these [community] languages were put forward. These held that such teaching would lead to intercultural tolerance, to understanding, and these completely unsupported but tenaciously clung-to assertions were added to dogmatic statements about how the teaching of these languages as language maintenance would overcome educational disadvantages experienced by migrant children.

Even granted their suspect nature, these ideas were not translated into school practice due to a six-month delay in having the committee's report accepted by the following Liberal government after it was tabled in federal parliament in mid-1976. The Liberal government had its own agenda to promote and commissions of inquiry to set in motion. By the time their recommendations became government policy, the CTMLS ideas had been shelved (a common fate for government reports).

Meanwhile, the multicultural bandwagon rolled on, but did little to change the fixation on ESL. Even when acceptance of the new ideology was symbolized by a change of name, the ESL approach dominated. For example, the Victorian Association of Teachers of English as a Second Language changed its name to the Victorian Association for Multicultural Education. However, the organization still put its emphasis on teaching English as a second language to immigrant children and on their first language maintenance in school; the organization gave little or no attention to cultural enrichment.

Several similar developments and educational conferences during the mid-1970s revealed how difficult it was for educators to come to terms with the new ideology. Meanwhile, tensions were clearly building among immigrant groups and ethnic organizations fuelled by expectations encouraged by the social reformist climate of the times under the Labor government.

The formation of the Australian Ethnic Affairs Council (AEAC) in January 1977 was one response to growing ethnic group restiveness and claims for "ethnic rights, power, and participation" (Storer 1975). The AEAC's pluralist blueprint, *Australia as a Multicultural Society* (Australian Ethnic Affairs Council 1977) enshrined three principles that were to become key ideological symbols with a strong rhetorical appeal. Ethnic groups could expect to maintain their *"cultural identity,"* expect to be accorded *"equality . . . as equal access to social resources,"* and expect to play their part in promoting the *"social cohesion"* of Australia. The dominant metaphor was a dramaturgical one: *"Multiculturalism means ethnic communities 'getting into the act' "* (Australian Ethnic Affairs Council 1977:204, italics in original).

The tenor of *Australia as a Multicultural Society* was predominantly utopian and in places (like the later Galbally Report) theoretically flawed in its treatment of key concepts such as culture and race. Reportedly, much of the publication was thought up by two leading sociologists of the day, Jerzy Zubrzycki and Jean Martin, then presented to members of the council and virtually rubber-stamped. Parts of the utopian vision of Australian society owed much to Zubrzycki's Eurocentric background in sociology and penchant for grand theory in the tradition of Talcott Parsons, his theoretical and chronological contemporary.

The next phase, *pragmatic multiculturalism*, was ushered in by the Review of Post-Arrival Services and Programs for Migrants chaired by a criminal defence lawyer (Galbally 1978). In November 1978, the prime minister, Malcolm Fraser, on behalf of the ruling Liberal government and with bipartisan support from the Labor party, adopted the multicultural model and proclaimed Australia a multicultural society by fiat.

The major characteristic of this period was the way in which culture became a surrogate concept for socio-economic or class issues in the prevailing discourse. The key achievements of the period [and of the Galbally Report – addition mine] in terms of programs were the establishment of the "self-help" ethos through support for ethnic schools, grant-in-aid for welfare to community groups and the initiation of the multicultural education program designed for "all students in all schools." (Lo Bianco 1988:27)

This ethos and kinds of support were legitimated by appeal to the three ideological symbols proposed by the preceding AEAC report. In time, ethnic community leaders were to assiduously campaign for even greater provisions, thereby generating the ethnic growth industry that became a feature of the 1980s, producing what Rimmer (1988) has termed "fiscal anarchy."

The Galbally Report contained a chapter setting out desirable directions for multicultural education (Galbally 1978: Ch. 9). This was based on the educational ideas espoused by the AEAC a year earlier and was aimed at improving the educational achievement of immigrant children. (The term empowerment had yet to evolve as the current rhetoric.) The AEAC had endorsed the principle that "policies and programs concerned with education for a multicultural society apply to *all* children, not just children of non-English-speaking background, and have ramifications throughout the curriculum" (1977:11–13). This was considered to be the "minimal response . . . compatible with the value of equality, on the one hand, and cultural identity, on the other" (1977:11).

The AEAC (1977:13) spelled out what this would mean for the educational system:

Schools should be given incentives to develop ethnic studies programs and to infuse the curriculum in general with the reality of the pluralist nature of Australian society, with the object both of enhancing the self-esteem of students of ethnic origin and giving *all* children a more authentic view of the nature of the society than the present mono-cultural education provides.

Several other educational aims were proposed: teaching English as a second language, bilingual education, community language education, support for ethnic ("Saturday morning") schools, and the importance of retaining immigrant (ethnic) heritages and histories.

A major thrust of both the AEAC's and the Galbally Report's agenda of educational provisions was the assertion that teaching about ethnic cultures in schools (a variant of culture contact theory, although it was not called that) would lead to reduced prejudice and discrimination against migrant children on the part of Anglo-Celtic pupils. As a consequence, it was asserted, without supporting evidence, that migrant children's cultural identity would be strengthened and lead to enhanced educational achievement. The thoroughly normative, ideological nature of the AEAC's assertion in this respect can be gauged by its admission that it knew "little about the association between the child's achievements and his sense of 'cultural identity'" (AEAC 1977:11).

Despite their suspect validity, these ideas were immediately taken up by the Commonwealth Schools Commission. This federal body was a hang-over from the social reformist days of the 1972–75 federal Labor government and had been retained by the following Liberal government. The Schools Commission was left-wing-oriented, with a strongly utopian and reformist view of education to the extent of advocating the use of education to bring about a restructuring of the whole society in line with still fashionable left-wing thinking in Britain (Bernstein 1970; Young 1971). Its main educational strategy was to make differential funding inputs into the system in order to bring about equality of outcomes.

Although subsequently the Schools Commission was to disown this ideology, having come under sustained attack for once holding it, the Commission's work over the remaining years of its existence was strongly influenced by a socialist and reformist agenda. It was the major funding body for curriculum innovations and programs in all schools, which in other mundane administrative matters were still controlled by the states, and had a major role in setting the guidelines for all education systems in its triennial reports, published until 1985.

These ideological and practical influences were apparent in the Multi-cultural Education Program (MEP). This was formulated by the Committee on Multicultural Education (1979), set up in haste by the Schools Commission to formalize the recommendations of the Galbally Report. The MEP was provided with considerable financial backing so that funding could be given to schools through two major initiatives: a small grants scheme to encourage curriculum development on a limited scale in schools, and large-scale funding for projects of national significance.

LEVELS OF STUDENT EMPOWERMENT

It was to take another five years before the results of the MEP would be officially evaluated (the Cahill Report, discussed in this section). Prima facie at least on paper, the MEP and AEAC educational ideas should have had several advantages over the previous exclusive ESL approach, provided they could be implemented in schools. Lo Bianco (1988:29) explains how they were an advance on earlier thinking:

First language maintenance came to be advocated both because it led to a strengthening of English acquisition and, also, intrinsically, for its own sake. This was true of both immigrant non-English languages and also Aboriginal non-English languages. . . . Language learning came to be seen as part of a cultural enterprise: learning one's own language or the language with which one's family identified for reasons of securing personal and group identification and learning languages for reasons of taking steps towards increasing social interaction between different, and linguistically divided, groups in the same society.

How successful this new approach was in terms of increasing children's options and ligatures was debatable. The previous phase had been dominated by the logic of teaching English as a second language as a counter to the previous assimilationist thinking, and with equality of opportunity for immigrant children in school, in society generally and subsequently in the workforce, as the dominant ideological motif. The new multicultural phase planned to augment this with a culturalist emphasis.

However, although basically sound in principle, it was an idea based more on faith than fact. Few teachers could cope with the concept of culture and how it might inform their pedagogy and curriculum. For this, the naive and theoretically flawed pronouncements on culture by the Galbally committee could be thanked. It had advanced thinking no further than the definition of culture proposed by Tylor in 1871. The emphasis on cultural pluralism led to numerous tokenistic celebrations of ethnicity in "spaghetti and basket-weaving terms" in schools, but little that addressed the root cause of immigrant disadvantage in the structure of Australian society and how immigrant children might be taught through a form of "radical multicultural education" to cope with it (Bullivant 1986a).

The claims for teaching immigrant cultures in schools with the aim of reducing prejudice (culture contact theory) and increasing children's self-esteem to raise their educational achievement were based more on pious hopes than on soundly researched evidence. As I have analyzed elsewhere (Bullivant 1986b, 1987a), both approaches are seriously defective, culture contact theory in particular having no credibility as an educational approach. Despite such criticisms and a general unease among many teachers with the approach advocated by the Schools Commission, the naive culturalist emphasis persisted in schools long after it should have been discredited and abandoned.

Pluralism in crisis

The culturalist emphasis extended into the next phase which saw multi-culturalism go through several turbulent years during the early 1980s. A major economic recession was developing in 1981–82, exacerbated by a prolonged drought. The Liberal government failed to cope with the growing crisis and was voted out of office in March 1983, to be replaced by the Labor government headed by Prime Minister Bob Hawke. Challenges to the multicultural ideology from academics and even members of the mass Anglo-Australian public were endemic and led to a reorganization of ethnic support bodies and feverish attempts through a nationwide series of public meetings organized by Professor Zubrzycki during 1981–82 to reformulate the ideology (see Australian Council on Population and Ethnic Affairs 1982; Bullivant 1984:Ch. 3, 1986c).

In 1984, a major public attack against immigration and multiculturalism by the noted Melbourne University historian, Geoffrey Blainey, became a cause célèbre. It revealed how strong was the groundswell of mass public opposition to multiculturalism and the immigration program that had been allowing increasing numbers of Asians into Australia for some years. The official ideology of pluralism was evidently in crisis; this may have been symptomatic of a deeper legitimation crisis brought about by mass public dissatisfaction with government institutions (Habermas 1976) into which the country's political order was sliding (Bullivant 1989b).

One of the new Labor government's priorities was to initiate reviews of the ideological state apparatuses and multicultural programs that had been put in place after the Galbally Report. Among these was the Schools Commission's Multicultural Education Program. Its manifest deficiencies had led to the Schools Commission's initiating a national survey of its results to date (Cahill et al. 1984). This report showed that, despite some successes, multicultural education had not even been attempted in the majority of schools. Altogether a total of 2,871 projects and small grant schemes had been funded in only 14 percent of Australian schools – an indication of how relatively little coverage of the whole education system the MEP had achieved. Of more importance for the discussion of this chapter is the fact that the major emphasis of the projects was "on community language programs (especially in Italian) and in cultural awareness and sensitization programs (whose overall value must be doubted)" (Cahill 1984:xii). As the Cahill Review comments (1984:xii): "The central finding of the Review . . . was that whilst the Program has resulted in many achievements, it has not as yet brought about substantial and lasting change in the Australian schooling system."

LEVELS OF STUDENT EMPOWERMENT

The evidence from the Cahill Review showed that linguistic provisions for all students had not developed much beyond what they were before the MEP was started. In the area of bilingual education, which had been supported by both the AEAC and Galbally committee, the Cahill findings were unequivocal (Cahill 1984:xiii):

There is . . . little support amongst the nation's teachers for the aspiration that the Australian schooling system should make its students bilingual. Whilst there is sympathy amongst teachers for languages other than English, only 34 per cent of teachers agree that such programs ought to become a normal part of the primary school curriculum. There is little support that all students study a language until year 12, but there is considerable minority support that it be mandatory until year 10.

While some success had occurred at the primary level in teaching Languages Other Than English (LOTE), a major finding was that the MEP had little impact on increasing LOTE study at the secondary level (Cahill 1984:345). This has obvious implications for the linguistic empowerment of students who might wish to pursue language-oriented careers in Australia. Of most importance was the finding that there is a drop-off of students from language study so that by the year 12, or Higher School Certificate level, only a small minority of students are studying a language other than English. It is at this level that success in examinations has a major bearing on proceeding to tertiary study, the main passport to professional careers.

Also of interest was the finding that students who were interviewed most often nominated Italian, French, or German as the languages they would like to speak well. In a society located in the Asia-Pacific region, one would have imagined that some Asian languages would have been more useful as possible preparation for occupational socialization.

Even the ability of schools to foster immigrant students' cultural ligatures came under question, though not in those terms. One of the aims of the MEP had been to foster the home language proficiency of immigrant students through community language maintenance programs in schools. But as the Cahill Review commented (Cahill 1984:346):

> Much naivete exists about the home language proficiency of children from non-English-speaking backgrounds and about the level of language proficiency achievable in programs of relatively short duration . . . [in the case of Italian] they were little more than language sensitization courses of one hour or less in duration . . . most primary schools (but with some exceptions) were reluctant to increase this commitment.

Neo-multiculturalism

The period 1987–88 saw major changes to the whole multicultural enterprise when the ideology of multiculturalism entered a new phase, what I term *neo-multiculturalism*. This can be traced directly to economic worries caused by the devaluation of the currency, mounting overseas debt, and adverse balance of trade, all exacerbated by the share market crash of October 1987. In essence, one major thrust of neo-multiculturalism is that multiculturalism is now clearly seen in instrumental terms as a way towards economic recovery. While continuing to give token recognition to social justice at the level of the individual, it puts much more stress on macrolevel goals and the "national pragmatic self-interest" (Lo Bianco 1988:27).

CHANGES TO THE MULTICULTURAL INFRASTRUCTURE

This new ideological direction was accompanied by sweeping changes to the multicultural ideological state apparatuses and programs during 1987–88. In the 1987 federal budget, the Schools Commission's Multicultural Education Program was scrapped and funding for ESL programs halved. The latter decision was immediately challenged by the ethnic community lobby of "professional ethnics" (whose undue influence had been criticized by the Cahill Review) and part of the funding was restored.

The Australian Institute of Multicultural Affairs, established in 1979 by the Galbally Report, was disbanded and a small core staff transferred from Melbourne to Canberra, where they became the nucleus of the subsequently much enlarged Office of Multicultural Affairs (OMA). This is within the prime minister's department and under his direct patronage, advised by a minister assisting the prime minister for multicultural affairs. To advise OMA and set the agenda for future multicultural directions, the prime minister also established a twenty-two member Advisory Council on Multicultural Affairs (ACMA) comprised almost exclusively of prominent ethnic public figures and one or two academics, but with no recognized expert in education among them. During 1988, one of ACMA's primary tasks in cooperation with OMA was to prepare and circulate nationally a discussion paper to promote public debate about future directions in multiculturalism (Office of Multicultural Affairs and Australian Advisory Council on Multicultural Affairs 1989).

The economic emphasis was further evident in other bureaucratic reshuffling that took place in 1987. This led to the establishment of the Department of Employment, Education and Training (DEET) and the Department of Immigration, Local Government and Ethnic Affairs (DILGEA). Both were to have consequences for the future directions and even survival of multiculturalism.

THE NEO-MULTICULTURAL IDEOLOGY – TOWARDS
NATIONAL EMPOWERMENT

OMA's neo-multicultural brief was quickly made explicit in its newssheet, *Focus for a Multicultural Australia* (March 1988:3). In the words of its then director, Peter Shergold, OMA exists among other things to promote multiculturalism as "an economic imperative" that will have a "valuable role to play in responding to the economic challenges that currently confront Australia . . . and pursuing a more just and equitable society." What he termed the "economics of multiculturalism" gave a clear indication of how far the ideology had departed from the original, naive ideas of its founders in the mid-1970s.

Multiculturalism demands that we examine more closely the challenge of managing a culturally diverse labour force; the human costs involved in restructuring manufacturing industries with large immigrant workforces; better use of immigrant skills, education and entrepreneurial drive by teaching English and recognizing overseas qualifications.

The multicultural rhetoric reasserted itself, however, when the director pointed out that the prime minister

has stressed that the roads to equity and efficiency are virtually identical. The cultural and social justice aspects – whether applied to immigrants, Aboriginals or other Australians – mean that conformity to a particular cultural stereotype should not be the price demanded in return for equality, equity or participation.

A further development endorsed by OMA was the National Policy on Languages, which was tabled in federal parliament at the end of 1987. The policy aims to maintain and increase Australians' command of both English and other languages, particularly Asian languages. The logic behind this is also driven by the economic imperative: As the OMA newssheet pointed out (p. 3), "seven of Australia's top 10 export markets in 1986–87 were non-English speaking countries, accounting for almost half of Australia's exports. Knowing the language means better understanding of the customer and market."

FURTHER PLURALIST CRISES

Faced with growing mass public concern over the way the immigration policies were operating, DILGEA set up the Committee to Advise on Australia's Immigration Policies (CAAIP) under the chairmanship of S. FitzGerald. Its report (CAAIP 1988) was published in 1988 and immediately precipitated another crisis in both the immigration policies and multiculturalism.

The essence of CAAIP's thinking was quite clear. Future immigration policy must be governed more by economic criteria to improve the calibre and skills of the workforce. During its consultations around Australia, the committee had found that many people had attitudes about immigration that reflected confusion, anxiety, criticism, and skepticism. The committee's general conclusion was that there is considerable "anti-immigration" feeling. The committee was also very critical of multiculturalism, which was seen by much of the mass public as "social engineering" actually promoting injustice, inequality, and divisiveness.

Predictably, the report raised a storm of opposition from diverse sources: OMA, the ethnic community lobby and professional ethnics, refugee organizations, government bodies, and even the then Minister for Immigration, Local Government and Ethnic Affairs, Mr. Holding, who had commissioned the report in the first place. As one way of bolstering the faltering ideology, the Advisory Council on Multicultural Affairs published *National Agenda for a Multicultural Australia* in July 1989 (Office of Multicultural Affairs and Australian Advisory Council on Multi-cultural Affairs 1989). It lamented that Australia falls far short of the requirements for a cohesive and distinctively Australian society and rec-ognized that there is significant mass public opposition to multicultural-ism. Nevertheless the agenda enshrined equity, efficiency, and respect for cultural diversity as the ultimate objectives of multiculturalism. The in-clusion of the pragmatic concept of efficiency sat uneasily with the other principles, in which clear ideological echoes of the 1977 AEAC and 1978 Galbally thinking could be detected.

MUDDLED THINKING IN THE NATIONAL AGENDA

A major section of the National Agenda related to promoting multi-cultural education in schools and tertiary education (see pp. 35–36 of the agenda) as a way of reducing prejudice and discrimination. Such a recom-mendation was either naive or clearly ideological and revealed how out of touch ACMA was with what had been happening in the real world of education. This was all the more surprising as ACMA would have been able to consult both the Cahill Report and my own *Getting a Fair Go*, a report on discrimination and prejudice in high schools prepared for the Australian Human Rights Commission in 1986 (Bullivant 1986b, 1987a). Although the research was based on a small sample of seven high schools in metropolitan Melbourne and obviously cannot be generalized beyond them, the latter report showed clearly that multicultural educa-tion was not wanted by either ethnic parents or their children because it was a distraction from what they viewed as the main purpose of educa-tion, namely passing examinations in academic subjects and getting qual-ifications for future careers. Multicultural education was criticized as being irrelevant even by some ethnic leaders in two of the seven schools surveyed.

A major section of the report also reviewed the work of eminent theo-rists both in Australia and other countries who have pointed out the failure of multicultural education and its underlying culture contact and self-esteem theories to increase intercultural understanding and thereby reduce prejudice. Yet all these ideas were again proposed by ACMA.

The National Policy on Languages

Given the theme of this chapter, the National Policy on Languages is of special relevance, as it has the potential to set in motion programs that would empower both immigrant and Anglo-Celtic-Australian students. To what extent is this likely to occur?

Lo Bianco (the prime mover and author of the policy) has commented that the conceptual basis of the National Policy on Languages is "socio-political language planning" (Lo Bianco 1988:29). After a lengthy gestation period, the policy was completed by the end of November 1986, and received prime ministerial endorsement in April 1987. It went through the usual parliamentary procedures, and funding for the policy was confirmed at the end of 1987. At the same time, the government announced the composition of yet another committee, which would oversee the implementation of the policy. This is the Australian Advisory Council on Languages and Multicultural Education (AACLAME). The inclusion of multicultural education is significant and indicates that the government has not abandoned the utopian aim of trying to foster multiculturalism through the educational system.

The policy comprises several programs, each of which receives separate and, by Australian standards, generous funding and allocation of separate administrative support. In summary, the programs are as follows (Lo Bianco 1987, 1988):

- Expansion of ESL for new immigrant arrivals;
- Funding for Australian Second Language Learning;
- An Adult Literacy Action Campaign to improve levels of adult literacy;
- Asian Languages Teaching and Asian Studies in schools and tertiary institutions through tagged funding;
- Multicultural and Cross-Cultural Supplementation Programs to boost inter-cultural and multicultural studies in tertiary institutions through tagged funding;
- A National Aboriginal Languages Project;
- A Language Testing Unit;
- An Australian Advisory Council on Languages and Multicultural Education.

In the teaching/learning area, the policy is driven by three imperatives:

Firstly: goals of educational equity leading to programs in community languages for language maintenance and intercultural goals leading to programs in community languages as second languages.
Secondly: the demonstrable relationships between the language needs of the society and its present economic directions leading to programs in the teaching of languages of economic and geopolitical significance.
Thirdly: the general educational value of languages, deriving from the traditional cultural and intellectual goals of second language learning and leading to a general justification for widespread learning of any language (Lo Bianco 1987:36).

There is a strong element of the rhetoric that seems to be an inevitable concomitant of any policy formulation of this type in Lo Bianco's comment that "these three imperatives are expressed as four E's in the Policy: Enrichment; Equality; Economics; and External" (Lo Bianco 1987:36). As will become apparent in the next section, the inclusion of equality is particularly worrying.

Like the multicultural ideology before it, the multilingual emphasis has led to the development of major institutional agencies. One such in mid-1990 was the multi-campus Languages Institute of Australia, with Lo Bianco as director. This was established to conduct the innovative research and teaching necessary to implement the goals of the National Policy on Languages. As the Monash University's vice-chancellor stated in the university's weekly newssheet *Sound* (4 May 1990), when announcing Lo Bianco's appointment as director: "The Languages Institute of Australia ushers in a new era in language policy in this country. In the context of the rapid internationalization of the Australian economy and the remarkable concentration of economic power in non-English speaking countries, the EEC and Japan especially, it is imperative that Australia is linguistically prepared for the modern world."

The institute is based at Monash University, which is situated in a southeast suburb of Melbourne. The institute is multi-institutional, comprising centers for language and society (at Monash University), a language testing unit (University of Melbourne and Griffith University in Brisbane, jointly), a language acquisition research centre (University of Sydney and University of Western Australia in Perth, jointly), and a language and technology centre/clearinghouse unit (University of Queensland). It is planned to establish teaching and curriculum centers in other important urban centers in Australia, which will guarantee the institute's national coverage. Monash is also the base for the National Centre for Community Languages in the Professions (among several other centers), which is cross-linked with the National Languages Institute.

Is macroempowerment possible through multiculturalism?

As will be apparent, the emphasis has now shifted from individual empowerment to macroempowerment. The need for neo-multiculturalism is being driven by wider social forces rooted in the whole structure and culture of Australia, which is itself rooted in a vibrant Asia-Pacific region and inevitably linked to its sociopolitical, economic, and strategic forces.

If Australia wants to survive and prosper in such a highly competitive world, it will need to restructure its workforce, become more outward looking in its basic ethos, more competitive, and more aware of the importance of encouraging excellence in all fields of endeavor, especially education; and thus less egalitarian and inevitably more tolerant of elitism developing among those who have the drive and vision to succeed. Australia must also become linked with and contribute to the world system of knowledge-generating, knowledge-utilizing networks.

Some of the measures to achieve these goals are contained in the National Policy on Languages, which is being legitimated by the convenient ideology of multiculturalism that happens to be in place at a time when the policy has evolved. But it could well have been some other ideology – and needs to be if many of the objectives now being advocated to improve Australia's economic performance are ever to succeed.

I have proposed that educationists should be guided by what I term the philosophy of *pluralist reconstruction* (Bullivant 1986b, 1987a, 1988). This means that every person in Australia, particularly those in schools and regardless of their ethnic background, must be encouraged to achieve to the maximum of their academic potential in order to contribute to the knowledge base that has emerged as the foundation for economic and political success in knowledge-based societies due to the cybernetic revolution since the 1970s. If this means that some students from ethnic groups succeed through academic achievement at the expense of Anglo-Celtic-Australian students, so be it.

In the area of foreign language learning, I strongly doubt whether difficult languages such as Japanese can be learned sufficiently well in the short term, intensive programs that are planned so that Japanese-speaking Australians would be able to play a part in Australia's economic revival, in which speed is a priority. Instead, I have suggested that much more can be done to train Australian representatives in cross-cultural communicative competence (Bullivant 1990) by applying a variation of general culture assimilator theory developed by Fiedler et al. (1971) and Brislin et al. (1986).

But other difficulties stand in the way of macrolevel empowerment, as long as the multicultural ideology is used to legitimate the new language policies and other developments that have been put in place. Multiculturalism contains the seeds of its destruction by hanging on to out-moded egalitarian cliches that are dysfunctional for economic improvement, no more so than in education. It is this that makes one question whether the National Policy on Languages operating through the education system can in fact empower Australia as a nation at the macrolevel.

At the university level, submissions for grants to include multicultural education in the curriculum have to compete with more trendy highfliers such as biomedical research, engineering, and similar capital-intensive research claimants. University politics of grantsmanship can easily subvert the intentions of an outside body, no matter how worthwhile they might appear on paper. Thus hopes by ACMA and the National Policy on Languages that tertiary-level resources will be diverted to multicultural and cross-cultural education are unrealistic. Some may be, most will not be, there being little mileage in multicultural education and attendant concerns.

In addition, a single federal educational system has not yet evolved, as progress is held back by a cumbersome structure of state education systems. There is no agreed national curriculum and assessment procedure. Teachers' unions exert stultifying control over what goes on in schools and are driven by an ideology which enshrines egalitarianism as the prime Australian value and actively discourages teachers from fostering excellence and accelerated learning in their pupils for fear of encouraging elitism.

Even more serious is the failure of the AACLAME and National Policy on Languages to take into account the findings of the Cahill Review, discussed above. Given that so many teachers are against bilingual education, that community languages are not taught seriously, and that even second language learning has gone into serious decline, especially at senior levels, it is sheer wishful thinking that the education system will speedily bring about the changes that are claimed to be essential for the economic recovery of Australia.

The assumption that even a reformed education system stressing language skills and intercultural understanding can achieve macrolevel economic empowerment is also faulty. It fails to recognize the lessons of the failure of educational reform movements in the United States, Britain, Canada, and finally Australia in the 1960s and 1970s, which led Bernstein (1970) and Halsey (1972) among others to conclude that educational reform to overcome deficits among children that are socially and structurally based had not succeeded, and in particular that education cannot compensate for society.

This is especially true of a society such as Australia's. The deep structural and cultural causes of its economic and social malaise are far more complex than something that is amenable to being reformed through education. Disregarding the several external economic influences that have played a part in the nation's economic problems, many internal forces are inhibiting progress. These are inefficient workforce structures and practices; a complacent manufacturing and managerial organizational culture; the virtual failure of the high technology "sunrise industries" – that at one time were claimed to be Australia's salvation – due to businesses' and government's inability to capitalize on local inventions and reluctance to invest in locally made technology, the majority of which is sold overseas and subsequently purchased back at inflated prices; the overwhelming egalitarian, hedonistic, and "she'll be right" national ethos and metaideology; the control over government exerted by the Australian Council of Trade Unions and the union movement in general that so frequently impedes necessary economic and structural reforms. These are only some of the impediments that language education cannot address. The macroempowerment of the Australian nation will not be achieved by that route, nor will it be by adherence to an outmoded multicultural ideology.

Conclusion

Despite this pessimistic scenario, there are more recent (1992–93) signs in the Australian political context that caution one against making prognoses about the country's future developments. Some of the signs have to do with changes in the political leadership in 1991 and the succession to leadership of Prime Minister Paul Keating. Reportedly he has less enthusiasm for multiculturalism and associated matters, which consequently get less priority in the mass media and policy making than was the case under his predecessor.

Whether the Labor or Liberal party gains power in federal elections, either will face basically the same pressing problems. Australia is still battling to recover from a recession that has bordered on a true depression, with at least 12 percent of the labor force out of work. Some estimates put the figure much higher. The country is burdened by a massive overseas debt that can only be reduced by increasing exports through more efficient production and reducing imports. Faced by these kinds of concerns, focusing on language policy seems almost irrelevant at best, or tantamount to rearranging the deck chairs on a sinking Titanic at worst.

Yet one of the new growth areas being fostered to aid recovery, particularly through the TAFE (Technical and Further Education) sector in tertiary education, is the hospitality and tourism industry. Considerable emphasis is placed on teaching Japanese language to TAFE students, who will ultimately provide the labor force for that industry – Japanese tourists forming a large proportion of those coming to Australia. Courses in Japanese and to a lesser extent Indonesian and Mandarin Chinese are proliferating in secondary schools; one or two notable examples in the Melbourne area have hundreds of students taking Japanese.

Whom these kinds of developments will empower is debatable. True, students will hopefully develop valuable skills that enable them to provide the kinds and levels of service discriminating tourists demand. But there is now evidence that Japanese tourist organizations in such places as the Queensland Gold Coast are using either Japanese locals or "imported" Japanese nationals to staff hotels that are Japanese-owned or in which Japanese companies have a controlling interest. Despite this, there is impressionistic evidence to suggest that well-trained TAFE students with Japanese language skills are still in great demand by hotels and other organizations in the recognized tourist areas of Australia.

All those who do not enter an industry in which Japanese and other foreign language skills will be used may still benefit from knowledge of a foreign language, namely by learning about the culture and lifestyles of societies in the Asia-Pacific region. Given Australia's past history of xenophobic and chauvinistic attitudes towards foreigners, particularly Asians, any leavening of this national mind-set can only be an advantage to Australia's relationships with other countries in its immediate region – which one hopes would be reciprocated. In this respect, acquiring a foreign language will lead to a level of empowerment that hopefully transcends narrow national concerns.

References

Althusser, L. 1971. Ideology and ideological state apparatuses. In L. Althusser (Ed.), *Lenin and philosophy and other essays*. London: New Left Books.
Apple, M. W. (Ed.). 1982. *Cultural and economic reproduction in education*. London: Routledge and Kegan Paul.
Australian Council on Population and Ethnic Affairs. 1982. *Multiculturalism for all Australians: Our developing nationhood*. Canberra: AGPS.
Australian Ethnic Affairs Council (AEAC). 1977. *Australia as a multicultural society*. Submission to the Australian Population and Immigration Council on the Green Paper, *Immigration Policies and Australia's Population*. Canberra: AGPS.
Bagley, C., and G. K. Verma. (Eds.). 1983. *Multicultural childhood education: Ethnicity and cognitive styles*. Aldershot: Gower.
Banks, J. A. 1986. Multicultural education, development, paradigms and goals. In J. A. Banks and J. Lynch (Eds.), *Multicultural education in Western societies* (pp. 2–28). Eastbourne: Holt, Rinehart and Winston.
Berger, P. L., and T. Luckmann. 1971. *The social construction of reality*. Harmondsworth: Penguin University Books.
Bernstein, B. 1977. *Class, codes and control*. 2d ed. London: Routledge and Kegan Paul.
Bourdieu, P., and J.-C. Passeron. 1977. *Reproduction in education, society and culture* (R. Nice, Trans.). London: Sage.
Brislin, R. W., K. Cushner, C. Cherrie, and M. Yong. 1986. *Intercultural interactions: A practical guide*. Beverly Hills: Sage.
Bullivant, B. M. (Ed.). 1973. *Educating the immigrant child: Concepts and cases*. Sydney: Angus and Robertson.
  1981a. *The pluralist dilemma in education: Six case studies*. Sydney: George Allen and Unwin.
  1981b. *Race, ethnicity, and curriculum*. Melbourne: Macmillan.
  1984. *Pluralism: Cultural maintenance and evolution*. Clevedon, Avon: Multilingual Matters.
  1986a. Towards radical multiculturalism: Resolving tensions in curriculum and educational planning. In S. Modgil, G. K. Verma, K. Mallick, and C. Modgil (Eds.), *Multicultural education: The interminable debate* (pp. 33–47). Lewes: Falmer Press.
  1986b. *Getting a fair go: Case studies of occupational socialization and perceptions of discrimination in a sample of seven Melbourne high schools*. Human Rights Commission Occasional Paper 13. Canberra: AGPS.
  1986c. Multicultural education in Australia: An unresolved debate. In J. A. Banks and J. Lynch (Eds.), *Multicultural education in Western societies* (pp. 98–124). Eastbourne: Holt, Rinehart and Winston.
  1987a. *The ethnic encounter in the secondary school: Ethnocultural reproduction and resistance – theory and case studies*. Lewes: Falmer Press.

1987b. Ethnic politics in Australia: The social constructions of pluralism. *Ethnic and Racial Studies* 10:110–19.

1988. Missing the empirical forest for the ideological trees. *Journal of Intercultural Studies* 9:58–69.

1989a. The pluralist dilemma revisited. In G. K. Verma (Ed.), *Education for all: A landmark pluralism.* Lewes: Falmer Press.

1989b. The pluralist crisis facing Australia. *The Australian Quarterly* 61:212–28.

1990. In-service teacher education for intercultural competence: An alternative to multicultural education in Australia. Paper presented to the 36th World Assembly of the International Council on Education for Teaching, September, Singapore.

Cahill, D., and Review Team of the Language and Literacy Centre, Phillip Institute of Technology, Coburg. 1984. *Review of the Commonwealth multicultural education program.* Report to the Commonwealth Schools Commission. Canberra: AGPS.

Cashmore, E., and B. Troyna. 1990. *Introduction to race relations.* 2d ed. Lewes: Falmer Press.

Committee on Multicultural Education. 1979. *Education for a multicultural society.* Report to the Schools Commission. Canberra: Schools Commission.

Committee on the Teaching of Migrant Languages in Schools. 1976. *Report.* Canberra: AGPS.

Committee to Advise on Australia's Immigration Policies (CAAIP). 1988. *Immigration: A commitment to Australia.* Report of the CAAIP. Canberra: AGPS.

Connell, R. W., D. Ashenden, S. Kessler, and G. Dowsett. 1982. *Making the difference: Schools, families, and social division.* Sydney: George Allen and Unwin.

Corson, D. 1990. *Language policy across the curriculum.* Clevedon, Avon: Multilingual Matters.

Dahrendorf, R. 1979. *Life chances.* Chicago: University of Chicago Press.

de Lacey, P. R., and M. E. Poole. (Eds.). 1979. *Mosaic or melting pot: Cultural evolution in Australia.* Sydney: Harcourt Brace Jovanovich.

Edelman, M. 1977. *Political language: Words that succeed and policies that fail.* New York: Academic Press.

Edwards, J. (Ed.). 1984. *Linguistic minorities: Policies and pluralism.* London: Academic Press.

Fiedler, F. E., T. Mitchell, and H. C. Triandis. 1971. The culture assimilator: An approach to cross-cultural training. *Journal of Applied Psychology* 55.

Foster, L. E. 1988. *Diversity and multicultural education: A sociological perspective.* Sydney: Allen and Unwin.

Foster, L. E., and D. Stockley. 1984. *Multiculturalism: The changing Australian paradigm.* Clevedon, Avon: Multilingual Matters.

Galbally, F. 1978. *Migrant services and programs.* Report of the Committee of the Review of Post-Arrival Programs and Services for Migrants, vol. 1 (May), vol. 2 Appendices. Canberra: AGPS.

Gould, J. 1964. Ideology. In J. Gould and W. L. Kolb (Eds.), *A dictionary of the social sciences* (pp. 315–17). London: Tavistock.

Gramsci, A. 1971. *Selections from the prison notebooks of Antonio Gramsci* (Q. Hoare and G. N. Smith, Eds. and Trans.). London: Lawrence and Wishart.

Grassby, A. J. 1973. *A Multi-cultural society for the future.* Canberra: AGPS.

1974. *Credo for a nation.* Immigration Reference Paper. Canberra: AGPS.

Habermas, J. 1976. *Legitimation crisis.* London: Heinemann.

Halsey, A. H. 1972. *Educational policy: E.P.A. problems and policies.* London: HMSO.

Jakubowicz, A. 1984. State and ethnicity: Multiculturalism as ideology. In J. Jupp (Ed.), *Ethnic politics in Australia* (pp. 14–28). Canberra: George Allen and Unwin.

James, A., and R. Jeffcoate. (Eds.). 1981. *The school in the multicultural society: A reader.* London: Harper and Row, in association with the Open University Press.

Jeffcoate, R. 1984. *Ethnic minorities and education.* London: Harper and Row.

Kalantzis, M., and W. Cope. 1988. Why we need multicultural education: A review of the 'ethnic disadvantage' debate. *Journal of Intercultural Studies* 9:39–57.

LeVine, R. A., and M. I. White. 1986. *Human conditions: The cultural basis of educational development.* New York: Routledge and Kegan Paul.

Lo Bianco, J. 1987. *National Policy on Languages.* Canberra: AGPS.

1988. Multiculturalism and the National Policy on Languages. *Journal of Intercultural Studies* 9:25–38.

Lynch, J. 1983. *The multicultural curriculum.* London: Batsford.

Martin, J. I. 1976. The education of migrant children in Australia. In C. A. Price and J. I. Martin (Eds.), *Australian immigration: A bibliography and digest,* No. 3, 1975, Pt. 2 (pp. 1–65). Canberra: The Australian National University, Department of Demography, Institute of Advanced Studies.

1978. *The migrant presence.* Sydney: George Allen and Unwin.

Mullard, C. 1982. Multiracial education in Britain: From assimilation to cultural pluralism. In J. Tierney (Ed.), *Race, migration and schooling* (pp. 120–33). London: Holt, Rinehart and Winston.

Office of Multicultural Affairs and Australian Advisory Council on Multicultural Affairs. 1989. *National agenda for a multicultural Australia: Sharing our future.* Canberra: AGPS.

Polesel, J. 1990. ESL, ideology, and multiculturalism. *Journal of Intercultural Studies* 11:64–72.

Poole, M. E., P. R. de Lacey, and B. S. Randhawa. (Eds.). 1985. *Australia in transition: Culture and life possibilities.* Sydney: Harcourt Brace Jovanovich.

Rimmer, S. 1988. *Fiscal anarchy: The public funding of multiculturalism.* Policy Paper no. 15. Perth: Australian Institute for Public Policy.

Rizvi, F. 1986. *Ethnicity, class and multicultural education.* Geelong: Deakin University Press.

Smolicz, J. J. 1979. *Culture and education in a plural society.* Canberra: Curriculum Development Centre.

Storer, D. (Ed.). 1975. *Ethnic rights, power, and participation: Toward a multicultural Australia.* Melbourne: Clearing House on Migration Issues, Ecumenical Migration Centre, and Centre for Urban Research and Action.

Tomlinson, S. 1983. *Ethnic minorities in British schools: A review of the literature, 1960–82.* London: Heinemann.

1984. *Home and school in multicultural Britain.* London: Batsford Academic and Educational.

Troyna, B., and D. I. Smith. (Eds.). 1983. *Racism, school and the labour market.*

Leicester: National Youth Bureau.

Tylor, E. B. 1871. *Primitive culture.* London: John Murray.

Verma, G. K. (Ed.). 1989. *Education for all: A landmark in pluralism.* Lewes: Falmer Press.

Willis, P. 1977. *Learning to labour.* Farnborough: Saxon House.

Young, M. F. D. (Ed.). 1971. *Knowledge and control: New directions for the sociology of education.* London: Collier-Macmillan.

9 Five vowels or three? Linguistics and politics in Quechua language planning in Peru

Nancy H. Hornberger

At the conclusion of the First Workshop on Quechua and Aymara Writing, convened in Lima, Peru, in October 1983, the participants included among their recommendations the revision of the official Quechua alphabet in use in Peru since 1975 to include three (i, a, u) rather than five (i, e, a, o, u) vowels (see Hornberger 1993 for more information on the workshop).[1] During the workshop and in the years following, in a series of meetings and publications, this language-planning decision has been the focus of a heated debate, involving multiple interest groups and a wide range of arguments, and reflecting long-standing dissensions in the process of the standardization of Quechua. As in many language-planning cases around the world, what might at first appear to be a trivial matter of language corpus planning turns out to have far-ranging social, cultural, and political implications.

This chapter explores those implications and the ways in which Quechua language use and Quechua language planning in Peru are both a reflection of sociocultural and politico-economic divisions in Peruvian society, and a vehicle for seeking to challenge those divisions. After briefly describing the background and emergence of the controversy and introducing the interest groups involved, this chapter will explore the main points of controversy and the various arguments presented by the different interest groups. A concluding section will discuss future directions and implications of this debate for language education.

---

1 I was a participant at the 1983 First Workshop on Quechua and Aymara Writing in Lima while carrying out dissertation research in Peru with support from the Inter-American Foundation and a Fulbright-Hays Dissertation Research Abroad Fellowship; and at the 1987 workshop sponsored by the Las Casas Center for Rural Andean Studies in Cusco while carrying out research on Quechua use in three urban highland Peruvian settings with support from the University of Pennsylvania Research Foundation. For the other workshops and meetings reported here, I rely on documentary evidence. I am grateful to these institutions for their support, and to Rodolfo Cerrón-Palomino, Luis Enrique López, Inés Pozzi-Escot, and David Weber for their comments on an earlier draft.

Background of the controversy: the status of Quechua in Peru

Peru has always been multilingual and pluricultural. The languages of the Incan empire included not only the "general language," Quechua, but also Aymara and Puquina as major languages, as well as 200 or more other languages and dialects. With the advent of the Spanish colonial power in the sixteenth century, Spanish replaced Quechua as the official language. Despite increasing pressure, especially after the revolt of Thupa Amaru was crushed in 1789 and repressive measures were enacted against them, the indigenous languages were weakened but not altogether destroyed. After independence from Spain in 1821, Spanish continued unquestioned as the national language, but there were large numbers of monolingual vernacular speakers and growing numbers of bilinguals.

Today, Peru counts among its 14.5 million inhabitants over the age of 5 approximately 73 percent monolingual Spanish speakers, 22 percent Quechua speakers (of which about 35 percent are monolingual), and 2.5 percent Aymara speakers (of which about 31 percent are monolingual). Speakers of other indigenous languages and of foreign languages make up the other 2.5 percent of Peru's population (Instituto Nacional de Estadística 1984:164).

Peruvian scholars have recently drawn increasing attention to the fact that it is not enough, when describing Peru's multilingualism and pluriculturalism, simply to note the existence of diverse groups. One must also recognize that noncommunication, inequality, and linguistic conflict are an integral part of that multilingualism. Pozzi-Escot (1987b) reviews the history of noncommunication in Peru, from pre-Columbian to present times, noting that in the present, Peru is once again approaching the use of a common language, as in Incan times, but is now doing so at the cost of bilingualism rather than by fostering it. She notes, as have others (Cerrón-Palomino 1980:13), that bilingualism has proven to be nothing more than a route from vernacular monolingualism to Spanish monolingualism; that the proportion of monolingual speakers of indigenous languages in Peru has decreased from 35 percent of the total population in 1940 to 9 percent in 1981, whereas monolingual Spanish speakers have increased from 47 percent to 73 percent of the total population during the same period; and she asks, pointedly, whether this loss of Peru's multilingual "face" is a conscious choice or simply a careless and soon to be irredeemable mistake (Pozzi-Escot 1987b:58).

López (1989) and Ballón (1989) describe the relation among the indigenous languages and Spanish in Peru as one of diglossia, following the usage of Catalan sociolinguists who extend this term beyond Ferguson's original (1959) definition to mean "a conflictive social situation in which one or more linguistic varieties are subordinated to another which enjoys greater social prestige in terms of the functions which it fulfills in a particular society" (López 1989:100, translation mine). López demonstrates that such a situation is leading not only to reduced functions for the indigenous languages, but also to the increasing influence of Spanish in the lexicon and grammar of the indigenous languages.

Chuquimamani offers a concrete example of this dual tendency arising from the situation of conflict between two languages. Chuquimamani (1988) notes, as have others (Hornberger 1988a:81ff.), that many Quechua speakers who have migrated from the rural community to the city disown their language and take on Spanish in their quest for social ascent, expressing themselves in the singularly revelatory statement, "Yo no intinti quichua," in which they deny, in heavily Quechua-influenced Spanish, that they understand Quechua. It is not just a city phenomenon, however; even in the rural areas, many are ashamed to speak Quechua. Furthermore, many speak a Quechua heavily mixed with Spanish loan words: Chuquimamani documents a 25 percent rate of Spanish loan words in four interviewees' discourses on childbirth, despite the fact that this is a topic for which Quechua terms do exist.

Language policy and language use reflect the sociocultural and politico-economic divisions of society; they can also, however, be vehicles for challenging those divisions. This was precisely the intent of the three language-related planning efforts of the 1970s in Peru. The Education Reform of 1972 sought the "full participation of all members of the society" and specified bilingual education as one means to achieve this (*Compendio* 1975:3–144). The National Bilingual Education Policy of 1972 sought to "promote, in the vernacular language communities, a critical interpretation of their socioeconomic reality in order to bring about their spontaneous, creative, and conscious participation in the process of structural change directed toward the elimination of mechanisms of dependence and domination" (Ministerio de Educación 1972, translation mine). The 1975 Officialization of Quechua made Quechua an official language of Peru, coequal with Spanish, and specified that it would be taught at all levels of education beginning in 1976 and used in all court actions involving Quechua speakers beginning in 1977. The Quechua commission appointed to implement this law developed a basic general Quechua alphabet and oversaw the development and publication of six dictionary-grammar sets for the six varieties of Quechua in Peru.

The 1979 Constitution of Peru retreated from Quechua officialization, designating only Spanish as the official language of Peru, whereas Quechua and Aymara are "in official use in the zones and form that the law establishes"; and the other indigenous languages are the "cultural patrimony of the nation" (Article 83, translation mine). Nevertheless, the expanded uses of Quechua and Aymara in new domains had already been set in motion by the three policies, especially in bilingual education programs in Alto Napo, Ayacucho, Cusco, and Puno (see Hornberger 1988a, 1988b, and Pozzi-Escot 1989:21–40 for more information on these language policies).

The emergence of the controversy

In the years following the officialization of Quechua, the institutions that had been engaged in teaching literacy and in developing materials and texts in Quechua and Aymara had confronted a series of problems in applying the official Quechua alphabet. To resolve those problems, as well as to define an official alphabet for Aymara, the First Workshop on Quechua and Aymara Writing (I Taller de Escritura en Quechua y Aimara) was convened in Lima in October 1983. Especially significant was the decision to consider Quechua and Aymara together, even though they are genetically unrelated indigenous languages. The decision was neither an arbitrary nor a coincidental one, but arose from the belief that it would be both "necessary and useful to analyze both systems in contrast to each other in view to a common solution" (López, personal communication, 16 September 1990).

Although the organizers of the workshop were linguists, they took care to include among the participants not only scholars of the languages, but also native speakers as well as teachers and others with experience in writing the languages. The workshop met for three days and issued final recommendations on a range of issues, including orthographic rules and the treatment of Spanish loan words. Here, however, we are interested only in their recommendation that both the official Quechua and Aymara alphabets include three vowels (i, a, u).

Three of the four plenary papers raised the question of five or three vowels for the Quechua alphabet, and a considerable proportion of the general discussion on all three days was devoted to it. Many of the arguments that were to characterize the debate during the coming years were presented at the workshop. The decision for three vowels did not come easily. Nevertheless, the workshop participants did approve it, along with the recommendation that the permanent Coordinating Commission appointed by the workshop draft and propose legislation that would complement the above-mentioned Article 83 of the 1979 Constitution. The eventual outcome of the commission's efforts was the adoption by the Peruvian government of a resolution approving in full the workshop's recommendations on the Quechua and Aymara alphabets and rules of orthography and punctuation (Ministerial Resolution #1218–85–ED on 18 November 1985) and a law and a resolution establishing an Academy of the Aymara Language (Law #24323 of 4 November 1985 and Supreme Resolution #252–86 of 30 December 1986).

The official adoption of the three-vowel alphabet was to become the focus of heated debate in a series of meetings and publications in the following years. In November 1986, one year after the official adoption, the four-day national Workshop Seminar on Curricular Programs for Bilingual Education was held in Cusco. In the course of the seminar, following the presentation of the opening papers and of the experiences of the bilingual education projects represented there, a spontaneous debate arose over the question, "Why use three vowels for Quechua?" (Debate 1987).

The following year (13–15 February 1987), also in Cusco, the Peruvian Academy of the Quechua Language held the First National and International Congress of Quechua and Aymara Academies and issued a document registering the congress's approval of the five-vowel alphabet by majority vote. However, a dissenting document by congress participants rejected both the process and outcome of the congress's consideration of the issue and, furthermore, denounced the disunifying role of the Summer Institute of Linguistics (SIL or, in Spanish, ILV) through its direct influence on the regional Quechua academies in Ancash, Huánuco, Junín, and Cajamarca (Primer Congreso, 1987:581–85; see the following sections for more discussion).

For three days in April of the same year, some 200 educators, anthropologists, linguists, and others met under the auspices of the National Institute of Culture (Instituto Nacional de Cultura) in Lima. A report on the meeting in the newspaper *La República* focused on the role of writing in Andean society, and included not only an account of the Puno Bilingual Education Project and a plea for greater use of Quechua in education, but also an exposition of the value of language academies that denounced the Peruvian Academy of the Quechua Language for using Spanish, not Quechua, in its deliberations and minutes (Cerrón-Palomino 1987; Jung and López 1987b; Pozzi-Escot 1987c).

A few months later, in July 1987, back in Cusco, the Andean College Program of the Bartolomé de Las Casas Center for Rural Andean Studies – a research and publication center of the Catholic Church – sponsored a workshop on Language, Culture, and the Southern Peruvian Andean Region. The workshop was directed toward scholars and students, government officials, politicians, and syndicate leaders, and had as its objectives: to consider the cultural and linguistic situation of the region in the light of insights from linguistics and the social sciences; to formulate criteria to direct political action with respect to the languages and cultures of the region; to raise the consciousness of base organizations as to the socioeconomic and cultural implications of the multilingual and pluricultural reality of the region; and to contribute to the consolidation of a regional and national conscience valuing languages and cultures. Here, again, the three-versus-five-vowel controversy erupted at the first evening's panel discussion.

Interest groups in the controversy

The organizers of the events summarized in the preceding section already suggest the main interest groups involved: Peruvian linguists convened the workshop on writing, bilingual education project personnel sponsored the workshop seminar on bilingual education, and the Peruvian Academy of the Quechua Language called the congress of academies. The alternating location of the events, between Lima and Cusco, is another indicator of interests represented: Lima, the capital of the country, is the seat of government and of the country's economic and intellectual elite; whereas Cusco, ancient capital of the Inca Empire, is located in the midst of the highland Quechua-speaking region of the country and has been the historic seat of pro-Quechua activism over the four centuries since the Spanish conquest.

A word of introduction about each interest group and a brief outline of their socioeconomic, educational, regional, and ethnic differences will be helpful here. Many of the Peruvian linguists who have been most active in the language-planning arena are or have been professors at San Marcos University, the oldest and most prestigious of Peru's universities. All have been actively involved in bilingual education projects, most importantly, the Experimental Quechua-Spanish Bilingual Education Program of Ayacucho, begun in 1964, and the Experimental Bilingual Education Project of Puno, begun in 1977 (for more information, see Pozzi-Escot 1972; Zúñiga, Lozada, and Cano 1977; Chavarria 1987; Pozzi-Escot 1987a:50–54; and Zúñiga 1987 on the former; and López 1987; López, Jung, and Palao 1987; Hornberger 1988a; and López 1988 on the latter).

The other major bilingual education project participating in these language-planning discussions has been that of the North American-based international Summer Institute of Linguistics, which has been working in Peru since 1946. The objective of this missionary body, in Peru as in the rest of the world, is to translate the Bible into every existing language to enable every person on earth to have access to the Word of God. In Peru, as elsewhere, the task of Bible translation has involved the SIL in developing writing systems for hitherto unwritten languages and in providing bilingual education for hitherto nonliterate populations (cf. Townsend 1972). As a matter of policy, the SIL undertakes work only under official agreement with the national government; in Peru there has been a close affiliation between the SIL and the Ministry of Education since SIL's earliest beginnings. The current contract (by Supreme Resolution #24–90–ED of the Peruvian government) specifies that one of SIL's activities in Peru is "the elaboration of a writing system for each language, in order to provide for its practical use and facilitate its future preservation" (translation mine). Most of the SIL's earlier energies were directed toward the many languages of the Amazon region in northern Peru, although they sponsored a Quechua-Spanish bilingual education project in Ayacucho for five years beginning in 1965; more recently, they are working in Quechua in Ancash, Cajamarca, Cerro de Pasco, Huánuco, Junín, Lambayeque, and San Martín (see Burns 1968, 1971 on Ayacucho; Larson et al. 1979; Pozzi-Escot 1987a:45–50; and Romero and Weber 1987 on the SIL bilingual education work in general).

The Peruvian Academy of the Quechua Language, founded in Cusco in 1953, is dedicated to the promotion of Quechua, through such activities as speaking it in public events; publishing Quechua writings (e.g., *Inka Rimay*); teaching Quechua; the awarding of the National Cusco Prize for a Quechua Novel, Poem, Story and Drama; and a project to publish a unified international Quechua grammar and dictionary (*Inka Rimay* 1985:56–65). Founding member and two-time president of the academy, Faustino Espinoza Navarro is a self-taught scholar of the Quechua language, a well-known public speaker in Quechua, and author of Quechua publications (e.g., *Qosqo* 1963; *Machu Pikchu* 1978). He is known in Cusco as *El Inca* 'The Inka' for his part in creating and playing that role in the annual *Inti Raymi* 'Festival of the Sun', which he also helped to found in 1944.

Socioeconomic status, educational background, regional affiliation, and ethnicity are differentiating characteristics among these interest groups, though as with any sociological characteristics, the reality is far more complex than any broad generalization would imply. The generalization that the SIL linguists enjoy the highest socioeconomic status and the Quechua academy members the lowest, based on the relative wealth of the United States, Lima, and the Peruvian highlands respectively, masks the fact that the North American missionary endeavor is a far cry from the affluence of other sectors of North American society; or that a Lima linguist's professional salary may provide far less means than the landholdings of an academy member, particularly in this time of excruciating economic crisis in Peru. The generalization that the SIL linguists tend to be trained outside Peru, or that the Peruvian linguists tend to have a higher level of education than the Quechua academy members, belies the fact that many Peruvian linguists have done graduate study or obtained graduate degrees in the United States or Europe and that some of the academy members hold advanced degrees. In addition, one's level of education need not be dependent only on years of formal study. Again, the generalization that the regional affiliations of the three groups are foreign, capital city, and Department of Cusco, respectively, oversimplifies the sense of affiliation that they may have. None of the three groups adopts a parochial affiliation to only the region of their origin: The academy members look beyond the Cusco Quechua region to the rest of the Quechua-speaking world; the Peruvian linguists look beyond the capital to the nation as a whole and even the Andean nations as a group; and the SIL linguists couple their global and country-of-origin perspective with a focus on the national perspective within which they work. In the same way, each group's ethnicity is as much a matter of whom they identify with as of whom they are identified with. The Peruvian linguists are identified primarily with the Spanish-speaking *criollo* 'creole' coastal culture, and the academicians with Quechua-speaking indigenous highland culture. However, this does not preclude the Peruvian linguists' being ideologically closer to the indigenous highland populations than their academy counterparts. Similarly, foreign SIL linguists generally try to identify with the local Quechua ethnicity and ensure that their work incorporates genuine voices of indigenous Peruvians; they usually learn to speak the local Quechua variety.

Perhaps the differences among these three groups are best summed up in the terms by which they refer to the fourth, in many ways invisible, interest group; that is, the Quechua-speaking population of Peru. As the Peruvian linguists/bilingual education specialists insist on pointing out to the Quechua academy members, they themselves most often refer to the Quechua speakers as *campesinos* 'peasants' whereas the Quechua academy members use the term *indígenas* 'indigenous people' (e.g., Debate 1987:170, 172). In part this difference is simply a reflection of the difference in generation between the two groups: The younger generation, the Peruvian linguists/bilingual education specialists, have adopted the term introduced after 1968 by the Revolutionary Government specifically to replace the term indígena, whereas the older generation, the Quechua academy members, have not. However, both the government's terminology planning and the interest groups' use of the terms also reflect ideological stances based on socioeconomic, regional, and ethnic differences: Campesino identifies Quechua speakers primarily by their socioeconomic position in society whereas indígena defines them primarily by linguistic and cultural characteristics; campesino is a term legislated upon the highlands from Lima whereas the term indígena has a certain regional historical force deriving from the indigenist movement of the early twentieth century (Tamayo Herrera 1980).

SIL linguists, on the other hand, most often refer to the Quechua-speaking population as Quechua speakers (e.g., ILV 1983:3), vernacular speakers (e.g., ILV 1983:5), native speakers (e.g., ILV 1983:6), readers (e.g. Debate 1987:148), or users (e.g. ILV 1983:9), all terms that the other two groups use as well. Consistent with SIL's goals in Peru, the emphasis in this choice of terms is not on Quechua speakers' cultural, political, or economic identity, but on them as speakers, readers, and writers of the language.

Points of controversy

The different interests these groups represent inform and influence the arguments they make in the three-versus-five-vowel debate. The main points of controversy in the debate are as follows: the structure of the language, the language-planning process, the basis of authority on the language, and the defense of the language's purity, authenticity, and autonomy. We will take up each point of controversy and the various arguments around them in turn.

The structure of the language

The arguments about the language's structure revolve around two issues: the rule for the use of *e* and *o;* and the relationship between written and spoken language. The crux of the linguistic argument is that Quechua has only three vowel phonemes, /i/, /a/, and /u/, with [e] and [o] occurring as allophones of /i/ and /u/ when in the proximity of the uvular consonant /q/ (or its aspirated or glottalized counterparts, /qh/ and /q'/). The Peruvian linguists, therefore, argue that, on the basis of the phonemic principle in designing alphabets (whereby each sound that is distinctive to the native speaker is represented by one and only one letter; cf. Pike 1947:208), the Quechua alphabet should have three vowels (*i, a, u*); the native speaker will automatically pronounce the written *i* as [e] and the written *u* as [o] when they occur in proximity to *q, qh,* or *q'* (Debate 1987:179; Jung and López 1987a:588; López Flores 1987:9–11).

The Quechua academy members' focus is elsewhere, however. On the basis of their accumulated thirty years of writing practice using a five-vowel Quechua alphabet (see Hornberger 1993 for more on the alphabets), the academy members have formulated the rule from the other end. For them, the rule is that for writing Quechua, *e* and *o* go with *q,* and *i* and *u* go with *k;* thus, if you change the *e* in *qella* 'lazy' to *i,* you must also, by the writing rule, change the *q* to *k,* yielding *killa* 'moon', a different word altogether. In order to write *qella,* they argue, they need all five vowels since, in Cusco at least, they pronounce all five (Debate 1987:165).

Cerrón responds that it is not only in Cusco that all five are pronounced, but also, for example, in Puno, Ayacucho, Ancash, and Cajamarca (Debate 1987:161, 166). This brings us to the second argument related to language structure: the relationship between spoken and written language. For the Peruvian linguists, the important point is to distinguish writing from pronunciation (Debate 1987:162–63). Cerrón uses the comparison of Cusco Spanish pronunciation of *acto* 'act' as [ajto] rather than [akto] and of *apto* 'apt' as [afto] rather than [apto] to make the point that there is not an exact correlation between writing and pronunciation (Debate 1987:163).

Academy members, on the other hand, start from the premise that one should not write one way and pronounce another (Debate 1987:166). Furthermore, they argue that Quechua has been written with five vowels ever since the Colonial period (Debate 1987:179), and they are totally accustomed to using *e* and *o* (Debate 1987:171).

The SIL linguists appear to fall somewhere between the Peruvian linguists and the academicians. On the one hand, they recognize that Quechua had only three vowel phonemes in the past and that the ideal alphabet for any language follows the phonemic principle. On the other, they also place great weight on native-speaker preference when there is a conflict between linguistic precision and native-speaker acceptance; and they emphasize the evidence for five vowel phonemes in several Quechua varieties.

The language-planning process

The last argument raised by the academy members hints at the second point of controversy, the language-planning process itself. On the one hand, Peruvian linguists/bilingual education specialists, Quechua academy members, and SIL linguists alike argue for a decision based on already existing implementation and native-speaker acceptance, but on the other, they cite different implementation precedents. The academy members cite 400 years of Quechua writing using five vowels since the Spanish arrived and began to write Quechua. The Peruvian linguists/bilingual education specialists cite their numerous publications using three vowels, noting that they are practically the only ones who produce written material in Quechua (Jung and López 1987a:591; also Primer Congreso 1987:583–84). The SIL linguists cite the preferences of the new native-speaking readers and writers they work with (who, however, have presumably been influenced by their SIL training). Furthermore, whereas the academy members report that they are totally accustomed to the use of the five vowels and the SIL linguists report that native speakers clearly prefer the use of five vowels (ILV 1983:9), the Peruvian linguists/bilingual education specialists point to evidence from the bilingual education projects that the three vowel alphabet works (Debate 1987:174): Children reading Quechua have no trouble reading the three vowels and pronouncing *e* and *o* near *q*, whether they are just learning to read for the first time or already know how to read in Spanish (Jung and López 1987a:586, 588).

Similarly, linguists/bilingual education specialists and academy members are all dissatisfied with voting as a means of making language-planning decisions, but they register their dissatisfaction over different votes. The sequence of meetings and conflicting decisions in the three-versus-five-vowel debate demonstrates just how unsatisfactory voting is as a means of reaching agreement, as one or another of the interest groups has challenged on procedural grounds the validity of decisions reached.

Basis of authority on the language

The third point of controversy in the three-versus-five-vowel debate is the basis of authority on the language. The Peruvian linguists/bilingual education specialists – most of whom are not fluent speakers of either Quechua or Aymara – defend the need for specialized scientific study to inform language-planning decisions. The SIL linguists derive their authority from their study of the language and their pedagogical work and literature production with native speakers. On the other hand, the Quechua academy members see the ability to speak Quechua as fundamental to having the authority to make planning decisions, and they periodically challenge the authority of the non-Quechua speakers. Indeed, I heard only one participant use extended Quechua discourse in the discussion at the language and culture workshop (Cusco, 20 July 1987), and the use of Quechua in these discussions is all too infrequent.

For the Peruvian linguists, authority to decide on the language rests not on their ability to speak it, but on their scholarship in it. When one workshop seminar participant, believing the *Diccionario Políglota Incaico* to be a colonial document, mentions it as dating from 1614, Cerrón-Palomino asserts that it in fact dates from 1905, further proving his knowledge of it by identifying the author of the Cusco section by name. Similarly, Cerrón is emphatic that it is one thing to speak a language and quite another to know it (Debate 1987:166–68, 175). The academicians also base their authority on scholarship (as well as on speaking the language), and they are not necessarily convinced that the Lima linguists' studies are more scientific than their own.

The third contested basis of authority, in addition to speaking and scholarship in Quechua, is the historicity of Cusco Quechua. The members of the Quechua academy take Cusco Quechua to be the mother language of all the Quechua varieties, basing their view on the political and social history of the Inca Empire. The linguists, on the basis of historical linguistic analysis, archaeological evidence, and Andean social history, establish the earliest origins of Quechua in the central part of Peru. They view Cusco Quechua to be only one of several varieties belonging to later evolutions of Quechua (Parker 1963; Torero 1974). For the Cusco academy members, Cusco Quechua is the standard against which to measure all Quechuas, and they challenge the Lima linguists' knowledge of Quechua when it is based primarily on exposure to Puno Quechua (through the bilingual education project in Puno). The Lima linguists, on the other hand, seek to convince the Cusco academy members with linguistic evidence that Puno Quechua may represent an older form of Quechua than that spoken in Cusco (Debate 1987:173, 175). Their purpose in doing so is not to denigrate Cusco Quechua, but to argue that regionalism should play no part in their joint efforts to defend the Quechua language (Debate 1987:160).

Defense of the language's purity, authenticity, and autonomy

The defense of the Quechua language's purity, authenticity, and autonomy is the final point of controversy in the three-versus-five-vowel debate. Cerrón-Palomino states that the Peruvian linguists base their decisions not on whim or disloyalty to Quechua, but rather on respect for the language itself, the search for the truly authentic Quechua that is not contaminated by contact with Spanish, and the attempt to be as objective as possible in analyzing Quechua (Debate 1987:160, 162, 174).

The Peruvian linguists' defense of Quechua includes vigilance for its purity from the influence of Spanish. They argue that writing Quechua with five vowels imposes Spanish conventions on Quechua (Jung and López 1987a:590) and makes Quechua subservient to Spanish, which they view as another form of colonialism (Debate 1987:164; López Flores 1987:12–13; Primer Congreso 1987:583). They assert that the highest authority on pronunciation must be the Quechua speaker who is not exposed to any foreign linguistic influence; and they note that the native Quechua speakers who have produced books in Quechua for the bilingual education projects have no trouble using three vowels (Jung and López 1987a:591, 1987c).

The Peruvian linguists/bilingual education specialists affirm that they seek the standardization of that authentic Quechua; that is, not the Quechua of the bilingual *mestizo*, but the Quechua of the rural sector, the monolingual campesinos. Authenticity will be found in those who have not been conditioned by the pressures of the Western world (Debate 1987:170, 171, 174, 178).

For the Peruvian linguists/bilingual education specialists, guarding Quechua's autonomy includes defending Quechua against what they regard as antiscientific analyses. Thus, when Faustino Espinoza suggests that the origin of Quechua is in onomatopoeic sounds, imitating the languages of animals (as others have claimed about the origin of human language in general), Cerrón-Palomino objects that such a theory leaves Quechua open to attack as being nothing more than the language of wild animals and birds, as Peruvian Hispanicist intellectuals often maintain (Debate 1987:175, 177).

Defending Quechua's autonomy not only includes adopting an objective stance toward analyzing it, but also seeking ways to build its range of use. Carmen López calls for a stance that would seek to make Quechua a vehicle of national communication, not only in the schools, but also in the university, on television, in the newspapers, and in government offices (López Flores 1987:13). The Peruvian linguists/bilingual education specialists are also conscious of sustaining and promoting Quechua use at an international level. They suggest that the use of the three-vowel alphabet can contribute to Quechua standardization at both the national and the international level, since it is understandable not only in Cusco, Puno, and so on, but also in Alto Napo (Peru) and in Ecuador, where only three vowels are pronounced (Jung and López 1987a:590).

SIL linguists also recognize the importance of the goals of unification/ standardization among Quechua varieties and preservation of Quechua language and culture, but it is fair to say that they take a view that is both more locally oriented and more bilingual. For Weber, the autonomy of Quechua depends not on its standardization according to one uniform norm, but on first recognizing and developing the functional range of Quechua in its regionally distinct varieties. He suggests that it is precisely the regional distinctives of each variety that serve as symbols of ethnic solidarity for Quechua speakers, and that to undercut those distinctives by unification/standardization would erode the fundamental reason for Quechua speakers to speak Quechua (Weber 1987:11–22). Furthermore, applying insights from the case of Nahuatl and Spanish in Mexico (Hill and Hill 1980), he argues that to impose restrictions on borrowing from Spanish into Quechua projects a purist attitude that may ultimately have the effect of hastening the death of Quechua (Weber 1987:23–33). The bilingual view of SIL linguists is also evident in an SIL document circulated at the 1983 workshop, which cited not only unification and preservation of Quechua as possible goals for writing Quechua, but also literacy for both monolinguals and bilinguals, the facilitation of Spanish as a second language acquisition by Quechua monolinguals, and the facilitation of Quechua as a second language acquisition by Spanish monolinguals (ILV 1983:3).

For the members of the Peruvian Academy of the Quechua Language in Cusco, defending Quechua's purity, authenticity, and autonomy means something slightly different from that of either of the above approaches. Like the Peruvian linguists, they are vigilant against incorporation of Spanish lexicon; indeed, many of them command an extremely rich Quechua vocabulary, born of years of collecting words from the most remote areas of the highlands. Like the Peruvian linguists, too, some of them accept that the basis for study of Quechua must be the indigenous

Quechua speaker (Villasante in Debate 1987:169, 176; but cf. Farfán, p. 171, who invokes the mestizo as the model). At the same time, however, sharing the SIL's more bilingual view, they explicitly include themselves among Quechua speakers and argue for language-planning decisions to be responsive to their needs as well (Debate 1987:171). From their perspective, different from that of either the SIL or Peruvian linguists, however, the purity and authenticity of Quechua have more to do with freedom from contamination from Lima and fidelity to Cusco norms than with freedom from Spanish influence and bilingual speakers, or with fidelity to the various local varieties of Quechua.

This relates directly to their view of Quechua's autonomy, as well. They are wary, with good historical reason, of domination by Lima; and they perceive the activism of the Lima linguists as nothing more than a "new domination under the pretext of science" (Espinoza Navarro, Workshop on Language, Culture, and the Southern Peruvian Andean Region, Cusco, 20 July 1987). From their perspective, the fact that the Ministry of Education approved the recommendations of the 1983 workshop despite the objections of Cusco representatives is evidence that the ministry is being manipulated by the Lima linguists (Debate 1987:169).

Fishman has noted that "all ethnocultural entities have elites of their own, and these are often the most reluctant to change the status quo vis a vis writing systems" (1988:283). It is difficult to enforce a change of writing system on the inertia of older readers and writers, he says, especially when no dramatic change in social function, ethnic identity, or social status goes along with the change. Considered in this light, it is not surprising that the academy members, many of whom have, after all, been writing Quechua for longer than members of the other interest groups, should resist a change in their writing system; there is no perceived benefit, indeed, there is instead the threat of domination from Lima.

Future directions and implications for language education

There have been moments when the three-versus-five-vowel controversy has led to direct attacks, in both word and deed, by one interest group on another.[2] At times, the debate appears to be at an insurmountable im-

---

2 As we have seen, the Cusco Quechua academy convened its own congress to take another vote on the decision they had participated in in Lima in 1983; in turn, Cerrón-Palomino challenged the academy's activities. The SIL has apparently used its influence with education officials in the departments where it is working in Quechua to modify the three-vowel Quechua alphabet; in turn, representatives at the First Congress dissented from the proceedings of the congress and denounced the SIL for

passe. As long as the debate remains unresolved, Quechua language educators are left with three choices, all of them unsatisfactory, given the aim of creating a community of Quechua readers and writers. One choice is for educators to continue their educational efforts following the dictates of their own views, regardless of what other educators do, with the inevitable result being a nonstandardized Quechua alphabet. Another choice is for educators to try to adapt their efforts to the changing dictates of the ongoing debate, running the risk and considerable expense of repeated republications of educational materials revised to conform to whatever alphabet is currently in official status, as well as unnecessary confusion for Quechua learners. A third choice is for educators to freeze all educational efforts or materials production until the debate is resolved.

Each of the three main interest groups in the debate is directly involved in language education and has in fact faced these choices. The Peruvian Academy of the Quechua Language has continued their Quechua teaching and publication through the debate, without deviating from their use of the five-vowel alphabet. The Puno bilingual education project underwent the expense of revising and republishing their texts and reorienting their teacher training and classroom instruction to conform to the three-vowel decision made at the workshop in Lima. The Summer Institute of Linguistics imposed a several-year moratorium on publications in Quechua, lifting it in late 1990 to allow publication in orthographies approved by departmental offices of education (Weber, personal communication, 2 October 1990).

Each of these decisions has obvious detrimental effects on the availability, consistency, and quality of Quechua language education and materials for Quechua learners. At another level, though, whatever alphabet is eventually decided on will also carry implications for Quechua learners – implications having to do with who the learners will be, the ease and efficiency of their learning, and the direction their learning will point them toward with respect to ethnic identity and social integration. The arguments raised in favor of and against the decision for three or five vowels suggest these implications. The choice for three vowels implies the

its disunifying action during the congress and for its systematic opposition to the 1985 official alphabet, especially in the departments of Ancash, Junín, and Huánuco (Primer Congreso 1987:584). Cerrón-Palomino has recently written that, shortly after the 1983 workshop, "the two above mentioned institutions [the Cusco Quechua academy and the SIL] disavow[ed] their word, in a clear stance of sabotage to all attempts at achieving the unification of writing in Quechua" but that "despite the disloyal and chauvinist attitude of the Cusco academy, whose posture in no sense reflects the feelings of the real users of Quechua, as well as the assimilationist and dissociating activity of the foreign institution [SIL] (which seeks to impose language-planning criteria in a strictly national matter), the revised alphabet was approved" (Cerrón-Palomino 1989b:114–15, translation mine).

rural monolingual Quechua speaker as primary target group and an autonomous, cross-regional, and cross-national community of Quechua readers and writers as goal; whereas the choice for five vowels implies the urban, bilingual Quechua-Spanish speaker as primary target group and communities of Quechua readers and writers linked perhaps more directly to the Spanish-speaking Andean world than to each other as goal. The sociopolitical ramifications of language education in this case are similar to those facing educators of English as a second or foreign language around the world, who are caught between English as a language of social empowerment and English as a language of cultural imperialism (Eggington 1993), and who face debates as to whether the local or international variety of English should be taught (cf. Tollefson 1991).

Given the far-reaching implications of the three-versus-five-vowel debate for Quechua language education and Quechua learners, it is crucial that the Quechua-speaking population as a whole, the fourth and most important interest group, no longer be left out of the decision-making process. At various points in the debate, both the Peruvian and the SIL linguists/bilingual education specialists have reiterated the importance of the participation of the Quechua-speaking population. The Peruvian linguists denounced a decision-making process that affects Quechua speakers who are not adequately represented (Jung and López 1987a); the SIL linguists noted that for all the alphabets they have worked in, the opinion of the readers has always been an important factor (Romero and Weber 1987:148). The problem is that in this language-planning debate, the Quechua-speaking population has been more often invoked than truly represented.

When they are represented, their voices are compelling. There is a certain honesty about the Cusco Quechua academy members who speak for themselves as Quechua speakers and do not claim to speak for anyone else. Cerrón-Palomino, the only Quechua speaker among the Lima linguists active in the language-planning debates, is also the most eloquent of them. What is needed in these discussions are more voices like these, more voices of Quechua speakers themselves.

These voices will be many and varied, and they should be. If Quechua language planning is to succeed at challenging the politico-economic and sociocultural divisions in Peruvian society, then it must begin by challenging those divisions within itself. It must incorporate all Quechua speakers, both monolingual and bilingual speakers, both campesinos and indígenas, both SIL-educated and Ayacucho or Puno project-educated teachers and readers, both Lima linguists and Cusco academy members.

Indigenous language speakers have resources to counter language conflict. Chuquimamani reports that when his interviewees were confronted with their own speech (on a tape recording), they self-corrected and reduced the number of Spanish loans they used; furthermore, when a wider group listened, they made "purist" commentaries and suggested replacements and even neologisms for the Spanish loan words. He notes that the mechanisms of creativity and development are present, but need activation by a clear motivation and by reflection on the language and its use (1988:176).

Quechua speakers, long used to linguistic conflict, have the linguistic and cultural resources to resolve this language-planning controversy; given a real opportunity to do so, they will have the motivation as well. To give them the chance, however, they will have to be incorporated into the decision-making process, not as absent interest group, nor as token, but as decision makers.

References

Ballón Aguirre, Enrique. 1989. La identidad linguocultural peruana: Bilingüismo y diglosia. In Luis Enrique López, Inés Pozzi-Escot, and Madeleine Zúñiga (Eds.), *Temas de lingüística aplicada: Primer Congreso Nacional de Investigaciones Lingüístico-Filológicas* (pp. 77–93). Lima, Peru: Concytec/GTZ.

Burns, Donald H. 1968. Bilingual education in the Andes of Peru. In Joshua Fishman, Charles Ferguson, and Jyotirinda Das Gupta (Eds.), *Language problems of developing nations* (pp. 403–13). New York: J. Wiley and Sons.

1971. *Cinco años de educación bilingüe en los Andes del Perú 1965–1970.* Lima, Peru: Instituto Lingüístico de Verano.

Cerrón-Palomino, Rodolfo. 1980. La cuestión lingüística en el Perú. Paper presented at the IV Andean Linguistics Workshop, Albuquerque, New Mexico. Published in 1982 in *Aula Quechua* (R. Cerrón-Palomino, Ed.), pp. 105–23. Lima, Peru: Ediciones Signo Universitario.

1987. Las academias de la lengua: ¿Para qué sirven? *La República*, 11 April, Suplemento de Ciencia y Tecnología, p. 9.

1989a. Language policy in Peru: A historical overview. *International Journal of the Sociology of Language* 77:11–33.

1989b. *Lengua y sociedad en el Valle del Mantaro.* Lima, Peru: Instituto de Estudios Peruanos.

Chavarria, Clotilde. 1987. Proyecto experimental de educación bilingüe Quechua-Castellano en Ayacucho. In *Seminario Taller sobre Programas Curriculares para Educación Bilingüe: Informe final*, pp. 140–46. Lima, Peru: Ministerio de Educación – INIDE.

Chuquimamani Valer, Rufino. 1988. Una muestra del conflicto lingüístico nacional en el habla de los sollocoteños: El caso del parto. In Luis E. López (Ed.), *Pesquisas en Lingüística Andina* (pp. 163–80). Peru: CONCYTEC/UNA-Puno/GTZ.

Compendio de decretos leyes y resoluciones de educación. 1975. Lima, Peru.

Debate: ¿Por qué el uso de las tres vocales en quechua? 1987. In *Seminario Taller sobre Programas Curriculares para Educación Bilingüe: Informe final*, pp. 160–80. Lima, Peru: Ministerio de Educación – INIDE.

Eggington, William. 1993. On the sociopolitical nature of English language teaching. *TESOL Matters* 2(6): 4.

Espinoza Navarro, Faustino. 1963. *Qosqo: Poemas del inka.* Cusco, Peru: Ediciones Inka-Rimay.

——— 1978. *Machu Pikchu: Poemas del inka.* Cusco, Peru: Wiraqocha Biblioteca.

Ferguson, Charles A. 1959. Diglossia. *Word* 15:325–40.

Fishman, Joshua A. 1988. Ethnocultural issues in the creation, substitution, and revision of writing systems. In B. A. Rafoth and D. L. Rubin (Eds.), *The social construction of written communication* (pp. 273–86). Norwood, N.J.: Ablex.

Hill, Jane, and Kenneth Hill. 1980. Mixed grammar, purist grammar, and language attitudes in modern Nahuatl. *Language in Society* 9:321–48.

Hornberger, Nancy H. 1988a. *Bilingual education and language maintenance: A southern Peruvian Quechua case.* Dordrecht/Providence: Foris Publications.

——— 1988b. Language planning orientations and bilingual education in Peru. *Language Problems and Language Planning* 12(1): 14–29.

——— 1993. The First Workshop on Quechua and Aymara Writing. In Joshua A. Fishman (Ed.), *The earliest stage of language planning: The first congresses phenomenon,* pp. 233–56.

ILV (Instituto Lingüístico de Verano). 1983. Consideraciones sobre el alfabeto general del quechua. Paper circulated at the I Taller de Escritura en Quechua y Aimara, October, Lima, Peru.

Inka Rimay: Organo de la Academia Peruana de la Lengua Quechua. 1985. Cusco, Peru: Academia Peruana de la Lengua Quechua.

Instituto Nacional de Estadística. 1984. *Censos nacionales VIII de población III de vivienda (12 de julio de 1981). Resultados definitivos de las variables investigadas por muestreo. Nivel nacional.* Vol. B, 1. Lima, Peru: Instituto Nacional de Estadística.

Jung, Ingrid, and Luis Enrique López. 1987a. Aportes del proyecto de educación bilingüe-Puno a la discusión en torno al alfabeto quechua. *Allpanchis* 29/30:585–92. (In Primer Congreso de la Lengua Quechua y Lengua Aymara, Cusco, 13–15 Febrero 1987.)

——— 1987b. Bilingüismo en 40 escuelas: Para quechuas y aimaras. *La República,* 11 April, Suplemento de Ciencia y Tecnología, pp. 7–8.

——— 1987c. Las dimensiones políticas de una escritura: El caso del quechua en el Perú. *Allpanchis* 29/30:483–509.

Larson, Mildred, Patricia Davis, and Marlene Ballena Dávila. 1979. *Educación bilingüe: Una experiencia en la amazonía peruana.* Lima, Peru: Instituto Lingüístico de Verano.

López, Luis Enrique. 1987. Balance y perspectivas de la educación bilingüe en Puno. *Allpanchis* 29/30:347–81.

——— 1988. El proyecto de educación bilingüe de Puno: De contextos y ajustes. *Revista Peruana de Ciencias Sociales* (Lima, Peru) 1(3): 9–28.

——— 1989. El bilingüismo de los unos y los otros: Diglosia y conflicto lingüístico en el Perú. In Enrique Ballón Aguirre and Rodolfo Cerrón-Palomino (Eds.), *Diglosia linguo-literaria y educación en el Perú: Homenaje a Alberto Escobar* (pp. 91–128). Lima, Peru: Concytec/GTZ.

López, Luis Enrique, Ingrid Jung, and Juan Palao. 1987. Educación bilingüe en Puno: Reflexiones en torno a una experiencia . . . que concluye? *Pueblos Indígenas y Educación* (Quito, Ecuador) 1(3): 63–106.

López Flores, Carmen. 1987. *¿Por qué es mejor escribir con tres vocales en quechua?* Lima, Peru: Ministerio de Educación – INIDE.

Ministerio de Educación. 1972. *Política nacional de educación bilingüe.* Lima, Peru: Ministerio de Educación.

Parker, Gary J. 1963. La clasificación genética de los dialectos quechuas. *Revista del Museo Nacional* (Lima, Peru) 32:241–52.

Pike, Kenneth. 1947. *Phonemics: A technique for reducing languages to writing.* Ann Arbor: University of Michigan Press.

Pozzi-Escot, Inés. 1972. *Plan para la castellanización de los niños quechua-hablantes en el Peru.* Lima, Peru: Centro de Investigación de Lingüística Aplicada (Working Paper no. 14).

1987a. La educación bilingüe en el Peru: Una mirada retrospectiva y prospectiva. In Luis Enrique López (Ed.), *Pesquisas en lingüística andina* (pp. 37–77). Peru: CONCYTEC/UNA-Puno/GTZ.

1987b. La incomunicación verbal en el Perú. *Allpanchis* 29/30:45–63.

1987c. Quechua en las aulas: Escritura y escolaridad en la zona andina. *La República,* 11 April, Suplemento de Ciencia y Tecnología, pp. 10–11.

1989. Reflexiones para una política nacional de lenguas y culturas en la educación. In Luis Enrique López, Inés Pozzi-Escot, and Madeleine Zúñiga (Eds.), *Temas de lingüística aplicada: Primer Congreso Nacional de Investigaciones Lingüístico-Filológicas* (pp. 21–54). Lima, Peru: Concytec/GTZ.

Primer Congreso de la Lengua Quechua y Lengua Aymara. 1987. *Allpanchis* 29/30:581–92.

Romero, Ezequiel, and David Weber. 1987. Programa de educación bilingüe del Instituto Lingüístico de Verano. In *Seminario Taller sobre Programas Curriculares para Educación Bilingüe: Informe final,* pp. 147–154. Lima, Peru: Ministerio de Educación – INIDE.

Tamayo Herrera, José. 1980. *Historia del indigenismo cuzqueño, siglo XVI-XX.* Lima, Peru: Instituto Nacional de Cultura.

Tollefson, James W. 1991. *Planning language, planning inequality: Language policy in the community.* London: Longman.

Torero, Alfredo. 1974. *El Quechua y la historia social andina.* Lima, Peru: Universidad Ricardo Palma.

Townsend, W. Cameron. 1972. *They found a common language: Community through bilingual education.* New York: Harper and Row.

Weber, David. 1987. *Estudios quechua: Planificación, historia, y gramática.* Yarinacocha, Pucallpa, Peru: Ministerio de Educación, Instituto Lingüístico de Verano (Serie Lingüística Peruana no. 27).

Zúñiga, Madeleine. 1987. El reto de la educación intercultural y bilingüe en el sur del Peru. *Allpanchis* 29/30:331–46.

Zúñiga, Madeleine, Minnie Lozada, and Lucia Cano de Gálvez. 1977. *Diseño de un programa experimental de educación bilingüe quechua-castellano.* Lima, Peru: Centro de Investigación de Lingüística Aplicada (Working Paper No. 34).

Index

In cases of references to work involving co-authors, only the name of the first author appears in this index.